HUNGARIAN REVIVAL

Political Reflections on Central Europe.

Aspekt non-fiction no 2

LÁSZLÓ MARÁCZ

HUNGARIAN REVIVAL

Political Reflections on Central Europe

1996 Aspekt

Marácz, László

Hungarian Revival : Political Reflections on Central Europe / László Marácz;
[transl. from the Dutch: D.E. Butterman-Dorey]. - Nieuwegein : Aspekt. - Ill.,
foto's. - (Aspekt non-fiction; 2) Vert. van: Hongaarse Kentering. Een politieke
beschouwing over Midden-Europa. - Nieuwegein : Aspekt, 1995. - (Ciceroreeks; nr. 3).
Met lit. opg., reg.
ISBN 90-75323-11-5
NUGI 654
Trefw.: Hongarije ; geschiedenis ; Midden-Europa.

Orginal title: Hongaarse Kentering
1995 Uitgeverij Aspekt b.v., Nieuwegein
P.O.Box 7081/3430 JB Nieuwegein/The Netherlands
Tel: +31-306051196 fax: +31-306056409 e-mail: Aspekt@knoware.nl
Foto omslag: 'Bloedige dinsdag' in Tirgu Mures, maart 1990
Frontpage: Bloody tuesday, Tirgu Mures, March 1990
Backpage: Xander Colee
ISBN Dutch version: 90-75323-06-9
ISBN English version: 90-75323-11-5

(c)1995/1996 László Marácz

Alle rechten voorbehouden. Niets uit deze uitgave mag worden verveelvoudigd, opgeslagen in een automatisch gegevensbestand of openbaar gemaakt, in enige vom of op enige wijze, hetzij electronisch, mechanisch, door fotokopieën, opnamen of enig andere manier, zonder voorafgaande schriftelijke toestemming van de uitgever.

All rights reserved. No part of this book may be reproduced in any form or by any means without permission of the copyright-holder.

CONTENTS

NOTE TO THE ENGLISH EDITION BY MICHIEL KLINKHAMER	9
FOREWORD BY LÁSZLÓ TŐKÉS	11
INTRODUCTION	17
PART I: THE HUNGARIANS	29
Western images of the Hungarians	31
Introduction	31
Historical Western images and stereotypes of the Hungarians	33
Negative images and stereotypes	33
Positive images and stereotypes	36
Positive and negative images and stereotypes	38
Hungarian images and stereotypes before, during and after the First World War	40
The Hungarian self-image	53
How many Hungarians live in the Carpathian Basin?	62
The Hungarian language and myths of ethno-genesis	64
Hungarian history	76
Trianon research	79
Research into the élite	80
Conclusions	81
The emergence of a new Hungarian self-image	83
The open Hungarian culture	84
Integrational power and tolerance	86
Mental-moral imperatives	91
Willingness to compromise	93
The drive for freedom	97
The Hungarian language	99
Mental and material cultural heritage	104
PART II: TRIANON AND ITS CONSEQUENCES FOR THE HUNGARIANS	113
Hungary before the First World War	115
The background to the First World War	117
The road to Trianon	126

The Trianon secrets	133
The losses of Trianon	143
Hungary during the interbellum	149
New Central European states	149
Ethnic engineering	154
The freeing of the Hungarians	167
Ethnic cleansing	170
Returning to hell	174
Anti-Hungarian ethnocide	177
Croatia: the annihilation of a Hungarian community	185
Lesser Yugoslavia: Hungarians as cannon fodder for Serbian generals	192
Slovakia: ethnic cleansing with the aid of administrative means	201
Subcarpathia: the obstruction of Hungarian autonomy	209
Transylvania: the anatomy of a pogrom	213
PART III: TOWARDS A NEW CENTRAL EUROPE	241
The Trianon apologia	243
Asymmetries	245
Neutralization	258
The status quo	267
Hungarian revival	277
Hungarian heroes	277
The Hungarian diaspora	281
Hungary awakes to reality	283
The Hungarian struggle for self-determination	287
The Balladur Pact and the ensuing opposition	298
Europe's hinge: Hungary	311
Lesser Hungarian particularism	311
Global Hungarian potential	316
Greater Hungarian strategy	322
The international perspective	332
NOTES	339
BIBLIOGRAPHICAL NOTES	357
INDEX OF NAMES	359

Note to the English edition by Michiel Klinkhamer

In the few months since its publication *Hungarian Revival* has provoked much lively discussion in the Netherlands. Apart from the controversy in the press that started in January 1996, when a review appeared in the NRC Handelsblad written by Peter Michielsen, the paper's East Europe editor, there was also a debate on 21st February 1996 at Amsterdam University's Institute for Russian and East European Studies entitled: *'Hungarian Revival: science or politics?'*. I was one of the participants in the debate. The main objection raised by colleagues of Dr. L. Marácz, author of the book, and voiced by the assistant professor was that the point of view defended in the book is nationalistic. In the discussion that followed, it emerged that there was neither clarity nor consensus on the meaning of this concept. If one understands by nationalism, striving to unite all members of a nation within the borders of one state, then this book could rightly be called anti-nationalistic. It warns of the dangers that would arise if certain Central European states, such as Slovakia, Serbia and Rumania, inhabited by a diversity of nationalities, tried to impose the essentially Western European concept of creating a homogeneous nation state. Apart from that, the book also rejects the not really topical issue of Hungarian nationalism. The author believes that the solution to the problem of the Hungarian national communities must lie in respecting human rights and autonomy. Several variants of autonomy are discussed in the book. The solutions found to this question will, to a large degree, determine the European internal structure and character of the future. How we treat our national communities in Europe is, in fact, a structural matter. *Hungarian Revival* is a merciless chronicle and analysis of the persistent policy of compulsory assimilation imposed on Hungarian communities living in Hungary's neighbouring countries. It is a plea for the preservation of the Hungarian nation as a spiritual and cultural entity. Peacefully objecting to what amounts to cultural genocide may not be called, under any pretext, nationalism.

The second point of criticism was that the book might be termed one-sided and thus, by implication, unscholarly and untrue. Indeed, matters are often viewed from the Hungarian perspective. The book complements other views already well represented in academic studies in the field (see bibliographical notes). It may be regarded as helping to balance the spectrum. Furthermore, access is given to much extremely valuable source material and scientific notions that were completely repressed during the communist era are given their rightful place once again. In that respect, the book might be regarded as compensating for lost time and as providing a programme for further research.

I found it necessary to voice the points of view mentioned above, which formed the essence of my argument during the debate in which I opposed former lecturers of mine. The theoretical argument employed during the debate that had proved its validity before the wall fell in Berlin is, to my way of thinking, no longer enlightening and constructive today, nor is it a useful instrument for describing and understanding the facts. The only scientific criterium for testing the essence of *Hungarian Revival* which underlies the author's justified and undisguised indignation is, to determine whether the facts and arguments put forward by the author are correct or not. I, thus, invite the reader to apply this criterium within his own framework of interpretation.

Drs. M. Klinkhamer,
Amsterdam, Spring 1996

Foreword by László Tőkés

A modern approach to the Trianon question

The Hungarian nation is busy preparing to celebrate the fact that, in 1996, it will be **1100** years ago since Hungarians first settled in the Carpathian Basin. Where the millennium-centenary celebrations are concerned we cannot speak solely of Hungary, the country, because more than a quarter of the nation, that is to say, approximately three and a half million Hungarians, live outside the country's borders in Rumania, Slovakia, Serbia, the Ukraine and in other neighbouring countries. Since the time of the Paris peace agreements, established after World War I by the prevailing powers, these Hungarians have been turned into marginalized minorities. In addition, more than two-thirds of the land area that used to belong to Hungary was given to surrounding 'national' states which were either created at the time of the agreements or assumed at that time the dimensions of a state.

The prime reason for marking the mille-centennial is not, however, to bewail the bygone days of the Hungarian nation's faded glory but rather, in the first place, to highlight the present problems of shrunken Lesser Hungary and the current state of affairs within the amputated parts of the nation where a struggle for survival is going on. In the context of a united Europe it also provides us with the opportunity to draw up a **national strategy** that is aimed, as much as possible, at the future and is introduced in the interests of perpetuating and reviving the nation distributed on both sides of the county's borders. This objective and this perspective is what justifies our investigation into Trianon at the sad time of the 75th anniversary of the peace agreement.

The dividing up of Hungary, initiated in 1920 in the interests of great powers and various nations, was continued and consolidated by the new peace agreements that developed after the Second World War (1947). During the almost fifty-year-long period of Soviet-communist dictatorship, people in Hungary and the successor states were hardly even allowed to mention the subject of having lost land because of Trianon. Molestation, persecution or even imprisonment awaited anyone who dared to broach this 'sensitive' subject whether from an historic angle or from any other point of view. Ultimately, it is thanks to the changes initiated in Central and Eastern Europe in 1989 that we are able to raise the 'Trianon question' at all. Thus, we at least regained one of the basic human rights, namely that of being able to (relatively) speak out freely and recall the past: the freedom to consider history.

This newly won freedom can only be relative because historic recollections and reflections are intricately intermingled with **politics.** What first has to be clearly established is the fact that it is not the disadvantaged Hungarian side that made the theme of Trianon politically topical in a negative way, but rather the small-nation great-nationalism of the states that divided up the Hungarian territory of the Austro-Hungarian Monarchy amongst themselves. We may in fact unreservedly assert that unlike the period of Hungarian revisionism that characterized the climate during the inter-war years, Hungary has completely abandoned the idea of wanting to win back its amputated regions. There is no single Hungarian political party either inside or outside of Hungary that now includes **revision** in its political programme as a serious option.

Nevertheless, Budapest and Hungarian minorities in surrounding countries are continually being accused of having revisionist intentions, notably by Rumanian and Slovakian nationalists and by the fake democratic Rumanian and Slovakian authorities. They furthermore accuse the Hungarians of wanting to win back the Rumanian **Transylvania** and the Slovakian **Upper Lands**.

The anti-Hungary propaganda smear campaign that fits neatly into the general process of communist reconstruction aims at achieving **political prestige** by stimulating nationalism and cultivating animosity towards minorities. Such smear campaigns also provide cheap electioneering material whilst at the same time masking the actually catastrophic economic and internal political relations.

What can remembering Trianon signify for the Hungarian nation? Above all else, does the country definitely and completely wants to claim its **right to commemorate** which is after all an essential aspect of its rights. To Hungarians, Trianon signifies a defeat as heavy and as catastrophic as that suffered for instance in 1526 at Mohács against the Turkish State. We should surely view it as unnatural that, due to relatively minor political considerations and fears, a nation should be prevented from commemorating and grieving about its own fateful historic defeats and disintegration. It is surely schizophrenic that Rumania has introduced a national holiday to commemorate the symbolic day when Transylvania was lost while Hungary, by contrast, burdened with a loser's twisted feelings of guilt is even expected to conceal the names of her own war victims. Trianon must be given its rightful place in the chronology of tragic events in our turbulent history.

Apart from the symbolic significance and the natural human need to commemorate and to feel ennobling reverence we should particularly emphasize the **consequences of Trianon**. It is now commonly recognized that the bad imperialistic peace agreements which smothered the conflagration of the First World War bore the seeds of potential danger and partly led to the Second World War. Similar implications, though different in form and degree, are still relevant today. Events since 1989 would seem to prove that post-war peace agreements of the sort referred to above have offered no permanent and stable solution (in our region at least) for relations between neighbouring peoples and nationalities. **Security** and **stability** are also under threat in this area of Europe, to mention just for a change some other place than the war zones of southern and Eastern Europe. Trianon remains unchangeably topical.

Bishop László Tőkés

The detrimental effects of Trianon are still being felt in the Carpathian Basin today. The repercussions are felt especially by the Hungarians who have been artificially separated from each other and by Hungarian national communities that have fallen prey to strange nationalistic oppressors. For Hungarian minorities in Rumania, Slovakia and Serbia the effects of Trianon are accumulating like some kind of a haunting and unfinished past and assimilation, expulsion, decrease in population, loss of territory, constant repression and destruction are becoming the order of the day. Hence the reason that we have to keep on talking about Trianon until the catastrophic consequences of it for our people and our region finally come to an end. Other than adopting an unrealistic revisionistic political approach, the only way that we can at present see of **escaping** from the structural crisis situation created by the unjust and for the Hungarian nation, disastrous Trianon Peace Treaty, is by offering **autonomy** to the Hungarian national communities. To be more exact, we have in mind a **system** of different **autonomous forms** which will guarantee the Hungarians living in the amputated areas in diaspora, or together in large numbers or even, in some places, as absolute majorities that they will be able to preserve their identity and survive the dominance of the nationalistic systems of the majority groups that are forcing them to assimilate and waste away.

In the last 75 years our expansionistic oppressors have not allowed us to 'forget' Trianon. We hope - and to that end we fight a peaceful struggle - that instead of receiving peace edicts that lead to war we will at last be able to arrive at lawful, democratic and just solutions that are based on consensus and will bring true peace and safety to our whole region within the 'broad' perimeters of a united Europe that has been hoped for so long.

                       24th August 1995
                       Bishop László Tőkés
                       Honorary Chairman of the RMDSZ

Introduction

The fall of the Berlin wall brought Central Europe back to life politically, economically and culturally. The collapse of communism contributed to the disintegration of the Cold War geopolitical power constellation established after the Yalta Peace Treaty (1945). However, the toppling Berlin wall also dragged the Trianon system with it in its fall. The Treaty of Trianon (1920) - the Versailles Treaty of the East - that has determined the structure of the power constellations in Eastern Europe for the last 75 years is now on the verge of falling apart. It is not only the Soviet-Russian imperium that has collapsed but also the artificial national dictatorships of former states such as Czechoslovakia and Yugoslavia that have now disintegrated. The state, national, cultural and geographical patterns that characterized Central Europe before the First World War are re-emerging as the force and dynamism of the Wilsonian right to self-determination and autonomy for national communities asserts itself.

The consequences of the Treaty of Trianon imposed on Central Europe by Western powers, notably France and Great Britain, were first felt in Hungary, the country on the continent of Europe with the oldest constitutional monarchy. In 1920, Hungary lost two-thirds of its territory and millions of its people suddenly became second class citizens in successor states such as Czechoslovakia, Yugoslavia, Rumania and Austria. Today members of the Hungarian communities in these states are still confronted by a ruthless kind of uncompromising psychological and physical terror which in past decades has taken on the form of genocide in the sense of the United Nations Convention on the Prevention and Punishment of the Crime of Genocide dated 9 December 1948. According to Article II of this Convention, genocide means any of the following acts committed with intent to destroy, in whole or in part, a national, ethnical, racial or religious group as such:
a. Killing members of the group;

b. Causing serious bodily or mental harm to members of the group;
c. Deliberately inflicting on the group conditions of life calculated to bring about its physical destruction in whole or in part;
d. Imposing measures intended to prevent births within the group;
e. Forcibly transferring children of the group to another group.

Although the situation of the Hungarian communities in Central Europe conforms with this definition of genocide which is predominantly qualitative and not quantitative I will avoid using this term throughout the text because it arouses too much emotion. Instead I will employ ethnocide or cultural genocide. Such political treatment of Hungarians was and still is accepted by the West, probably because in terms of Western power politics Hungary has a marginal role. Trianon successfully disrupted the relatively good relations that had up until then existed between the various nations and ethnical groups of people living in the Carpathian Basin, the former Hungarian part of Central Europe. For Hungarians, Trianon was traumatic because it led to humiliation and to the 'fragmentation' of their country. For other peoples, Trianon constitutes a psychosis because they very well know that it is because of Trianon and the later 'peace' conventions that they have been so richly rewarded at Hungary's expense. People in Hungary's neighbouring countries are plagued by the fear that one day the Hungarians will band together and claim the right to self-determination that has been withheld from them for so long because of Trianon.

In this book, it will be argued that on the basis of internationally recognized moral, cultural and political standards it is now high time to innovate change in this intolerable situation. Not only is it necessary to find a satisfactory solution to the Hungary question for all the parties involved but also for Europe as a whole. As long as hotbeds of national and ethnic unrest exist in the heart of Europe, peace and safety for people living on the continent of Europe will be under threat.

Hungarian Revival is constructed like a triptych, the three individual parts of which closely interrelate. The first part introduces **the Hungarians, the second part deals with Trianon and its consequences for Hungarians** and in the third part the way to **the formation of a new Central Europe** is outlined. The three separate but closely related themes together constitute the *Hungarian-complex*. A thorough analysis of the complex of historical, political, cultural, geographical, social and linguistic variables, certain specific factors and manipulation and distortion of the Hungarians will give a deeper insight into the role that has been played by Hungarians in Central Europe in the past and into the part that they might well play in the future. Thoroughly analyzing the Hungarian-complex is like creating a window to a new era that since the fall of an inhuman, anti-liberal power political system - that of communism - is coming towards us with great dynamism and at great speed. In the future, it will no longer be possible to base international politics on purely power political considerations people will also have to take into account humane, moral-cultural, economic and communicational values, as the fall of the wall in Berlin so clearly demonstrated. For Hungarians everywhere mental-moral imperatives and values, cultural and historic ties, tolerance, the drive for freedom, willingness to compromise; the struggle for emancipation, human rights, autonomy and self-determination; opposition to national egoism; mental power, communication and information technology and the global dispersion of Hungarians will be the main aspects and determining factors in the next century. These qualities and values will merge and cristalize in Hungarians enabling them to take on a global 'guiding role'.

In part one, the reader will get to know the Hungarians by becoming acquainted with their history, national and cultural identity, their Western perception and their newly emerging self-image. The analysis will highlight the fact that the West hardly knows and understands Hungary and the Hungarians. The Western image of Hungary derives from a collection of stereotypes and prejudices that are either too positive or too negative. The Western view of Hungarians is a constantly fluctuating one. In that respect, it is a view that falls most readily into the so-called barbarian category, the way in which, since olden times, all cultures which fell outside the Western sphere of influence were collectively viewed. Because of Trianon the Western image of Hungary has been predominantly negative throughout this century. This demonstrates how close the tie is between image-forming and political power. Hungarians are still branded as 'nationalist', 'irredentist', 'revisionist' and 'anti-Semitic' 75 years after Trianon and 50 years after the end of the Second World War. The labels have stuck despite the brave Hungarian uprising of 1956 when, unarmed, the Hungarians fought to liberate themselves from the powerful Soviet Union and its communist ethics, despite the fact that in 1989 the Hungarians took the lead during the political upheavals in East Europe and despite the fact that in neighbouring countries Hungarians helped instigate the fall of national-communist mini-dictators such as Ceausescu, the 'Rumanian genius'. The fall of communism in Central Europe has given Hungarians renewed access to their own national identity, history and culture. The suppression of Hungarian national identity of the last century and a half has led to deliberate falsifying, distorting, twisting and manipulating of views of Hungarian history, society, culture and language. The identities of Hungary's neighbouring peoples have also been subjected to distortion and manipulation which means that they too have mythologized self-images. It is this collection of self-images that has legitimized Trianon and also a dangerous kind of anti-Hungarian expansionism in the Carpathian Basin.

Now, for the first time in a long while, the Hungarians have the opportunity to examine the characteristics of their own national identity and to contribute to breaking down the mythologized self-images of people in their neighbouring countries. These will be the terms for establishing peaceful and lasting relations between the peoples of the Carpathian Basin. The transparency of the Hungarian culture and history provides the basis for a new Hungarian self-image founded on elements which are integral to Hungarian culture, language and history itself. Here the central keynotes are mental-moral imperatives, constitutionalism, tolerance, integration, the drive for freedom and willingness to compromise. What being Hungarian actually involves will spontaneously emerge when this mental-cultural state is recognized.

The second part of the book examines **Trianon and its consequences for the Hungarians**. The background to the First World War will be analyzed. It will be argued that the Allied camp, the Entente, France and Great Britain (and Russia) also contributed considerably to the outbreak of the 'Great' War and to the repercussions this had for Central Europe. Since they were part of the Austro-Hungarian Dual Monarchy the Hungarians stood firmly in the camp of the Central Powers led by Germany. The French view of Europe, which very much mapped out the power balance in Central Europe after the First World War, aimed at completely eliminating Germany's power over Europe. This point of view automatically entailed minimalizing the importance of Hungary, Germany's 'natural' ally. The confederates of the Little Entente: Czechoslovakia, Yugoslavia and Rumania planned to surround Hungary and, by annexing Hungarian areas, trap the Hungarians in a deadly stranglehold grip. In Central Europe, a cluster of nationalistic states was established. They poured all their energy into 'internal' imperialism the main objective being, to rid themselves of their Hungarian 'minorities'. The Second World War brought slight relief for the Hungarians but did nothing to help restore a kind of independence in Central Europe that might benefit the peoples of that area. Likewise, Soviet-Russian occupation did nothing to improve the lot of people in Central Europe. Since Trianon the successor states of Czechoslovakia, Yugoslavia and Rumania and since 1989 the post-communism successor states of Slovakia, Rump Yugoslavia (Serbia), the Ukraine, Rumania and, to a lesser degree, Austria, have tried in all sorts of ways to get rid of their Hungarian 'minorities'. The Hungarians have been exposed to the whole possible repertoire of genocide practices: anti-Hungarian administrative restrictions, actual 'apartheid' legislation, language bills aimed at curbing the use of Hungarian, restrictions on Hungarian education. Furthermore, there have been restrictions for Hungarians employed in public service, agriculture and property restrictions, bans on Hungarian co-operatives, societies and institutions, restrictions for Hungarians wanting to own property. Through deportation Hungarian areas have been territorially restructured, non-Hungarian settlements have been established and there have been centrally stimulated and co-ordinated anti-Hungarian hate campaigns and psychological warfare. Times of war, such as recently in ex-Yugoslavia, and the anti-Hungarian pogrom in Marosvásárhely (Tîrgu Mures) in March 1990, have seen the attempted mass murder of Hungarian people. Even though Hungarian national communities have been at the receiving end of a tremendous amount of anti-Hungarian *ethnic engineering*, 75 years on from Trianon none of the Hungarian communities in any of the various states have been effectively broken down.

In the third part of the book we shall consider the possibilities for restructuring and creating a **new Central Europe**. The territorial and political restructuring of Central Europe began immediately after the collapse of communism. This in turn led to the disintegration of various states, the creation of certain new states and claims lodged by national communities for autonomy and the right to self-determination. Until now Hungarian national communities have been excluded from such developments. Western politics and public opinion sticks rigidly to the Trianon constellation arrangement which compels Hungary to go along with degrading 'compromises' that do not safeguard the rights of Hungarian national communities in surrounding countries. Apart from all the negative Western stereotype notions and ideas used to hide what the situation is really like in the Carpathian Basin there is also a rich assortment of Trianon apologias which effectively mask from view the Hungarian lot. Retaining 'logical' structures is something that plays a signficant part in all this. Asymmetries stating that 'non-Hungarians have rights that are withheld from Hungarians' or misconceptions such as the one that Hungarians form 'minorities' while in the Carpathian Basin they are in the majority. Alternatively, Hungarians are neutralized by being classified as 'extremist' when all they are doing is standing up for their rights in absolute conformity with the norms and regulations of internationally recognized organizations such as the United Nations or the Council of Europe. A cursory glance at any of a number of articles in international papers and journals or statements, declarations and reports drawn up by international negotiators will suffice to convince the reader how deeply rooted the anti-Hungarian apologia is in Western political culture.

So it is that the West, or at least a number of Western states, inadvertently support a dangerous sort of state nationalism in Slovakia, Serbia, Rumania and the Ukraine that is gravitating from the periphery towards the central part of the Carpathian Basin; encroaching at the expense of the Hungarians who live there on their own native soil. Despite all the national disunity and the fact that Hungarians are now being threatened by expansionary state nationalism they have remained the only loyal discussion partner of the international community of free and democratic states in the Central European region. If autonomy is achieved among Hungarian national communities, this will contribute to stability and cohesion in Central Europe and will be a factor stimulating possible political, economic and cultural prosperity in the region. In my opinion, the West can, therefore, no longer afford to remain insensitive to Hungary - a country that in 1996 will be 1100 years old - and to Hungarians and should, therefore, start to support Hungary in accordance with its own Western norms. In this way the West could contribute to the regeneration of the Carpathian Basin and the region would once again be able to function as 'a European hinge': a link between West and East, thus perpetuating a 1000 year old tradition. A strong and clearly defined Central Europe would also be conducive to stimulating reconciliation between the Western and Eastern Christian spheres of influences. Without political and cultural stability in Central Europe the continent will be weakened by internal strife and the cultural-moral allure of the European continent will fade. Subsequently, in the next century Europe will not be able to compete on an even footing with other continents in the global race. A radical revising of Western policies on Central Europe may, therefore, be delayed no longer. For their part, Hungary and the Hungarian people themselves will have to fight for emancipation and decisively turn forty years of communism into something mentally and morally cathartic. In this area change is already clearly evident. The fight for political emancipation, equal human rights and autonomy for Hungarian national communities and the evident mental-moral catharsis among Hungarians is taking on ever more self-conscious forms. It is now only a question of time before the Hungarian question, like other emancipation struggles on the international political agenda, will be rightfully dealt with.

Hungarians call themselves *magyars*. Until 1920 the terms *Hungarian* and *magyar* were separate concepts. All the country's citizens were known as *Hungarians*. That included not only ethnic Hungarians but also Germans, Slovaks, Rumanians, Ruthenians etc. The name *magyar* was reserved for ethnic Hungarians. Today, the *magyars* are mostly concentrated in the central area of the Carpathian Basin. This area forms a continuum composed of the territories of the Hungarian state and the areas of the border regions with Austria (Burgenland), Slovakia, the Ukraine (Subcarpathia), Rumania (West Transylvania), Rump Yugoslavia (North Vojvodina), Croatia (Baranya) and Slovenia (the Mura region). Some 800,000 other Hungarians, known as *székelys* 'Szeklers' live compactly in an area which is historically known as *székelyföld* 'Szeklerland' situated in the heart of Transylvania at the foot of the Carpathians. The Szeklers are ethnic Hungarians. In the Hungarian kingdom of the past they defended the country's southern borders and in exchange received special royal privileges. In the past, the Rumanians manipulated census figures in order to make it look as if there were fewer Hungarians living in Rumania. One of the ways in which they did this was by counting Szeklers as non-Hungarians which is why the term Szekler-Hungarian is still used today. The only real Hungarian minority is that of the *csángós* Csango-(Hungarians). They number approximately 200,000 and live on the other side of the Carpathians, in the Rumanian region of Moldavia near the city of Bákó (Bacau).

In this book, *Carpathian Basin* is used to denote the whole south-east region of Central Europe that is surrounded by the Carpathian Mountains and the Adriatic coastline, roughly speaking the area that was historically Hungarian and which, in 1920, was drastically reduced to its present size. Until 1920 Slovakia did not exist and the area that is now more or less covered by Slovakia, together with the Ukrainian Subcarpathian region was called *Felvidék* 'the Upper Lands' in Hungarian. Since the Second World War and the annexation of *Kárpátalja* 'Subcarpathia', also known in Slavic as Ruthenia or Ukrainian-Carpathia, by the Soviet Union the name *Felvidék* 'the Upper Lands' is reserved for Slovakia. The area *Kárpátalja* 'Subcarpathia', denotes the area that was historically Hungarian and that is now part of the Ukraine. After the First World War, the north-west region of Hungary which was incorporated into Austria came to be known as *Burgenland*. In Hungarian the name *őrvidék* 'Watch Area' has recently been coined for *Burgenland*. Until Trianon the name *Délvidék* 'the Southern Lands' denoted the whole historic area (excluding Croatia) that in 1920 was annexed partly by former Yugoslavia and partly by Rumania, namely: *Mura-vidék* the 'Mura area' in Slovenia, the *Baranya* in Slavonia, *Bácska* in Serbia and the *Bánát in Serbia/Rumania*. Today the name *Mura-vidék* 'Mura Area' is used to indicate the area of Slovenia that was formerly Hungarian and the *Baranya* 'Baranja' is the name given to the area of Hungary that now forms part of Croatia. *Vajdaság* 'Vojvodina' in Lesser Yugoslavia (Serbia) incorporates *Bácska* and the Serbian part of *Bánát*. The other part of *Bánát* is in Rumania. Until Trianon *Erdély* 'Transylvania' was the name of the historic area of 'Siebenbürgen'. This area is smaller than the area that was given to Rumania in 1920. Today, apart from the historic area of Transylvania *Erdély* 'Transylvania' consists of the regions of East Hungary and the so-called *Részek* 'the Parts or the Partium'. On the whole, I have endeavoured to keep as close as possible to the regional names given above though in some places it has been necessary to deviate. As indicated, it would be more correct to call the area annexed by Rumania in 1920, eastern East Hungary and the historic region of *Erdély* 'Transylvania'. In most cases though I have stuck to current usage by calling the whole area 'Transylvania'. Throughout the book place names in Hungarian areas are first given in Hungarian then the local name is given in brackets, for instance: Kassa (Košice), Kolozsvár (Cluj-Napoca). When only one place name is given it is usually the Hungarian variant.

For discussions on the material, facts and observations included in this book I would like to express my grateful thanks to: József Bakonyi (France), József Böröcz (Switzerland), Rezső Gracza (USA), Sándor Győri-Nagy (Hungary), Endre Jónás (Germany), Michiel Klinkhamer (The Netherlands), Bruno Naarden (The Netherlands), Zoltán Palotás (Hungary), Gábor Pap (Hungary), István Sebestyén-Teleki (Switzerland), Zsolt Szabo (the Netherlands) and Szabolcs de Vajay (Switzerland). The work of the Dutch historian Bruno Naarden was important when it came to comparing the Western image of Hungary with the barbarian concept which he elaborated as a paradigm when examining Western perceptions of cultures that fall outside of the Western sphere of influence. The studies of the American-Hungarian historian Stephen Borsódy helped to give clear insight into the history of national and ethnic relations in Central Europe. In view of the fact that this book contains political reflections on the situation in Central Europe and a position is chosen which favours the Hungarians I sincerely hope that I have not in any way misused history. Should this prove to be so then any criticism levelled by historians will be justified. Yves de Daruvar, the French-Hungarian anti-Nazi freedom fighter who served in the French army should be praised for the fact that he so unequivocally criticized the role played by France, the country he so loved, at the time of the outbreak of the First

World War and for the fact that he found France responsible concerning the Hungary question in Central Europe.

I am deeply honoured that Bishop László Tőkés for whom I have enormous respect agreed to write a brief foreword. Through his moral uprightness, his courage and his perseverance in matters of human rights and religious freedom and because of his unshakable faith in God and justice, László Tőkés has become a shining example for Hungarians and others who serve the cause of freedom. The fact that Transylvanian Hungarians have been able to produce someone of the calibre of Tőkés is proof enough that Hungarians have moved into a new era. I am certain that László Tőkés will be given his rightful place in history among others who fought for the emancipation of their people and who are so respected in the West such as: Gandhi, de Dalai Lama and Bishop Tutu.

Last but not least, I would like to express my indebtedness to the Dutch historian Perry Pierik, publisher of this book, who encouraged me to at last put in writing all the loose ends on issues relating to the lot of the Hungarians. I am especially grateful to him for his devotion, supervision and for the high speed at which he has worked. I hope that he will be satisfied with the final result.

Finally, I would like to mention that none of the persons referred to above or the Institute for Russian and Eastern European Studies of the University of Amsterdam may be held in any way responsible for the contents of this book. Only the author of this study is answerable for any mistakes, misapprehensions and blunders and for the possible consequences.

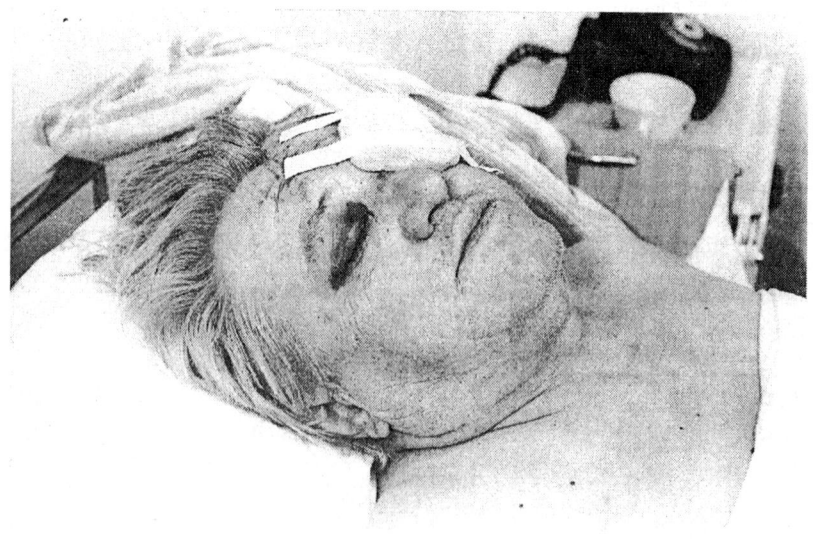

The writer András Sütő wounded and in hospital after having been attacked by Rumanian extremists.

PART I

The Hungarians

'One day my mother said:
"You could write a book about us you know."
"What do you mean?" I replied, my eyes opening wide,
and then, to add a comic twist I asked,
like a shopkeeper:
"What kind of a book would you like: happy or sad?"
"It must be a book that tells the truth," she answered.'

From the autobiographical diary notes of *Anyám Könnyű álmot igér* 'Mother promises me a peaceful night's sleep' (1970) by András Sütő, Hungarian writer living in Transylvania who was badly wounded during the anti-Hungarian pogrom in Marosvásárhely (Tîrgu Mures) 19th March 1990 (see photo).

Western images of the Hungarians

Introduction

The British academic Hugh Seton-Watson argues in his paper *What is Europe, Where is Europe?* that the origins of Europe may best be seen in terms of a dichotomy between the 'civilized world' and the world of the 'barbarians'. According to Seton-Watson this dichotomy is even more fundamental than the dichotomy between Christendom, in the sense of a community of peoples - a geographical area as distinct from a religious faith - and heathenism.[1] The two dichotomies of civilization and barbarism and true faith and infidelity were fused together in the late Roman Empire and in successive empires such as in Charlemagne's Europe. Hence, the image or traditional stereotype of a civilized Europe corresponding geographically to the area covered by the Roman Empire and of everything beyond being regarded as uncivilized or barbaric.

This dichotomy of Seton-Watson's between the civilized and the barbarian has proven to be a useful paradigm when it comes to studying the problems of national stereotypes and the images of exotic peoples and areas located outside of civilized Europe. Those who fit into the 'Western barbarian image', for instance, the peoples of China, Japan or Russia meet the following hypotheses:[2]

(1) the set of stereotypes and images is rather resistant
(2) the variants alternate between being negative and positive
(3) Western political decisions and attitudes determine the choices between these variants

I am convinced that the Western images and stereotypes of the barbarians also provide the insight and theoretical framework required for studying the Western images and national stereotypes of the nations and peoples of Central and Eastern Europe, an area that lies beyond the domain of Seton-Watson's civilized Europe and which corresponds to the region that lies along the Danube, on the other side of the Roman *Limes*. Central and Eastern Europe has been, and still is, very much ignored by the West and so it still remains a *terra incognita*. This view was beautifully illustrated by the late British Prime Minister, Neville Chamberlain, who, when justifying the *appeasement* politics adopted towards Hitler during the conference held in Munich in 1938 on the fate of Czechoslovakia, spoke of countries and peoples "far away" in Central Europe "of whom we know nothing".[3]

In this chapter, I shall be attempting to demonstrate that the Western images and stereotypes of the *Hungarians*, a people who have been and still are the object of much Western stereotyping, also fit the hypotheses of the Western barbarian image. This would support my claim that deeper levels of insight might be reached if Western images and stereotypes concerning Central and Eastern Europe were examined within this framework.

It should be pointed out that Western attitudes towards Central and Eastern Europe can be heterogeneous. The views of individual countries, such as France, Germany, Great Britain and the United States may differ depending on national interests, rightist or leftist political traditions in any one country or, for instance, because of denominational discrepancies. Though I am aware of these differences and will spell them out where necessary I shall generalize by referring throughout to the *West* since this echoes my opinion that there is such a thing as a general Western attitude towards this region.

The line of argumentation will be as follows. First of all, I shall discuss the set of the traditional Western images and stereotypes of the Hungarians. No one has, as yet, attempted to give a full general account of this topic. Only matters relating to specific periods or events in history have so far been examined. In my present study, I shall rely heavily on these various studies. The overview produced will not be exhaustive and the conclusions drawn will be merely tentative. We shall nevertheless see that, down the centuries, the stereotypes and images of the Hungarians adhered to in the West have been fairly persistent and have displayed positive and negative variants. In the second place, I shall demonstrate how the switching between positive and negative values is triggered off by changing political decisions and attitudes in the West. For these purposes we shall focus on the Hungary-image of the Western policy-making elites of before and during the First World War and from the inter-war years. When it comes to the question of the presumed relationship between Western political decisions and stances and the existing national images and stereotypes projected on Central and Eastern Europe, these particular periods in history are very relevant, because Western political and military intervention actually altered the geopolitical power balance in the region. The prevailing images and stereotypes of the Hungarians well illustrate this relationship. The images and stereotypes emerging in the post-1989 era will be discussed only briefly. I shall consider why the Western image of Hungary turned negative in the years following the fall of communism.

Historical Western images and stereotypes of the Hungarians

It would be a very difficult task to give a complete overview of the historical Western images and stereotypes of the Hungarians. In this introductory chapter, the discussion will, therefore, be limited to a few selected cases while keeping in mind that new cases may cause a different interpretation of the same facts. Even in a superficial study into the situation one quickly becomes aware of the existence of two distinguishable sets of Western images and national stereotypes of the Hungarians. There are both negative and positive images and stereotypes. Let us first look at some of the negative ones.[4]

Negative images and stereotypes

Some time before the 9th century, Hungarian tribes invaded Central Europe from the East arriving in a series of waves of migrations. The Swiss-Hungarian historian, Szabolcs de Vajay, has convincingly demonstrated that the final Hungarian conquest of the Carpathian Basin was all part of an ingenious political, diplomatic and military strategic plan extending, in fact, over a much longer period than has previously been thought. Instead of putting the official conquest date at 896 AD, one should realize that it continued from 822 to 1003.[5] The apparently uncoordinated and chaotic Hungarian military manoeuvres of the period, which penetrated deep into Western Europe, served to maintain the *balance of power*, especially within the German Holy Roman Empire that bordered on the Carpathian Basin where the Hungarians had settled.

Only the Holy Roman Emperor had the right to mobilize the empire's army. Both the German tribes which did not form a power basis for the emperor and the Hungarians were afraid that a strong united imperial army might form and turn against them. The doctrine of Hungarian foreign policy was, therefore, to form an alliance with the German tribes to counterbalance the emperor and his power base. The most obvious way of keeping these two factors of power in balance was by using preventive military force. Destructive military actions initiated by the Hungarians were directed at the German tribes and their territories and the aim was to weaken the emperor's power basis. At the same time, the Hungarians left the territories of their allies untouched. It was not, therefore, the same tribes that were constantly falling victim to these devastating attacks. It all depended on whether or not the tribe in question formed part of the emperor's power basis.

In Western historiography these preventive military operations on the western side of the *Limes* which were aimed at controlling the *balance of power* in the German Holy Roman Empire were described as 'plunderings' carried out by 'barbarians'. The alleged affiliation between the Hungarians and other tribes from the East, such as the Scythians, Avars and Huns who attacked the West centuries before the Hungarians arrived verifies in a very direct way the origins of the image of *Hungarians as barbarians*. This view of the Hungarians as a plundering, marauding, barbarian folk has been reiterated in many Western, and even Hungarian, textbooks and encyclopedia. By way of illustration consider the following text entitled 'Hungarian terror' to be found in the *Larousse Encyclopaedia of Ancient and Medieval History*:[6]

"The havoc wrought by the Hungarians can only be compared with that wrought earlier by the Huns. Harvests were burnt, cattle were slaughtered and houses and churches left in cinders. All men were killed, the children mutilated and the women tied to what was left of the cattle, which was then driven off to the raiders' camp. From the year 900 Hungarian raids were pressed to the borders of Italy, then into Saxony and Bavaria. From 912, they advanced farther still to Swabia, Thuringia, Lorraine and even Burgundy. In the end, the greatest attraction was, a country in which petty princelings waged absurd, ferocious internecine wars. The Popes, quickly succeeding one another and often debauched, joined in the conflicts. The body of one was disinterred, tried in public and thrown into the Tiber. Accordingly, the Hungarians had little difficulty in crossing the Alps, and from 921 to 926 they were ravaging North Italy and Tuscany. A few ventured as far as Nimes and even Narbonne. In these regions, their bands were as daring as the corsairs. The latter were unremitting in their activity. From their mountain posts north of St. Tropez, they even arrived on one occasion in mid-winter at St. Gall in Switzerland."

The memories of plundering, barbarian Hungarians who were reputed to eat raw meat and drink the blood of their enemies was even used to explain the etymology of the English and French word *ogre*: 'a monster and man-eater; serving to frighten children in fairy tales'. English and French linguists and historians have explained the etymology of this word by linking it to *Hongre*, the Old French for 'Hungarian'. The Hungarian linguist Eckhardt argues, however, that this etymology is incorrect because in French *Hongre* has never at any stage had the form *Ogre*. According to him *ogre* is more probably a derivative of the Latin *orcus* meaning 'underworld'.[7]

Negative western images and stereotypes of Hungarians also appeared during the Baroque and Enlightenment eras, after the Ottoman Turks had been banished from historic Hungary in 1699. More than 170 years of Turkish occupation and Hungary's functioning as a *cordon sanitaire* for the West against Turkish aggression had turned the Hungarian Kingdom into an utter ruin. One of the consequences of this was that Hungary was unable to keep up with the technological advancements and developments of the citizenry in the West. The negatives images of the Hungarians involve in this period the 'inferior Asian barbarians' and 'a rapacious, wandering horse-riding folk who had no place among the civilized German and Roman peoples of Europe'. 'Hungarian backwardness' is embodied by the Hungarian aristocracy and gentry that is caricatured as being *lusta* 'lazy' and *gőgös* 'arrogant'.

The Habsburg Court in Vienna and the German citizenry in Hungary did much to cultivate these negative images of the Hungarians. The Hungarians were portrayed as an uncivilized people with no proper culture of their own. Their only possible cultural assets derived from the Germans. Political motives lay at the root of these negative Habsburg/German images. After the Turks had been defeated in Central Europe, a power vacuum arose in the region. The Viennese Court saw this as a chance to expand its Habsburg Empire in an easterly direction and, thus, fill the power vacuum created by the Turks. The only force capable of standing between the Habsburgs and their aspirations to seize the Hungarian Crown was the Hungarian aristocracy, the traditional bearers of Hungarian identity. As a result, that caricatures were rapidly produced of the Hungarian aristocracy that were designed to hamper the regeneration and recovery of Hungarian national identity.

Positive images and stereotypes

According to St. Iotsaldus, author of the biography on St. Odilo (996-1049), abbot of the French abbey at Cluny, the two most important European rulers of the eleventh century - apart from Pope Sylvester II and the Holy Roman Emperor Otto III - were

King Stephen I (997-1038) of Hungary and King Sancho of Spain (1005-1035). This prominence had to do with the fact that both these Catholic rulers were instrumental in the 'making' of Europe as they founded, respectively, the Hungarian and Castilian states. St. Odilo was not only the initiator of a spiritual reform movement, but he was also someone who conceived a grand European plan. The abbot of Cluny sought to stabilize Europe and make it safe along the borders of the former Roman Empire, safe against the invasion of nomadic tribes from the east in the Carpathians and, in the Pyrenees, against Arab expansion from the south. In this concept of Europe, Hungary and Castile were crucial to the safety of Christian Europe. Furthermore, these states made it possible for the Catholic Church to expand to these parts of Europe. Both states also supported the spiritual reforms initiated in Cluny and made possible the reopening of important pilgrim routes. In the Hungary of St. Stephen, the existence of the road to Jerusalem was a certainty which was why the head of the Catholic Church, Pope Sylvester II, launched a campaign portraying Hungary as a 'living bastion and shield for Christian Europe'. This positive Western image of Hungary reappears when the Hungarians built a dam to prevent Turkish expansion into Central Europe.

In the Romantic period, an exotic image of 'freedom loving Hungary' emerged in the West that was accompanied by a set type of vocabulary, which included expressions such as: *csikósok* "cowboys", *betyárok* "outlaws", *huszárok* "hussars", *cigányok* "gypsies", *puszta* "puszta", *mulatság* "amusement", *csárda* "tavern in the puszta" and so on. German writers like Lenau and Schiller and composers, like Franz List, played an important part, when it came to transmitting exotic images of Hungary to the West. The romantic image of 'freedom-loving Hungary' had a political counterpart, namely 'liberal Hungary' resisting Viennese absolute centralism. This positive image came as a result of the National Renewal, the so-called Reform Period initiated by Count István Széchenyi (1791-1860). The progression from ignorance to a positive image was indeed striking after such a long period of neglect by the West, which had started with the defeat in the anti-Habsburg War of Independence of 1711 led by Ferenc Rákóczi II (1676-1735) and had continued until the time of National Renewal in 1815.

This positive image of a liberal Hungary was particularly popular among Western liberals who saw the Hungarians as champions of liberalism in Central and Eastern Europe: "In 1848, there was strong popular feeling among us against the Austrian regime, and very lively sympathy for Hungary, and our Foreign Secretary, Lord Palmerstone, fully shared both feelings..."[8] Lajos Kossuth, leader of the 1848/1849 anti-Habsburg Revolution and War of Independence and his close collaborators who went into exile after the Hungarians were defeated at Világos were celebrated as real heroes in the West, particularly in Great Britain and America.[9]

Positive and negative images and stereotypes

During the period of Ottoman occupation, which lasted from the fifteenth to the seventeenth century, Germany was very interested in how the war was going in Hungary, either because they were near to the Hungarian front line, or because they were involved in fighting against the Turks. It is curious to see that - as reflected in the study of Kálmán Benda - different images and stereotypes of the Hungarians were emerging simultaneously in German tracts and pamphlets of the time. One set of German stereotypes depicts Hungary as the 'shield of Christianity' and evokes metaphors from earlier, medieval times. There was deep resentment of the fact that, after the battle of Mohács (1526), Hungary had fallen prey to the pludering and murdering of the Turks. The Hungarians were praised for their *vitézség* "heroism", *bátorság* "bravery", *harciasság* "fighting-spirit" and *lovagiasság* "chivalry". The hero of this camp was the Catholic Count, Nicholas Zrínyi, who led the Christian resistance against the Turks.

The other set of stereotypes depicts the Hungarians as 'traitors, cowards, unreliable and impossible to control' and as people who collaborated closely with the Turkish heathens in order to manifest their hatred of the Germans.[10] This stereotype of Hungary was linked to the Hungarian Protestants of Eastern Hungary and Transylvania who cooperated with the Turks and called for religious tolerance so that Hungarian independence might once again be restored. The Transylvanian princes: János Zapolyai (1487-1540), István Bocskai (1557-1606), Gábor Bethlen (1580-1629) and Imre Thököly (1657-1705) were the ones who chiefly personified this Hungarian national movement and so they were the ones who were demonized.[11]

At the same time, a completely different Hungarian stereotype image was being projected in the Catholic papers and pamphlets being circulated by the German Catholic principalities. The positive and negative values of these images and stereotypes were reversed in the publications and pamphlets being dispersed in the Protestant principalities along the Rhine and in Brandenburg. These principalities were in favour of the Turks and against the Emperor and sympathized with the Hungarian national movement in Eastern Hungary and Transylvania.

To summarize, we may conclude from the examples above that two sets of Western images and stereotypes existed. There was the negative variant that portrayed the Hungarians as *inferior, backward, plundering Asians, as barbarian intruders into Europe* and there was the positive variant portraying the Hungarians as *heroically fighting to protect Christian Europe and defend liberal European values*. The images and stereotpes are rather persistent. Through the ages, the same images, or variations on the theme, recur. The West's image of Hungary, however, is rather unstable swinging as it does between the negative and positive variants. How these values are realized depends very much on the prevailing political decisions and attitudes in the West or on the decisions and views of a particular state or political camp. Thus, if Hungarian action conflicted with Western political interest or, more particularly, with the interests of a given Western state or political camp the negative variant would be triggered off. If, on the other hand, the Hungarians defend the interests of the West, or, more especially, those of a given Western state or political side, then the positive variant will surface. The conclusion, therefore, is that Western Hungarian images and stereotypes conform with the hypotheses of the Western images of the barbarians.

Above I have discussed the matter of the German papers and pamphlets produced during the era of Turkish occupation; a time in which the Western images of the Hungarians were both positive and negative. I will now go on to consider a *turning point* in values and its trigger more closely.

Hungarian images and stereotypes before, during and after the First World War

Before going on to look at the Western images of the Hungarians before, during and after the First World War let us first briefly look at the geopolitical situation in Europe in the second half of the last century and at Hungary's position within the European system of states.

The West, notably Great Britain and the United States, supported the Hungarian, anti-Habsburg Revolution and War of Independence of 1848/1849, even though they were reluctant to show this. According to the British historian, A.C. Macartney, this was because of the traditional British policy aimed at maintaining the balance of power "...that caused Britain also consistently to support the Austro-Hungarian Monarchy, although there was much also in the structure of the Monarchy which British progressives disliked. In 1848, there was strong popular feeling among us against the Austrian regime, and very lively sympathy for Hungary, and our Foreign Secretary, Lord Palmerstone, fully shared both feelings, but while willing, as he said, to do everything possible for the Hungarians, he refused to do anything for Hungary, because he held that Austria in the absence of Hungary would be too weak to fulfill her role of barrier against Russia and factor in the European balance of power, and that Hungary without Austria would be too weak to take her place."[12]

Hungary's isolation in 1848/1849 and the disappointment among Kossuth camp emigrants when the Western powers failed to support the Hungarian cause, prompted Hungary to drop its plans for separation from Austria. Instead, after a period of passive resistance, the Hungarian political leadership decided to push for a compromise with the House of Habsburg. The right moment for this finally arrived in 1867, after Austria had been defeated by Prussia in 1866. Because of the *Ausgleich* between the Emperor, Franz Joseph, and the Hungarian aristocrats, the Empire gained a dual structure. The head of state was Franz Joseph, Emperor of the Austro-Hungarian Dual Monarchy and King of Hungary (K. und k.). The Ministries of Foreign Affairs, Defence and Finance were incorporated, but apart from that Hungary's status remained equal to Austria's. Because of the Ausgleich the Hungarians were at the mercy of Vienna where all the Dual Monarchy's foreign policy was drawn up.

Dualism brought a long period of stability which in turn stimulated economic growth. At the same time, though, it perpetuated the conservative, semifeudal structure of the Austro-Hungarian Empire, such as the lack of universal suffrage in Hungary, that had been criticized by the Hungarian liberals of 1848. Dualism also disrupted equality among the different nationalities domiciled within the Empire. More and more the nationality question was leading to disintigration.

The Hungarians looked to Tsarist Russia with increasing suspicion and fear, for several good reasons. Firstly, because it had been with the help of the Tsarist army that the Hungarian War of Independence of 1849 had been crushed and secondly, because Russia had been the propelling force behind pan-Slavism in the latter half of the 19th century. The Russians turned pan-Slavism into an effective vehicle for gaining more control over the Slavic-speaking groups in the Balkans who had newly awoken to nationalism. The Hungarians were worried that pan-Slavism would stir up the Slavic-speaking nationalities in the south of the country and that Hungary's territorial integrity would subsequently come under threat. In European relations, it was the enlarged Germany of 1871 that was becoming the centre of attention. In the race for European hegemony, Germany soon started to rival the established powers of Great Britain and France. When the *DreiKaiserBund* of 1872 was being set up, Germany had first relied on the support of the two other continental powers of Austria-Hungary and Russia. How, one wonders, did the Hungarians view Bismarck's Germany?

My interpretation of events would counter the claim that in the second half of the last century Hungary willingly complied with Prussian Hohenzollerism and militarism.[13] Hungarian public opinion eyed Bismarck's rise to power in 1862 with concern. Hungary rejected both Prussia's interior politics, because they were considered anti-liberal and its foreign policy, because - Hungary considered Prussia too aggressive. The Hungarian newspapers condemned Prussia's war with Denmark of 1864 which aimed at annexing Schleswig-Holstein. Hungary supported Austria at the time of the Austro-Prussian war of 1866, even though there was friction with Austria. The Hungarians maintained that Prussia's victory would precipitate the ultimate fall of liberalism and constitutionalism in Germany. After the war of 1866, Hungary rejected Bismarck's proposal to reinstate the Hungarian constitution in order to avoid becoming dependent on Germany. It was for similar reasons that Gyula Andrássy, the Hungarian Prime Minister, rejected Bismarck's moves towards Hungary after the *Ausgleich* of 1867. Where the Franco-Prussian war of 1870/1871 was concerned, Hungarian public opinion was the same as that taken towards the Austro-Prussian conflict, that is to say, the stance was anti-Prussian. The liberal statesman, Baron József von Eötvös, noted that in Hungary the fall of Metz was treated like a second Mohács catastrophe. Even the Prime Minister, Kálmán Tisza, probably the most pro-German politician of the day, wrote in the autumn of 1870 that having Bismarckism throughout Europe would not be in Hungary's best interests. To conclude, it might be asserted that the leading Hungarian *Ausgleich*-generation politicians viewed Bismarckism with scepticism, because they saw themselves as liberals, were afraid of Prussian conquests and because they saw the Junker politician as a protégé of Russian Tsarism.

In short, the Western Great Powers of Great Britain and France did not support Hungarian independence in the time leading up to World War I. The Hungarians were too weak to defend themselves against pan-Germanism or pan-Slavism and the dilemma was that they had to choose between these two forces. They opted for the lesser of the two evils which was, in their eyes, Germany but they had no illusions about the future. The mood of the day was best captured in the quip much repeated in Budapest on the eve of the Great War: "If Germany loses, we lose too. If Germany wins though, we're lost."[14]

In the West, the images of Hungary that had been positive until the time of the First World War had turned negative. The image that had once portrayed Hungary as 'liberal and constitutional' had been replaced by images that depicted it as a 'cruel oppressor of Hungary's nationalities' and as 'a threat to peace in Europe' because of the alliance between Austria-Hungary and Germany. It is true that after 1870 dualist Hungary had embarked on an ambitious policy of Magyarization. However, this policy was not of the sort or duration as that often propagated in official, nationalistic historiographies of Czechoslovakia, Yugoslavia and Rumania. After 1871, dualist Austria-Hungary became allied to Imperial Germany. Anti-Hungarian views, however, gave an equally unfounded interpretation of the Hungarian alliance with Germany prior to the First World War. They turned a few decades of Hungarian reliance on German power, all originating from Hungary's vulnerable geopolitical position, into another millennial crime.[15] In view of the centuries of Hungarian rejection of the Habsburg variation of the German *Drang nach Osten* that had gone before, this was, of course, a real falsification of historic fact.[16]

According to the Hungarian historian Géza Jeszenszky, the book *Racial Problems in Hungary (1908)*, by the British historian and propagandist R.W. Seton-Watson, was responsible for the shift in the Western images of Hungary: "This book is practically a history of Hungary with special reference to the development of the nationality problem, and to the Slovaks in particular. For most British observers this book was the decisive argument against the Hungarians, and it was the mortal blow on the traditional British image of Liberal, Constitutional Hungary."[17]

Seton-Watson's book came in sharp reaction to the so-called 'Kossuth-myth' that had been cultivated in the Anglo-Saxon world since the time of the Hungarian anti-Habsburg Revolution and War of Independence of 1848-1849.[18] The leader of the Revolution, Lajos Kossuth, had been given asylum in Great Britain after the Hungarian army had been defeated. His stay in Great Britain did much to promote the stereotype image of Hungarians as champions of liberalism and independence. Kossuth himself was, however, a rather authoritarian personality, intolerant of Hungary's non-Magyar nationalities. Furthermore, Kossuth, the revolutionary, favoured radical political solutions, when it came to questions, such as the matter of total independence from Austria and the House of Habsburg. Because of his attitude he provoked moderate Hungarian politicians like Count Széchenyi. Influenced by the positive image of the Hungarians in this period, R.W. Seton-Watson first took, before his first trip to Austria-Hungary in 1906, a pro-Hungarian stance. As his son, Hugh Seton-Watson noted: "In the Hungarians he saw a nation which had made great sacrifices for the cause of liberty, and also had traditional links with Britain. Hungarian liberalism, the parliamentary style of which seemed to resemble the British, and Hungarian Calvinism, which had much in common with the Presbyterian culture of his native Scotland, attracted him."[19] When, during his travels,

Seton-Watson discovered that Hungary's political system was not as liberal as he had first thought it to be, his sympathy turned to virulent antipathy.

After the publication of *Racial Problems* Seton-Watson started to propagate Hungary's negative images and stereotypes fanatically. For instance, during a visit to Rumania in 1915, he declared in an interview given for the daily newspaper *Adevarul*: "What Prussian militarism is for us, Magyar hegemony is for you: these are the principal obstacles to European progress. We together with our French and Russian allies must fight the German danger; but you with the Serbs must put an end to the brutal and artificial domination of the Magyar race over all its neighbours."[20]

The turning point in the Western images of Hungary, the appearance of *Racial Problems in Hungary* in 1908 was, however, no coincidence. The book's wide reception had to do with the fact that in 1907 Great Britain had signed anti-German pacts with two other rival countries of Germany, namely, Russia and France. Because of this Hungary, in its capacity as a member of the *Central Powers* - the alliance led by Germany -, found itself in the enemy camp. In France, the turning point probably took place earlier than in Great Britain. After 1878, when Austro-Hungary became allied to Imperial Germany, France could no longer, as in previous centuries, rely on the Hungarians to support it in its rivalry against Germany. In earlier centuries, France had supported Hungarian anti-Habsburg/German uprisings in order to weaken the position of the Germans. The French's changing image of Hungary emerges from the following quote taken from a study by the French historian Bertrand Auerbach entitled *Les races et les nationalités en Autriche-Hongrie* that appeared in 1898: "...les Magyars commettent un anachronisme lorsqu'ils tentent de fonder une nation une et vivante sur les cadavres de nationalités..."[21] Political and military strategy was, therefore, what determined the changing image of Hungary in the West.

The negative attitudes of the West towards Hungary were generally shared by the decision-makers on the side of the victorious *Entente Powers*. Such sentiments were, for instance, reflected in the assertions made by Harold Nicolson, at the time a young British diplomat and negotiator who took part in the Paris peace talks: "My feelings towards Hungary were less detached. I confess that I regarded, and still regard, that Turanian tribe with acute distaste. Like their cousins the Turks, they had destroyed much and created nothing. Buda Pest was a false city devoid of any autochthonous reality.[22] For centuries the Magyars had oppressed their subject nationalities. The hour of liberation and of retribution was at hand."[23] Such anti-Hungarian attitudes definitely influenced the outcome of the Treaty of Trianon (1920). They became the prime justification behind the partitioning of historic Hungary.

Count Carlo Sforza, Italian diplomat and Minister of Foreign Affairs in the years 1920-1921, lists in his book *Makers of Modern Europe* a number of typical instances of negative Western images and stereotypes of Hungary. The book paints a portrait of the statesmen and diplomats who played a prominent part in the 'making' of a 'New Europe' after the First World War.[24] The portraits are based on Count Sforza's personal impressions and memories. He also devotes a whole chapter entitled *Tisza, The Magyar* to Count Stephen Tisza, Prime Minister of Hungary between 1910 and 1917. In the summer of 1914 after the heir to the throne, Franz Ferdinand, had been assassinated, Tisza tried to play a moderating role during Austro-Hungarian Crown Council debates and to prevent the outbreak of the First World War.[25]

The adjunct *The Magyar*, which draws attention to his nationality, would suggest that Tisza was not so much viewed as an individual but more as a representative of the whole Hungarian nation. This was underlined by Sforza's remark to the effect that: "Count Stephen Tisza, as I knew him in Hungary and Austria during the years preceding the World War, has always seemed the most typical embodiment of that Hungarian state of mind to me."[26] The title also draws attention to another dreaded enemy of the West, the barbarian king *Attila the Hun*. The linguistic structure of *Tisza the Magyar* corresponds to that of *Attila the Hun*. Here, Sforza is subtle in using language to imply links between the Hungarians and the barbarians.

Sforza's chapter on Tisza draws on almost every negative Hungarian image and stereotype of the period. The image of Hungary as a backward country with a self-centred political élite composed of Hungarian aristocrats who oppressed Hungary's 'commoners': "In the long spirited history, the Magyar aristocracy, and the Magyar gentry as well, never so much as suspected that it was fair, or might be politic, to exercise a little justice toward the subject races of St. Stephen's Crown, or to treat them with some degree of equality. Their Thousand-Year-Old Constitution has always been, is still today, a framework to keep up rights of a feudal country, against the Crown when there is need, against the nameless people always."[27] The image of Hungarians as provincial:"...he [Tisza] made him forget his Calvinism as soon as he found himself among his thoroughbred provincial Magyars. There, he felt his heart beat in unison with theirs; there, he threw off his mask, and the master of Hungary indulged in dancing *csárdás* till dawn, flourishing his handkerchief, doing in fact all those things that the other aristocrats spoke of with fondness to us strangers, but that they no longer knew how to do."[28] The stereotype image of chauvinistic Hungarians oppressing Hungary's non-Magyar nationalities: "Tisza always struck me as being more Hungarian than feudal, and that he so whole-heartedly favored the privilege system which he seemed to personify, because, unimaginative as he was, he never succeeded in seeing any other way of securing the life of his Magyarized Hungary."[29] The image of the Hungarian aristocracy and of the Hungarians as aggressive, hotheaded and inferior people: "Violent as all the other Magyars, and blind as they are to all that runs counter to them..." and "...he could when he thought it necessary, curb the white heat of his Magyars."[30] The stereotype of the Hungarians as unconditional supporters of German imperialism and militarism within

47

Europe: "...admirers of Germany, or better, of what was worst in Germany: Hohenzollerism, oppression of the Poles, the Hungarians were, of all the people, the most naïve and ardent supporters of pan-Germanism."[31] Naturally, Sforza had every good reason for beating on the anti-Hungarian drum after the First World War. In 1916, in the middle of the First World War, the country that Sforza represented had deserted the Central Powers, its allies, as we shall see in part two of this book. In exchange for territorial expansion, Italy had gone over to the side of the Entente which had promised that if they won the war, Italy would be free to annex South Tirol taking it away from Austria.

To summarize then, it may be said that the traditional, negative images and stereotypes of the Hungarians who were depicted as inferior, backward, aggressive Asian oppressors once again surfaced in the years leading up to the First World War and remained in circulation during and after the War. In this period, new variants were added to the existing collection of stigmas. The Hungarians were, for instance, labelled 'chauvinist' and called 'Magyarizers' and 'accomplices of the Germans'. The object of all the stereotyping were the Hungarian aristocracy, the leading political élite of the day, who it was considered, represented the Hungarians as a whole. This resurfacing of negative Western images of Hungary clearly connects with the fact that the Hungarians were in a different political camp from the Western Great Powers. After Great Britain, France and Russia had joined to form an anti-German coalition in 1907, R.W. Seton-Watson and his collaborators launched a campaign to promote anti-Hungarian images and stereotypes in the *Entente* countries.

These Western images and stereotypes were reinforced by the negative self-images of Hungarian progressives and left-wing extremists, such as the poet Endre Ady and his literary circle from the periodical *Nyugat* 'The West' and Oszkár Jászi and his scientific magazine *Huszadik Század* 'The Twentieth Century' which condemned Hungary for its alleged 'eastern backwardness' and aristocratic dominated feudal society.[32]

The emergence of a post-Trianon Hungarian national state did not alter the Western images and stereotypes of Hungary in the inter-war years. It would seem that more objective views, like the personal impressions of major Harry Hill Bandholtz, an American member of the Inter-Allied Military Mission, did nothing to change these ingrained anti-Hungarian views. Bandholtz was in Hungary from 10th August 1919 until 10th February 1920 and so he also witnessed the Rumanian occupation of Budapest. In his *Undiplomatic Diary* that was published in 1933 Bandholtz displayed great respect for the Hungarians: "The Hungarians certainly have many defects, at least, from an American point of view, but they are so far superior to any of their neighbours that it is a crime against civilization to continue with the proposed dismemberment of the country."[33]

In the interwar period, negative Western images and stereotypes were created by the following two factors. First, the West's perception of the Hungarians as an inferior and conservative people living in a political dreamworld remained unchanged. Characteristics of Hungarian political conservatism, such as *díszmagyar,* the gala-dress of the Hungarian aristocracy, the oligarchical oppression of the peasants, the lack of universal suffrage, Hungary's ancient constitution, the respect for the Holy Crown, attachment to the institutions of the Monarchy and legitimism were all regarded as something unique and exotic but also as something that was rather backward. In the second place, the Western Powers looked upon Hungary's struggle for revision of the Treaty of Trianon as disruptive and as a threat to European balance of power and peace. In the West, it was only British conservatives grouped around Lord Rothermere, then, owner of *The Daily Mail,* seriously supported Hungarian revisionism.[34] This fusing of political conservatism and the objectives of the revisionist movement led to the West's portrayal of the Hungarians as 'chauvinists', 'irredentists', 'revisionists' and 'revengists'.[35] In fact, old images survived with a few new variants.

During the Second World War, Hungary was an ally of Nazi Germany though the Hungarians were not willing to follow all the orders issued by the Nazis. After the war, however, the image of the Hungarians who were seen as subscribing to German hegemony again resurfaced in Europe. Hungary was once more branded 'the No. 1 satellite' and hailed 'the most faithful ally' of Nazi Germany, despite the fact that Hungary had refused to offer military and logistic assistance to the Germans in their move to crush Poland in 1939; despite the fact that on 17th August 1943 a secret agreement had been signed between Great Britain and Admiral Horthy's government, in Turkey, stating that Hungary would surrender to the Western Allies the moment they reached the country's frontiers; despite the fact that Hungary itself was occupied by Hitler's troops on 19th March 1944; despite all the assistance extended throughout the war to Allied (notably Polish and French) prisoners of war escaped from German POW camps; despite the open collaboration continuing between Hungary's Slovak, Rumanian and Croatian neighbours with Germany and finally, despite the suicide of the Prime Minister Count Pál Teleki in protest against the violation of Hungarian sovereignity.[36]

The book written by John Flourney Montgomery, United States ambassador to Budapest between 1933 and 1941, entitled *Hungary, the Unwilling Satellite* did nothing to really alter the image of Hungary as Nazi Germany's 'most faithful ally'.[37] In his book, which is based on personal impressions and experiences, Montgomery outlines the vulnerability of Hungary's geopolitical position before the Second World War. According to Montgomery, Hitler was livid with the Hungarians, because during the war they made absolutely no effort to help in the extermination of the Jews. As long as the Hungarians were in control of their own destiny, that is to say, until the Nazis had occupied the country in March 1944, they had been able to stave off the extermination of the Hungarian Jews.[38]

Raul Hilberg, author of the authoritative work on the Holocaust, *The Destruction of the European Jews* remarked that: "By 1944 only one important area was still intact. That area was Hungary, and 750,000 Jews survived within its borders. When the Hungarian Jews looked at a map of Axis Europe at the beginning of 1944, they could see that all around them Jewish communities had been attacked and destroyed" and "In March 1944 ... the Germans overran the the country and catastrophe overtook the Jews."[39]

Throughout the German occupation, Admiral Horthy remained Regent of Hungary, he accepted the ignominy of it all and did his best to save what could be saved. On 26th June 1944, Horthy issued a decree ordering that a stop should be put to the deportation of Jews from Budapest which was where most of the Hungarian Jews lived. The deporting of Jews had begun after the Nazis had seized power in Hungary installing a puppet regime composed of Hungarian fascists recruited from the Arrow Cross movement.[40] The national gendarmerie leaders, who were in collaboration with the Germans decided to ignore Horthy's decree and wanted to continue with the deportations. On 6th July 1944, Horthy issued a second decree ordering the Hungarian army, which included a tank division, to prevent the gendarmerie from allowing Budapest's remaining 200,000 Jews to be deported. The gendarmerie forces withdrew from the city, thus, evading armed conflict with the army and the deportation of the Jews was halted.[41]

During the time of the Soviet-Russian occupation of Hungary, the positive Western images of Hungary once again came to the fore. The Hungarian uprising of 1956 reinforced the image which saw Hungarians as brave, heroic defenders of European values and liberties, holding out against oppressive barbarism from the East. The Hungarian ability to survive even in adversity was what prompted the West to describe the Hungarians of the last years of the Kádár regime as constituting 'the jolliest barrack of the socialist camp'. Even these positive Western images of the Hungarians were sometimes still accompanied by the old negative Western images which persisted in labelling the

Hungarians as 'chauvinists' and 'irredentists'. Take, for example, the curious opinions of the influential American Senator, Daniel Patrick Moynihan, claiming that "in 1956 Cardinal József Mindszenty sought sanctuary in the American Embassy in Budapest, where he remained for fifteen years. He is remembered there as much for his bitterness toward Woodrow Wilson and for the Versailles Peace Treaty as for his anti-communism" and that "Hungarian public opinion was openly irredentist during the latter years of Marxist rule."[42]
The Hungarian stereotype dwells on conservative, undemocratic traditions, nationalism and anti-Semitism, the Hungarian national character of melancholia, Hungarians as a source of trouble in Central Europe and the Hungarians as being Germanophiles. The Westerners in influential positions who support the Hungarian cause are few and far between. Intensive contacts between Hungary and the West including, for instance, the massive training of Hungarian students at Protestant universities in Switzerland, Germany and the Netherlands between the 16th and 18th centuries, the political exiles of 1848/49 and 1956 who fled to the West and the personal reports of Western 'eye-witnesses' such as Harry Hill Bandholtz or John Flournoy Montgomery do not seem to have a corrective effect.

In recent years, since communism collapsed in 1989, the Western image of Hungary has again turned negative. Much of this is linked to the reviving of national traditions and identity which were suppressed in the communist period. Western politicians and decision-makers suspect and fear that such revivals will lead to revisionism and that Hungary will start to support Germany's increasing power in Europe. Various utterances made by Hungarian politicians, such as the one made by the late Prime Minister József Antall to the effect that he felt, in spirit, like the Prime Minister of fifteen million Hungarians and national events, like the reburial of Admiral Horthy, clearly stir up Western suspicion toward Hungary. This, in turn, triggers off the negative set of Western images and stereotypes of the Hungarians.

The Hungarian self-image

In the twentieth century, two major historic events have shaped the destiny of the Hungarian people. The first of these events was the signing of the Trianon Peace Treaty after World War I, in 1920, and the second was the fact of Soviet-Russian occupation of the country in the period after the Second World War. The Treaty of Trianon, which will be examined in detail in the second part of this book, destroyed the one thousand year old Hungarian state and divided the Hungarian nation into five parts which, in the second half of the last century had prospered under Austrian-Hungarian dualism. After Trianon, the Hungarians remained citizens, on their own native soil in the Carpathian Basin, of what was left of truncated Hungary but were also taken over by the successor states of Austria, Czechoslovakia, Rumania and Yugoslavia. The scattered 'limbs' of the Hungarian nation were forced to adhere to particularist systems, a situation which only eased up temporarily when before and during the Second World War the Hungarians were successfully reunited for a short while. For very many Hungarians their right to self-determination has been seriously restricted since 1920 with no guarantees that their basic human rights will be respected and they have been treated as 'minorities'. In the Carpathian Basin, on what is their own native soil, the Hungarians are in the majority.

When the Second World War ended, the Allied Powers handed Hungary over to the expansionist regime of Soviet-Russia. The Hungarians were forced to 'integrate' into the communist power block which by then extended over the whole of Central and Eastern Europe and was controlled by the Soviet Union. The main objective of this power apparatus fuelled by internationalist communist ideology was to obliterate Hungarian national identity and culture. A tyranny of oppression bore down on the civilian sector of Hungarian society, a society that had blossomed during the inter-war years and had come to radiate a degree of national consciousness. In 1956, when the Stalinist reign of terror led in Hungary by Mátyás Rákosi alias 'the bloodhound', a man everyone loathed, became unbearable the Hungarians finally revolted against the oppressor. After the uprising had been quashed, several hundred thousand Hungarians left their homeland and settled around the world thus giving rise to a huge Hungarian diaspora. It was only with Soviet-Russian backing that the communist nomenklatura was able to remain in power. In Hungary, the communist system gave rise to an 'atomistic' society which, power-politically, was an 'exact' replica of a feudal system. The Hungarian aristocrats who had previously ruled over and exploited the terrorized masses were replaced by the communist nomenklatura, led by party leader János Kádár and his adherents, the man who had been a traitor at the time of the Hungarian uprising.

Hungarians living across the border in the Upper Lands (Czechoslovakia), in Subcarpathia (the Soviet Union), Transylvania (Rumania), the Southern Lands (Yugoslavia) and in the Burgenland (Austria) were exposed to an even worse ordeal after the Second World War. In the successor states Hungarians were subjected to aggressive nationalistic anti-Hungarian oppression characterized by ruthless homogenizing and violent assimilation procedures. The Hungarian regions that had been divided up among the successor states after the First World War were to be permanently annexed. The objective underlying this assimilation policy was nothing less than to completely eliminate Hungarian communities in the various countries. Aided by the triumphant superpowers and under the blanket of international communism the Hungarian-haters were given the chance to realize their plans. It is indeed ironic that when the wall fell in Berlin and the iron curtain was abolished this enmity did not end. This is a point that will be returned to and expanded on in the next part of this book.

After the communist world had 'collapsed', the Hungarians in the Carpathian Basin found themselves marginalized on all fronts. The Hungarian 'élite', the people who had established the communist system of Kádár, the nomenklatura, had exchanged one-sided orientation to the East for one-sided orientation to the West. In the post 1989 period, internationalist communist ideology was mechanically replaced by an internationalist global view. These orientational and ideological changes did nothing to alter the existing internal power-political and micro-economic structures which most closely resemble feudal systems:

- citizens can bring little influence to bear on the exercise of power;
- the legal system does not work. For many citizens who might want to avail themselves of the system the financial threshold is too high. A sum of at least 5000 Hungarian forints is required to take a case to court, an amount which most citizens cannot afford. (In 1995, the average monthly wage was 15,000 Hungarian forints);
- several times people have failed to organize a referendum for which 100,000 signatures had already been collected as the constitution requires. For instance, the Horn administration composed of ex-communists and leftist liberals managed to block a referendum on the cancelled EXPO, the world exhibition planned for 1996;
- the media have become an elusive network partly backed by communist concerns, such as oil companies;
- the marginalization of the Hungarian people is bad for the general atmosphere in the country and partly accounts for the high number of suicides and cases of alcoholism;
- the Hungarians have hardly any economic assets to manage. Little of the property confiscated by the communists has so far been reprivatized so that owners have been unable to reclaim their rightful property;
- there is no strong independent trade union. The federal trade union is a wing of the Hungarian Socialist Party (MSZP), the party that succeeded the old communist party and is currently in power;
- the civic society is very much on the periphery;
- all major political decisions are made behind the scenes. It is often a politics of fait accompli that is employed;

- those who represent the interests of Hungarians on the other side of the border have little power to really influence any negotiations between Hungary and neighbouring states on Hungarian rights.
In the successor states, surreptitious anti-Hungarian regimes have been replaced by overtly anti-Hungarian regimes. These regimes are not afraid to mobilize voters with anti-Hungarian programmes. Furthermore, they are not afraid to follow up these programmes as was made only too clear when, in March 1990, an anti-Hungarian pogrom was organized in Marosvásárhely (Tîrgu Mures) that will be discusssed in more detail in part two.[43]

Until now the Hungarians have been unable to find a way to escape from their awful plight. Present Hungarian thinking goes little further than to promote the slogan 'return to Europe' which has no meaning. They hope that in 'fleeing' to Europe all the national problems caused by Trianon and the political-economic problems arising from communist mismanagement will somehow be miraculously resolved. Hungarian politicians have not yet grown weary of singing the praises of 'good' neighbourliness but, for their part, the surrounding countries are busy developing themselves at the expense of the Hungarians with tough expansionist politics that gravitate to the core of the Carpathian Basin.

When it comes to pushing back the Hungarians on all sides - even in Hungary itself - the whole gamut of indirect strategies is employed. Slovakia, for example, is making very effective use of ecological weapons that are being used to surround Hungary in this constant anti-Hungarian struggle. Constructing a new hydro-electric power station on the Danube at Bős (Gabčikovo) and re-directing the flow of the Danube in Slovakia's favour have provided the Slovaks with new sanctions to wield against the Hungarians. For their part, Hungary has taken no steps to prevent such destructive activities continuing on the native soil of the Hungarians in southern Slovakia, in the region known as Csallóköz (Žitny Ostrov), which means that Hungarian farmers in the area are now having water supply problems nor has Hungary protested at the changing of the Slovak-Hungarian border in favour of Slovakia. Such negligence will have great repercussions when Western Hungary's fresh water supplies are inevitably endangered. Meanwhile the campaign to encircle and isolate Hungary with the help of ecological weapons continues. The Slovaks have announced plans to construct a nuclear reactor on the Danube of a similar type to the one that melted down at Tsjernobyl. It is to be constructed at the border town of Mohi (Mochovce) which lies some 140 kilometres to the north of Budapest. If necessary they will use Russian funds to help finance the project. The Hungarians can, therefore, look forward to much radioactive wind blowing in their direction.

For 50 years now, the communist regime has been systematically trying to eradicate all traces of Hungarian national culture and identity. This destructiveness was most blatantly demonstrated when, in the fifties, the Hungarian security police, the AVH, used unbridled physical violence against its own civilian population. Many people were killed in the process or were interned in labor camps such as the one at Recsk because it was suspected that they harboured sympathies for Tito or the West, because it was thought they upheld Christian or democratic ideals or simply because they were Hungarians. Apart from the physical terror that did lessen somewhat during the last phases of communism there has always been the presence of a kind of psychological terror. This latter kind of terrorizing consisted mainly of propagandizing negative stereotypes and images of the kind described in the previous chapter.

In the media and in academic circles in communist Hungary the Hungarian people were portrayed as being inferior and aggressive. It was claimed that they had played a negative part in history which in turn had led to collective fascism, the Hungarian variant of this being known as 'Horthy fascism'. In fact, this was a term first coined by the propaganda mongers of the Rumanian dictator Ceausescu. (See the the study of the

Transylvanian Hungarian historian Lajos Demény below). Hungarian communists were later only too glad to adopt the slogan. Apart from seeking to really mutilate the Hungarian's image of themselves, the communists endeavoured to create a perpetually bad atmosphere in the country and amongst the Hungarians domiciled in the Capathian Basin hoping in this way to successfully repress them. The Hungarians were portrayed as 'all-time losers', as people who had always managed to be on the wrong side. They were said to be a pessimistic people prone to committing suicide, having abortions and abusing alcohol and they were sketched as lacking concrete ideas and ambitions for the future. The statistics published at regular intervals, whether they were right or wrong, were all aimed at reinforcing this negative image. Using tactics that Goebbels had once used, these 'facts' were reiterated until the Hungarians eventually started to believe in their inferiority. So it was that Hungarian culture became steeped in pessimism and misery. Pride of place was given to those who projected sentiments of desolation and isolation in word and or in writing and losers were given similar prominence. Hungary is full of statues to fallen revolutionaries such as Kossuth. In spite of a goulash-communist reputation for having been the 'jolliest barracks' to have conquered the world outsiders do not see Hungary as fun-loving but rather as a fairly introverted and socially pretty unstable country. These anti-Hungary stigmas and stereotypes stuck and today they still dominate the Hungarian self-image.

The Hungarians are not yet ready to forcefully regenerate a positive self-image born of self-knowledge and self-respect that draws inspiration from the Hungarian culture itself. This is something that is not yet possible and the reason why this is so will be examined in the next chapter. Even in this post 1989 era it is still taboo to carry out research into Hungarian national identity and culture. Such research activities are viewed as dangerous. Research institutes and individual researchers who tread this ground risk being shadowed by the intelligence services. The communist clique that weathered the political upheavals almost unscathed has no use for a revival of Hungarian culture and identity. The communists know though that in a country that is so nationally self-conscious they do not have a future. However, as I shall argue in the next chapter, Europe does have a vested interest in such developments, hence the reason why Europe must not resign itself to accepting the fact that Hungarian national culture and identity is persecuted.

Once again, just as in the communist period, the interests of Budapest go hand in hand with those of the extreme nationalist hardliners of Hungary's neighbouring states. According to this view reviving Hungarian identity and culture will bring problems with it. Such developments could lead to demands for Hungarian territorial revisions and affect the power and positions of ex-communist leaders in Budapest which is why everything and anything pertaining to Hungarian culture and identity is contested. Below I shall explain how it is that in Hungary no one is free to carry out research into characteristics of national identity such as into the number of people belonging to, the language, the history and the social structure of the country's ruling élite.

Before going on to systematically discussing these characteristics, first a few general remarks about national identity. What in fact is national identity? According to Anthony D. Smith national identity consists of the following components: (1) a common historic background, (2) shared myths and historic memories, (3) a common mass-culture such as, for instance, a common language, (4) a shared judicial system and (5) a common economic framework.[44]

National identity may further be linked to other types of identity such as class, religious and ethnic identity. Hence, the reason that national identity is essentially a multidimensional concept. In the past, Magyar (Hungarian) identity was preserved by the aristocracy which incidentally did not only consist exclusively of ethnic Magyars. National identity is not always by definition synonymous with the state or with the power-political framework as in most West European states where political and cultural community is one and the same. It may not be said to apply to the Basques for example. In political terms the Spanish and French Basques are correspondingly Spanish and French citizens inhabiting the territorial areas of different states but they are identified as Basques.

There is no congruence between the Hungarian state and Hungarian national identity. Hungarian national identity deviates in time and space from the Hungarian state. There were Hungarians before there was a Hungarian state. Before the Conquest of the Carpathian Basin - officially in 896 AD - and before the Hungarian state was founded, there was already such a thing as Hungarian identity. Hungarian national identity is, furthermore, not restricted to the territory of the present Hungarian state. Since the Treaty of Trianon, substantial numbers of Hungarians, those who inhabit the Carpathian Basin, actually live outside Hungary. At present, many Hungarians who still live in the places where they were born are now dispersed across seven different states (Austria, Slovakia, the Ukraine, Rumania, Lesser Yugoslavia (Serbia), Croatia and Slovenia). The Hungarian-American historian Stephen Borsody aptly called it 'a divided nation'.[45] Finally, because of the major political upheavals of this century diaspora of Hungarians have been scattered all over the world. Hungarian societies from some fifty different countries around the world belong to and constitute the World Federation of Hungarians. Together Hungarians may be said to inhabit a *global village*. In part three of this book, I shall enumerate the opportunities of such a *global village*.

During the years of communist rule, every effort was made to divest Hungarian identity and culture of all substance. Under communism, Hungarian identity was seen as mere folklore. At that time, two ideological concepts were fervently pursued: socialist internationalism and lesser Hungarian particularism which aimed at confining Hungarian identity to the bounds of the territorial area that constitutes the present Hungarian state. These ideologies became so deep-rooted that, even since the 'velvet revolution' of 1989, *Hungarian citizens* living outside of Hungary have not been given the right to vote. A Hungarian state that has a national policy should surely offer ethnic Hungarians anywhere in the world citizenship as soon as possible.

It was because of the communist regime that the institutions of lesser Hungarian particularism were able to gain a firm hold and since the 1989 changes it has proved difficult to eradicate these ideologies. The democratically elected Antall administration, much criticized for its 'nationalistic' policies, has not succeeded in setting up scientific research institutes able to continue serious research into the characteristics of national identity and culture. A shroud of obscurity and secrecy surrounds the whole question of national identity and culture. Research into the characteristics of national identity may only be carried out in a monolithic context, if at all. This would indicate that Hungarian society is not very democratic and is still very much dominated by a totalitarian political culture. Prohibiting research into the characteristics of national identity and culture will create serious integrational complications. Only nations that are strongly rooted in their own traditions and culture will be able to put up some resistance to the explosive uncontrolled growth of global culture. If European integration comes about for countries not firmly rooted in traditions and cultures of their own, the people of those nations will start leaving their homelands en masse thus saddling Europe with a migration problem of unprecedented magnitude. Such nations will be incapable of pushing through reforms in their own respective countries because they will lack the basis and the flexibility required to do this. Finally, one has to ask whether countries with a big deficit in the area of national identity will be able to count as being thoroughly European if one thinks of Europe in terms of being a set of different national identities. How can nations be expected to fight for a place within Europe if, in the area of national identity, they are lagging far behind?

How many Hungarians live in the Carpathian Basin?

On the matter of Hungarian self-knowledge an important question to be asked is: "How many Hungarians live in the Carpathian Basin?" Because of the lesser Hungarian ideology people were not and still are not allowed to carry out proper research in this area. The successor states are keen to statistically reduce their numbers of Hungarians. For Rumania, for instance, there was the uncomfortable fact that in 1920 the Rumanian majority in Transylvania was 53.8% while in the Carpathian Basin (Croatia excluded) the Hungarian population formed a majority of 54.5%. Since the time of Trianon, all the successor states have perpetually worked hard at falsifying their demographic statistics. In Hungary, this has happened since the time of the Second World War.

The periodical published by the Hungarian Statistics Office carried an article in its October 1991 issue that was entitled *Development of the population and the composition of native speakers in Transylvania*.[46] In his article: *The Rumanian Hungarians and the false data from the Statistics Office* Endre Jónás, a Hungarian-German statistician, sharply criticized this official body's methods and results.[47] According to Jónás, the two obvious objectives of the Statistics Office were, to artificially reduce the numbers of Hungarians and to likewise artificially inflate the numbers of Rumanians.

The Statistics Office claims that the natural increase in Transylvanian Hungarians between 1910 and 1956 was 1.023% and it estimates that there are at present some 2 million Hungarians living in the area. Jónás maintains that these statistics are unreliable for the following reasons. The Transylvania Hungarians, notably those living in the districts of Szabolcs, Szatmár, Bihar and Szeklerland are traditionally very fertile. On top of this the Hungarians have a higher natural fertility level than Transylvanian Rumanians and finally the Hungarians living in Transylvania have greater longevity than their Transylvanian Rumanian counterparts. On the basis of these data - we shall not go into the minute details - Jónás arrives at the conclusion that there are in fact 2,798,000 Rumanian Hungarians, 2,414,000 of whom live in Transylvania. There is, thus, a 28.5% discrepancy between Jónás' results and the figures issued by the Statistical Office.

There are three ways to artificially inflate the numbers of Rumanians and decrease the numbers of Hungarians. First of all, by falsifying the size of the gypsy population, the numbers of Csango-Hungarians (Hungarians living in Moldavia) and the total number of Jews or Yiddish native speakers. The Statistics Office obtains these figures from official Rumanian sources. Secondly, Jónás arrives at a total of 860,000 people who do not fall into the category of being Rumanian, gypsy, Hungarian or German. According to official figures these ethnic groups amount to a total of 650,000 people. There is a 26% discrepancy between the two estimates. In the third place, Jónás claims that there are 2.3 million gypsies in Rumania. The Statistics Office had simply counted these gypsies as ordinary Rumanians.

According to Jónás these official sources allow 763,000 Hungarians, 2,300,000 gypsies and 210,000 other non-ethnic Rumanians to simply disappear while at the same time the total number of Rumanians is increased to 3,273,000. Jónás concludes that since Trianon 25.8% of the Rumanian population constitutes a repressed minority which makes Rumania the last colonial imperium of Europe.

Let us now take a closer look at the way in which official Hungarian government bodies make use of statistical data relating to the number of Hungarians living in the Carpathian Basin. Two main studies have been carried out in this area, one of which was carried out by the geographical-cartographer Károly Kocsis and his assistant, Eszter Hodosi and is entitled *Hungarians on the other Side of our Border*.[48] The other study that was carried out by the historian Ferenc Glatz and his work group and is entitled *Minorities in East-Central Europe;*

Historical Analysis and a Policy Proposal. Both studies make use of the same more or less superficial data as that used by the Statistics Office. Kocsis estimates that there are approximately two million Hungarians domiciled in Transylvania and Glatz puts this figure at 2.1 million. Neither Kocsis nor Glatz explains how he arrives at his particular total and no effort is made to explore ways of arriving at other conclusions. Both of the books emanating from these two research projects are beautifully illustrated with good quality maps onto which the dubious data pertaining to the numbers of Hungarians dispersed throughout the Carpathian Basin are projected. One cannot help wondering why Hungarian scientists who have the most modern of research techniques at their disposal produce maps that are based on 'official' but manipulated statistics. In this way, such researchers impede the Hungarian self-knowledge while deliberately or unintentionally contributing to the amount of negative visual propaganda already being produced by the Serbs, Rumanians and Slovaks.

The Hungarian language and myths of ethno-genesis

Knowing and using a common language is one of the characteristics of national identity, but language alone is not enough to enable a country to call itself a nation. The Dutch and the Flemish share a common language, Netherlands, but they do not see themselves as people who belong to one and the same nation. The French, German and Italian Swiss speak different languages but they do see themselves as belonging to the same nation. So, if all these speakers of different languages are of the Swiss nation this would refute the paradigm of the German philosopher Herder, that 'nationality lives in language'. The theory clearly does not always apply. Though language is a feature of national identity it is not always a necessary prerequisite for the formation of a nation.

Whether or not they do form a nation, people who share a common language may always work together in an institutional framework in order to promote uniformity in matters of spelling, grammar and lexicon. This was precisely what Dutch and Flemish people had in mind when they set up the Netherlands Language Union. The Netherlands Language Union is an organization that is supported by the Mininstries of Culture in both countries. The relevant working parties do not consist only of government representatives but also of linguists, authorities on literary matters and people from the social sector.

Indeed, a Hungarian Language Union organized along the lines of the Netherlands Language Union referred to above should be founded as soon as possible. The fact that this has not yet happened indicates that authorities in Budapest feel no need to strengthen the status of Hungarian in the Carpathian Basin. Naturally, the Hungarians living in the Carpathian Basin have every right to be given the opportunity to enter into institutional debate on their own native language. Hungarian is not the exclusive prerogative of Hungarians living in Hungary. Once established there are many fascinating issues that such a Language Union could examine.

To start off with, such a proposed Language Union could try to establish why the Hungarian language spoken in the Carpathian Basin is so homogeneous. There are few dialectical differences in Hungarian. The institute could also examine the nature and effects of linguistic contacts between speakers of Hungarian and of the other languages spoken in the Carpathian Basin. For instance, Transylvanian linguists have observed that the long vowels of Transylvanian Hungarian are shorter than those of Hungarian spoken elsewhere which is a direct consequence of the influence of Rumanian. This is an important observation because vowel length in Hungarian determines word meaning. Hence, the shortening of vowels may cause difficulties in Hungarian communication. The Hungarian Language Union would have to consider how to counterbalance for this in the spelling system. The Language Union could decide to resolve the problem by having the longer vowel sounds represented by two letters instead of by a single letter with an accent as is the practice now.

A major shortcoming of the Hungarian constitution is that it does not actually stipulate what the country's official language is. The constitutions of most other European countries do make this explicit. According to authorities in the field this stems from Saint Stephen's principle that "having only one language makes a country weak and vulnerable." Saint Stephen's multi-lingual philosophy might sound good, but one should not forget that though his concept proved sound for a thousand years it was later to be disproved by Herder's theory and the French Revolution and by the homogeneous language nation envisaged by Trianon. The first edict of the French Revolution did not relate to 'freedom, equality and fraternity', but rather was a decree stating that the French language should be compulsorily spoken throughout the state. Unfortunately, in the modern age, it has proved impossible to run a country along the ideal lines once proposed by Saint Stephen. A tough language war is continually being waged around the European Union's round tables. It is a conflict that not only has to do with preserving national identity but which also has practical implications. For instance, in how many and which languages must manufacturers provide instructions for the consumer? Hungary's shortcomings in this area derive from the fact that its awareness of national identity is virtually non-existent.

In Hungary, the origins of the Hungarian language are studied practically only in connection with the Finno-Ugric language relationship hypothesis. The hypothesis that Hungarian - and thus according to academics the Hungarians - is related to Finnish, Estonian, Mordvinian and other small Eurasian languages has become a complete dogma. It was a theory first propounded by the German researchers Josef Budenz and Pál Hunfalvy in the mid-nineteenth century while they were doing research at the Hungarian Academy of Sciences within the Indo-Germanic framework. The latter Magyarized his real German name, Hunsdorfer by changing it to Hunfalvy. The two men appeared on the scene after the 1848/1849 Hungarian war of independence had been quelled which had taken place during the so-called Bach-era. It was a time when Hungarians were being made to toe the line by Vienna and were being ruled and germanized with a rod of iron by the Austrian governor Alexander Bach. In desperation Count Széchenyi wrote a letter to the presidency of the Hungarian Academy of Sciences, founded by him, for the purposes of studying Hungarian language and culture. In 1858, Szechényi complained after going into exile because of the defeat of the Hungarian army at Világos, saying:"And will this last real Hungarian institution be divested of its original character? Unfortunately, yes!"[49] Until the time when Budenz and Hunfalvy presented their views no Hungarian linguist or historian had ever disputed the relationship of Hungarian and the Hungarians to Scythian peoples such as the Huns and Avars.

The discovery of these Finno-Ugric linguistic links was used as a psychological blow to the Hungarians whose pride and fighting spirit had always partly derived from the inspiration they had gained from their supposed Scythian origins. Budenz and Hunfalvy were allowed to make use of the facilities at the Hungarian Academy of Sciences in order to create a new Hungarian identity that was to be established through the language. From that time on the Hungarians were to view themselves as Finno-Ugrian and anyone who presented scientific theories to challenge this theory was declared 'unscientific' by these gentlemen and their ilk. Those who even dared to work on a different language relationship theory were instantly hailed *csodabogár* (literally, "miracle flies") 'eccentrics'. The Finno-Ugric language relationship theory and the accompanying presumptions about identity were also embraced by the communist regime for the simple reason that such presumed origins corrupted and neutralized Hungarian identity as a political factor and thus gave political leverage.

The paradigm has been socially and politically endorsed. The Hungarian Academy of Sciences now only accommodates researchers who adhere to this paradigm which in itself is perhaps not such a bad thing. According to Kuhn, progress can only be made in a field of research once it has been proven that a paradigm offers no further possibilities.[50] After 130 years of research, it would seem reasonable to presume that this particular paradigm has by now been rejected and that theories to challenge it have piled up. Here below are just a few examples.

The Finno-Ugric theory is in the first place a lexical theory so in that respect it is a typical product of Western culture. Until the beginning of this century, Western language research centred predominantly on lexicological studies. Blinded by the Biblical maxim: 'in the beginning was the word' people in the West hardly paid any attention to grammatical structures. In the East, by contrast, the Indian scholar Panini had analyzed the grammatical structure of Sanskrit some 1000 years before Western academics got around to doing much the same thing.[51] Even from a lexical point of view the Finno-Ugric language theory is seriously faulty.

- The Finno-Ugric language theory is ill-defined. It is virtually impossible to isolate and examine lexical similarities which relate only to Finno-Ugric languages, but ignore other Eurasian languages such as Altaic languages, Mongolian, Turkish or Tungusic languages;
- It is nonsense to talk about Finno-Ugric phonetic laws when what one is really discussing is more a matter of phonetic tendencies. Notably in the field of Indo-Germanic language theory, where the phonetic law concept was first proposed, such theories seem to be untenable;[52]
- The lexical elements of the so-called original Finno-Ugric language are reconstructed in a random way. In all cases, the Hungarian lexical forms are said to derive from smaller Finno-Ugric languages such as the language of the Voguls and not the reverse. In view of the fact that Hungarians constitute by far the biggest group of 'Finno-Ugric' speakers and together form moreover a sizable state this is, to put it mildly, a poorly supported argument;

- The Swedish linguist, Björn Collinder, estimates in his *Comparative Grammar of the Uralic Languages* that the number of words of common 'Finno-Ugric' origin, that is to say, words which the languages classified as Finno-Ugric have in common is, at the most, 400.[53] This makes estimates produced by the Hungarian Academy of Sciences to the effect that 1000 'Finno-Ugric' words have common origins extremely high and certainly requires further motivation. It should, furthermore, be mentioned that the postulated common lexical roots do not occur in all Finno-Ugric languages;
- We have no written records of the original Finno-Ugric language which makes documenting the reconstructed Finno-Ugric vocabulary and the so-called 'phonetic laws' impossible. This is also admitted by Finno-Ugric linguists themselves. According to Péter Hajdu in his *Finno-Ugric Peoples and Languages*:"as there are no texts in basic Finno-Ugric idiom...the vocabulary of this language and its grammatical structure in its entirety and its details remains unknown. So the only thing we can do is to try to reconstruct a hypothetical Finno-Ugric basic idiom."[54] In addition, we have no historic sources to support notions about the communities presumed to have evolved after Finno-Ugric community, consisting of Ugrians, Volga-Finnish peoples and so on, fell apart;
- The Historical Hungarian Etymological Dictionary contains many basic words of unknown origin. One cannot help wondering why these words are not just recognized as being Hungarian. Does every Hungarian word have to derive from another language? According to the compilers of the Historical Etymological Dictionary, Hungarian has hardly any lexical similarities to languages such as Turkish and Sumerian but such parallels have been convincingly drawn in a number of other exploratory studies in this field.[55]

From a grammatical point of view, Hungarian is fairly isolated from other Finno-Ugric languages. Just like all the other Finno-Ugric languages, Hungarian is an agglutinative language, but this is something which is common to very many Eurasian languages. There are a number of fundamental grammatical differences between Hungarian and other Finno-Ugrian languages. For instance, verbal prefixation, a typical feature of the Hungarian language, is also something that is peculiar to Hungarian. Finno-Ugric language experts do acknowledge that Hungarian is syntactically isolated. Gyula Décsy who is affiliated to the University of Bloomington admits that this is true but refuses to attach any significance to the finding. He maintains that the years of wandering through the southern Russian steppes accounts for the many grammatical differences that have arisen between Hungarian and other Finno-Ugric languages. To his mind, this population migration trend accounts for the many alien elements and constructions that crept into the language. Décsy forgets, however, to indicate when and how these changes occurred.[56] The Finno-Ugrian gurus in Hungary, Péter Hajdu and Péter Domokos, have compiled a list of twenty typological phenomena in the various Finno-Ugric languages.[57] They even fail to attach any significance to the fact that not one of the phenomena listed occurs in all Finno-Ugric languages. One subsequently has to question the conclusive force of such 'Finno-Ugric' typologies. The opposite theory that it is perhaps because of the wanderings of the Hungarians that their language has retained its original elements is simply not considered in studies of this sort.

The only possible conclusion is that the basis for Finno-Ugric language relationship postulations is very thin. It has to be said that 130 years of research in the field within a big scientific institution: the Hungarian Academy of Sciences, has so far produced amazingly few results. Methodological problems have been accepted without question but fundamental problems remain unanswered. It is high time for the myth to be thoroughly reviewed.

An alternative research hypothesis into the origins of the Hungarian language might involve removing Hungarian from the Finno-Ugric language family first and presuming that there are only superficial similarities between Hungarian and these other languages. It would then be logical to compare Hungarian with languages with which we are certain it was in contact in the past such as the Turkic languages (Chuvash), Persian (Alanic), Russian and certain Caucasian languages. Such an alternative hypothesis would have to include and further develop research into the results of language contact and area studies. Not only lexical phenomena but also grammatical phenomena would have to be considered in such a study.

In Hungary, people subscribe dogmatically to the theory that Hungarian has Finno-Ugric origins. It is obviously more than just a language theory. The Finno-Ugric hypothesis has, for more than a hundred years now, been trying to give Hungarians a new identity as Finno-Ugrians, an identity to replace their Scythian or their own Magyar identity. The *Finno-Ugrian/Uralic reader* compiled by Péter Domokos is packed with phrases such as 'Finno-Ugric lira' and 'Finno-Ugric literature'.[58] The answer to the question: how can a constructed and abstract language theory possibly form the basis of any literary analysis? remains vague. It would seem that there is not only such a thing as 'Finno-Ugric' literature, but also such a thing as 'Finno-Ugric' peoples as may be deduced from the following communiqué released by the MTI, the Hungarian press office:

> "The advisory committee of the World Congress of Finno-Ugric Peoples which met in Csongrád on Sunday was attended by the Hungarian president Arpád Göncz. Twenty Finno-Ugric peoples were represented and preparations were discussed for the Second World Congress. The World Congress of Finno-Ugrian Peoples was first held in Komi in Russia in 1992. The next gathering is planned for 1996. Since our country will be celebrating the 1100th anniversary of the Conquest in that same year, the Hungarian division of the World Congress has decided that the congress should be opened at the Arpád monument in the National Park of Historic Monuments in Ópusztaszer.' (MTI, 4th July, 1994)

The Finno-Ugric language hypothesis, therefore, claims to be more than a language hypothesis, it also pretends to provide a theory on the origins of the Hungarian people and, thus, to make far-reaching claims about Hungarian identity. As this language hypothesis is not based on any scientifically proven facts we are dealing here with *inventing tradition* in the way described by the anthropologist Hobsbawm.[59] During the last century, many people in many cultures created myths about their identities and origins most of which aimed at glorifying their own culture and mobilizing nation-forming forces. The Finno-Ugric hypothesis fitted into such a category with the one major difference that the myth of Finno-Ugric identity and origins was not aimed at upgrading Hungarian culture, but rather at downgrading it. The Germans created these origins myths about the Hungarians and imposed them at a time when the Hungarians were at their most vulnerable. The objective of the Finno-Ugric myth was to link Hungarians with obscure nondescript peoples such as the Voguls and Ostjaks who had settled in the region of the Urals, thus, simultaneously implying that this must also be the region where the Hungarians had their deepest roots. Such projected origins directly conflicted with what Hungarian traditions, fairy tales, chronicles, gests, myths and sagas have always intimated about the origins of the Hungarians. In all these sources the Hungarians are said to descend from the patriarch Nimrod and to be allied to the great warrior peoples of the East, the Scythians, Huns and Turks. According to traditional beliefs the Hungarians derive from southern Eurasia, but according to the Finno-Ugric hypothesis they come from the northern regions of Eurasia. The Hungarian's relationship to the Scythians has been important in their history. The Hun-Hungarian continuity theory had always managed to mobilize the Hungarians in moments of dire need when circumstances had required them to defend their country and the Carpathian Basin from intruders. It was exactly this fighting spirit that the Germans and Habsburgers wanted to eradicate from Hungarian identity and they planned to do this by saddling them with a new and tame Finno-Ugric identity.

Attacking Hungarian identity was merely one side of the story. The Germans and Habsburgers saw to it that the national identity of the peoples who, during the course of the 19th century had gained national awareness and who lived in countries surrounding the Hungarians, was reinforced. This was a way of bringing further pressure to bear on the Hungarians. The Viennese Court supported the myth about the origins of the Slovaks, the myth of the Great Moravian Empire and that of the Rumanians, the myth about their Daco-Roman ancestory.[60] All other powers that have since tried to perpetuate a power constellation in the Carpathian Basin at the expense of the Hungarians have subscribed to these myths namely, the West after the Treaty of Trianon and Soviet-Russian communism after the Second World War. In Hungary itself, the Finno-Ugric myth was abandoned towards the end of the inter-war years by which time Hungarian confidence in national identity had been sufficiently restored.

The myths about the other peoples inhabiting the Carpathian Basin such as that of the Daco-Romans for the Rumanians and that of the Great Moravian Empire for the Slovaks are typical instances of *inventing tradition*. The Great Moravian myth states that the Slovaks were descended from the Great Moravians who, long before the 9th century, had established the so-called Great Moravian Empire. It is interesting to note that the southern periphery of this fictitious realm crossed right through the middle of what is now Hungary. The Daco-Roman myth claims that the present Rumanians are descended from the Dacians and the Romans and that the Rumanians thus inhabited what is now Rumania, including Transylvania, before the Hungarians. It is on these grounds that the Rumanians claim to be historically entitled to the land of Transylvania and to have a right to view the Transylvanian Hungarians as intruders. Clearly all these myths about origins simply aim to prove one thing, that certain peoples inhabited the Carpathian Basin long before the Hungarians and that they, moreover, occupied a far greater territory part of which is now inhabited by Hungarians. The Slovaks and Rumanians, therefore, use this argument to show that their ancestors lived in the Carpathian Basin first and to claim the 'right' to view and treat their own Hungarian inhabitants as 'intruders' and second class citizens.

These myths about the origins of the Slovaks and Rumanians cannot be substantiated with scientific arguments. What is curious, though, is that since the time of the Treaty of Trianon they have been given credibility in the Western world, notably by being reiterated in encyclopedias and textbooks. The Australian-Hungarian linguist, Lajos Kazár, summarizes all the academic criticism and arguments on this subject in his book: *Facts against Fiction: Transylvania - Walachian/Rumanian homeland since 70 B.C.?* (Sydney, 1993). According to Kazár the history of the present Rumanians and their forefathers, the early Vlachs, of before the 13th century A.D., is one of the most controversial subjects in encyclopedias and textbooks since the signing of the Treaty of Trianon (1920). In encyclopedias and history books, this question is dealt with under the headwords: Transylvania, Walachia, Moldavia or Rumania. This fact alone would suggest that it is high time to thoroughly and critically review information published about Transylvania.

On the basis of representative random sampling with the entry 'Transylvania' found in encyclopedias published since 1920, Kazár concludes that since the time of the Treaty of Trianon the size of Transylvania varies greatly from source to source. In quite a few descriptions it is given as being 60,000 square kilometres. The area that the Entente powers assigned to Rumania in 1920 actually covered 102,787 square kilometres. Such discrepancies alone should warn one of the potential inaccuracies to be found in the relevant texts.

When it comes to the matter of identifying the people now known as Rumanians who, until the second half of the 19th century were known as Vlachs, as 'Daco-Romans', the encyclopedias fall into two main camps. This latter name does not appear in historiographic writings until the 18th century. (a) Encyclopedias which accept the Daco-Roman continuity theory and the 'historic right' of the Rumanians to populate Transylvania and (b) encyclopedias that repudiate the Daco-Roman theory and the 'historic right' of the Rumanians to live in Transylvania.

Those who adhere to the (a) theory contend that the ancestors of the Vlachs/Rumanians, or at least some of their ancestors, were native to 'Transylvania', Walachia and Moldavia. These inhabitants had been sent by the Roman emperor Traianus to Dacia Traianus. It was reputed that together with the Dacians who had survived the terror of Traianus, the Latin speaking colonists and legionaries had formed a new people, the so-called Daco-Romans. Groups of these people were said to have settled in the areas which, after 270 A.D., were no longer part of the Roman Empire. It was believed that they had survived the devastation of migrating peoples by hiding themselves in caves in the Carpathian Mountains. Upholders of the (b) theory reject the claims of the (a) camp; that is to say, they repudiate the notion that the Daco-Romans existed and dwelt in the area later to become known as Rumania.

The (a) camp uses as its argument the fact that the Vlachs/-Rumanians speak a language with a Latin structure. It should, however, be pointed out that the lexicon of the language is predominantly non-Latin. According to the (b) camp, the language spoken by the Vlachs/Rumanians evolved in the south-west, southern region of the Balkan peninsula. In the Middle Ages, different Vlach states evolved in the region and even today there are still quite a number of ethnic Arumanian and Meglenitic Vlachs living there who are racially similar to the Rumanians.

As far as the (b) camp is concerned the Daco-Roman continuity theory fails to explain why no burial places have been found if the 'Daco-Romans' supposedly inhabited the region between the 3rd century and the beginning of the 13th century. This 1000 year hiatus applies not only to Transylvania, but also to Walachia and Moldavia. In none of these areas have churches or other religious locations been found where remains of the alleged 'Daco-Romans' might be unearthed. It is all very incongruent if one considers that Rumanian historiography asserts that these people were descended from the Romans and Dacians, people who were famous for their architecture and buildings and also when one thinks that the Daco-Romans living in what is now 'Transylvania' were converted to Christianity in the 4th or 5th century.

Obviously, both camps cannot be right which means that one of the types of encyclopedias must be circulating incorrect information. From an academic point of view such ambiguity is, of course, intolerable. The problem should be resolved as quickly as possible, because the 'Daco-Roman' myth and the 'historic rights' ensuing from that same myth have been generally circulated and accepted by people since 1920. As we all well know, no specific scientific discoveries were made in 1920 to substantiate the 'Daco-Roman' theory. The fact that this theory and the 'historic right' deriving from it is to be found in ever more encyclopedias and history books has nothing to do with scientific research, but rather with power-political decision-making in Trianon (1920). Equally important is the study of the early history of the Rumanian language relating the origin of this language to the Balkan peninsula. The only study in the West elaborating on this alternative hypothesis has been published by somebody writing under the pseudonym of André Du Nay.[61]

To conclude then, we may assert that the Finno-Ugric, Daco-Roman and Great Moravian myths and all the other myths about the origins of the peoples in the Carpathian Basin are inextricably intertwined. In the case of the Hungarians, though, the myth created aimed at stamping out national identity whilst in the case of the other peoples in the Carpathian Basin the myths were designed to elevate their status.

Hungarian history

The Finno-Ugric origins theory offers no insight into the early history of the Hungarians nor can it serve to enlighten matters about the Hungarian's mental-material cultural heritage. Official Hungarian historiography still supports the 'doctrine' of the communist ideologist of the fifties, Erik Molnár, who preached that on arriving in Europe the Hungarians had a primitive culture and occupied themselves more or less exclusively with hunting and fishing. According to the archeologist Gyula László the theory of the Hungarians having their Finno-Ugric origins in the Urals is unacceptable, because it is a postulation that conflicts with the over-population theory. László points out that in conjunction with food production methods it was only possible for eight to ten families to live on 100 square kilometres of land some 5000 years ago. It is, therefore, logical to presume that these peoples originated from many different areas. Research into early Hungarian history will have to account for these variables. In recent years, a number of Hungarian academics have carried out research, often at their own expense, into alternative hypotheses concerning the origins of the Hungarians.

For example in 1988, the Hungarian anthropologist, István Kiszely, carried out research into a Turkish speaking tribe known as the Ugars, who live in North-West China near to the city of Urumchi. Since the beginning of the 19th century, it has been known that the Ugars were in some way or another connected with the Hungarians. The Hungarian linguist Sándor Kőrösi Csoma (1784-1842) went in search of the Ugars whom he had heard about while travelling in Tibet. Kőrösi never managed to reach the area where the Ugars lived, but he did leave behind the first English-Tibetan dictionary and a book on Tibetan grammar. Kiszely, who had financed the expedition himself, found striking parallels between the cultures of the Hungarians and the Ugars as, for instance, in their mythological representations, ornamentation, music and war weapons. Kiszely concluded that the ancestors of these two peoples must at least have been in contact with each other. Kiszely maintains that one of the places where they might have originated from could have been the area from around lake Bajkal in the Tarim Basin.[62]

Another theory that is gaining popularity is the one that asserts that long before the Arpád Hungarian Conquest of the Carpathian Basin in 896 A.D. there were already Hungarians living in the Carpathian Basin. Gyula László maintains that there were at least two conquests and that the Avars were proto-Hungarians. This theory is confirmed in the *Tárih-i Üngürüsz*, a Turkish translation of the 'History of the Hungarians', that Sultan Sulijman I had translated by an interpreter in 1543 during the time of the Turkish occupation. The Hungarian source has been lost but the Turkish translation was found in Istanbul at the beginning of this century. Finno-Ugrians and later the communists, notably the party ideologist György Aczél, did everything in their power to prevent the *Tárih-i Üngürüsz* from being published. The *Tárih-i Üngürüsz* which dates from around the year 900 makes mention of the rather startling fact that the Hungarians of Árpád discovered Hungarian speaking people in the Carpathian Basin.[63] Further research must also be carried out into the actual Conquest itself. In the previous chapter, it was explained how it is that in the West the Conquest of the Carpathian Basin is viewed only in terms of stereotypes and images. Much the same can be said of Hungarian historiography on the matter. The episodes preceding and also following the Conquest are described as 'adventurous wanderings' and 'raids'. The Swiss-Hungarian historian, Szabolcs de Vajay, demonstrated that in military-diplomatic terms the Conquest of the Carpathian Basin and the establishing of a Hungarian state was a brilliant operation based on the concept of retaining *balance of power* in Europe. This version is still missing in Hungarian textbooks.

Similarly, little research has been carried out into ancient Hungarian belief systems. In Hungary, much research has however been carried out into shamanism which, of course, is also important but Arabian sources tell us that the Hungarians were 'fire worshippers', an Arab term of abuse for people who belonged to certain Persian religious movements. It would, therefore, seem important to examine these religious movements, if we are to gain a better understanding of

Hungarian culture. If the Hungarians were somehow influenced by Persian belief systems, then it would be logical to presume that long before they came to Europe they lived according to moral commandments.

In official academic circles, the old Hungarian runic writing is not generally the subject of study, only a handful of researchers are working on such studies outside the universities, in their own time and at their own cost.[64] People who do involve themselves in the study of runic writing are branded 'fascists' by the academic establishment. If Hungarian runic writing were studied more broadly this might not only produce interesting results on the early history of the Hungarians, but also on early Hungarian religious beliefs, results for research in the Hungarian language system, results for the development of writing and even for gaining insight into stenography. It has been discovered that the rules of runic writing are very similar to those of stenography.

Trianon research

In Hungary, research into the Treaty of Trianon (1920) virtually came to a standstill after the Second World War. Whenever Trianon research is carried out it is rarely from the Hungarian perspective. As we shall see in part two of this book, it was because dualistic Hungary had entered into unilateral union with the Germans that the consequences of the Treaty of Trianon turned out to be so bad for the Hungarians. Even the Hungarian 'progressives' and radicals like Mihály Károlyi and Oszkár Jászi, became unilaterally oriented. These politicians had placed all their hopes on the Entente Powers, but this had not paid off. Just like with the research of Oszkár Jászi, Trianon research currently being carried out in Hungary is far too preoccupied with the matter of the internal domestic and social problems of the Austrian-Hungarian regime of the time. Though these issues need to be examined they tell us nothing about the international relations of that period nor about the causes, effects and corollaries of Trianon. R.W. Seton-Watson and his colleagues took advantage of the internal social problems that were rife in dualistic Hungary and about which Oszkár Jászi and certain other Hungarians had become over-concerned. This was one of the factors that contributed to the weakening of Hungary's foreign political position.

Both the conservatives and the progressives were politically unilaterally oriented when it came to foreign affairs, but the geopolitical situation in Hungary really required a foreign policy on a much broader base as will be argued in part three. Hungary needs to strike a balance between East and West. It is, therefore, vitally important that Hungarians study Trianon in this light, so that similar anti-Hungarian power constellations can be dealt with more effectively now and in the future. The realization that in Hungary it is high time for Trianon research to commence clearly emerges from the statements made by Géza Jeszenszky, Foreign Affairs minister in the Antall administration and historian who studied in Budapest. Jeszenszky can only look at foreign relations in one way: "Hungaria semper fidelis. Hungary will always remain loyal to its European and Atlantic friends, even if the love remains unrequited. I only hope that they will not come to realize our true worth after our downfall."[65] Some of the Western politicians on whom Jeszenszky pins all his hope think quite differently about political relations in Central and Eastern Europe. Lord Carrington, for instance, is still very charmed by the Serbian butcher of the Balkans. In the *Utrechts Nieuwsblad* of 19th March 1994 he was reported to have said: "Milosevic always keeps his word."

Research into the élite

If a country's democracy is to be given any credibility it is necessary for its people to know exactly what kind of traditions have produced its leaders, who the leaders represent etc. This century has seen several terrorist regimes seize power in

Hungary. There has been white terror as well as red terror. In the last few decades, much research has been carried out into the wrong-doings of the white terror that reigned in 1920-1921, when admiral Horthy and his national army decided to put things to rights in Hungary. It was, however, strictly forbidden to investigate the red terror of 1919, a kind of terror that was again rampant in Hungary in the fifties. After the changes of 1989, the Hungarian state gave financial backing for the 1956 Research Institute to be set up. It is curious that the Institute has so far produced few 'revelations'. Neither the people employed by the institute, nor other researchers have access to the secret dossiers of the former communist intelligence service. It is, therefore, impossible to establish with any certainty whether or not people serving in the present government had sympathies with the old communist regime. Factual information about the scandalous acts during the period of red terror in the fifties is only to be found in the *Black Lexicon* written by Ferenc Kubinyi. The publication of this *Black Lexicon* was made possible by the financial support of Hungarians living in the West and, like samizdat literature, it circulates via the underground book market.[66]

Conclusions

In this chapter, I have explained how it is that in Hungary no one is free to carry out research aimed at tracing the characteristics of national identity. Such research is prevented by power-ideological filters, so that only research of a monolithic nature is indeed possible. One of the prerequisites of a free society, though, is, the freedom to carry out scientific research but, for the time being, in this extremely important area such freedom does not exist. For the Hungarians it is very important to openly carry out research into national identity and culture because, after such a long period of communist repression this will help them to regain their self-knowledge and self-respect and it will put them in touch with their own culture again. The sort of questions that are relevant are: how many Hungarians live in the Carpathian Basin, where do they live, what is the status of the Hungarian language, how does the Hungarian spoken in Hungary compare with that spoken by the Hungarian communities in the Carpathian Basin, what about the early history of the Hungarians, how did major events in Hungarian history happen and who constitute the Hungarian élite, etc.

Another reason why it is so important for research to be carried out into national culture and identity is, because of the overriding world-wide desire for uniformity that has gained influence during the past few decades. Countries that have weak national and cultural identities will automatically find it difficult to resist such a force and there is a danger that their cultures will fade away into a big global melting pot. No single nation is now able to escape from the pressure to modernize and the thirst to innovate, nor is that necessary. Such processes of change and modernization must be based on human knowledge, mental resources and cultural and moral values that have accumulated in societies over the centuries. What is important is that this knowledge and these collective values are preserved and adapted to suit the needs of a modern age. Even though the Hungarians in the Carpathian Basin are in a difficult position and their culture and identity has been oppressed they have the potential to become one of the most successful nations of the next century. Once before in the past the Hungarians had already successfully managed to innovate change in their culture. In the latter half of the last century, Hungary saw what was known as the Age of Reform which was initiated by count István Széchenyi and others and which brought about great changes in the country. In the next chapter, I shall show that the Hungarian culture and identity has great mental and informational potential which is what will make it be suited to a global ordering principle in the next century.

The emergence of a new Hungarian self-image

In the first chapter, I pointed out how little people in the West know about the Hungarians. The West merely has two groups of stereotypes and images to go on. In the second chapter, I demonstrated how badly the Hungarians understand themselves. During the course of time much of their self-knowledge has been lost, because since the Second World War the national and cultural identity of Hungarians living in Hungary has been systematically eradicated by communism and for Hungarians living outside of Hungary, in the Carpathian Basin, oppression exerted by tough, uncompromising nationalists has existed since the time of Trianon. The question is, what does it mean to be Hungarian. Here below is one definition of what being Hungarian involves:

Being Hungarian is a mental-cultural state, a general way of living determined by feelings of solidarity, a common past and fund of memories (the old myths, sagas, legends, ballads, fairy tales, the linguistic links, the symbolism, the Hungarian Holy Crown,...), and striving seriously for shared cultural norms (a love of freedom, common decency, tolerance, willingness to compromise,...), together with an individual sense of responsibility to think and act creatively in the interests of all Hungarians.

The Hungarians call this awareness of being Hungarian *magyarság* which, in Western publications is often translated as *Hongarendom* (Dutch), *Hungarianness*, *Ungarntum* (German). The word is created from the noun *magyar* 'Hungarian' and the suffix *-ság* which denotes collectivity. In the light of the above description, one can only reject such translations of the word *magyarság* as inaccurate, because what they suggest is an extremist ideology and that is not what the Hungarian word means. In Hungarian, it simply means all Hungarians, with the above-described qualities, put together.

The qualities that form Hungarian identity will be explained in more detail below. We shall be examining: the open Hungarian culture, the mental-moral imperatives of the Hungarian culture, including those which apply to the Hungarian Holy Crown, tolerance, the desire for justice and freedom, willingness to compromise, the Hungarian language and the knowledge gained from old Hungarian sagas, myths, ballads and fairy tales.

The open Hungarian culture

Being Hungarian, therefore, has nothing to do with the *Blut und Boden* ideologies developed in Western Europe, nor can it be limited to citizenship of the Hungarian state. Historic Hungary, the *Natio Hungarica,* which constituted the Hungarian nation up until 1848 and functioned with a system of nobility, embraced not only ethnic Magyars, but also all the other ethnic peoples of Hungary such as Germans, Rumanians, Serbs, Croats, Slovaks, etc. This ruling class which was culturally *Magyar* oriented, was ethnically very heterogeneous. The same applied to the serfs and farmers, a class also composed of people drawn from all of Hungary's ethnic groups. So, in ethnical terms the Hungarians are heterogeneous. Nationalistic interpretations of the history of Central Europe based on racial differentiations must, therefore, be rejected. The Hungarians have not been oppressing their 'nationalities' for a thousand years. Just like any other nationality Hungarians have been both the oppressors and the oppressed. In actual fact, the national historiography of the successor states which also gained ground in the West after the time of Trianon, as we saw in the last chapter, translated a social conflict that had existed within the antiquated structures of the Austrian-Hungarian double monarchy into a national conflict. It was not until the end of the last century that this national conflict came to light.

What is interesting is the fact that invariably important figures in Hungary's history were not ethnic Hungarians. Count Miklós Zrínyi (1620-1664), for instance, who had estates in the south of

Hungary and in Croatian-Slavonia was ethnically a Croat but first and foremost a Hungarian patriot. Zrínyi campaigned to liberate Hungary from Turkish tyranny. He fought not only on the battlefield, but also with his pen. In his most famous epic, *Szigeti Veszedelem* (1646) 'The Catastrophe of Sziget', he glorifies his great-grandfather of the same name whom he praises for his heroism, notably for the heroic deed of defending the castle of Sziget in the year 1566 against the advancing armies of the Turkish Sultan, Sulijman II. Zrínyi's great-grandfather meets his heroic death in this same battle. His last major work was *A török áfium ellen való orvosság* (1660) 'An antidote to the Turkish poison'. In this political treatise, Zrínyi argues that there is no single European power that will be prepared to support the Hungarians in their struggle against the Turks. They will have to push back the Turks on their own. Zrínyi's political thinking was to be very influential in later Hungarian uprisings.

The leader of the anti-Habsburg Revolution and the War of Independence of 1848/1849, Lajos Kossuth (1802-1894), was an ethnic Slovak. The Hungarian poet of this revolution, Sándor Petőfi (1823-1849), who was of Slovak-Serbian extraction *voluntarily* Magyarized his Serbian surname, Petrovics, by changing it to Petőfi. Through his simplicity and naivety Petőfi managed to appeal directly to the Hungarian soul in his poems and he also completely took on the Hungarian life-style. His work is permeated with a yearning for freedom which for him was more important than love. In 1849, the 26 year-old poet entered the realms of legendary by dying in the battle of Segesvár (Sigishoara) while serving in the army division of the Polish general Bem which resisted the Cossack army in Transylvania. After the quelling of the 1848/1849 War of Independence, thirteen generals were executed in Arad by the Austrian authorities, a number of them were ethnic Serbs and Germans. All these men had fought for Hungarian freedom. Being Hungarian is, therefore, definitely not an ethnic matter.

Integrational power and tolerance

Saint Stephen, the first Western and Christian king of Hungary, was responsible for integrating the peoples of the Carpathian Basin. He drew together the countries of the Hungarian Crown to form a strong and united state made up of a diversity of ethnic peoples and cultures but with a predominant Magyar component. Until 1848, Hungarian society had a feudal class structure and it was not organized according to ethnic principles. Organizing things along ethnic lines was alien to the Hungarian nature. It was not something that fitted in with the life-style and traditions they had brought with them from the steppes. In the steppes, bonds had often been formed which cut across ethnic barriers but were in the interests of the whole tribe. This experience stood the Hungarians in good stead for later (in the Carpathian Basin) and for being able to become an integral part of a state. Tolerance and hospitality was to become an important moral principle of the Hungarian state and this was the maxim that Saint Stephen passed on to his son, Duke Imre "... a country with one language and one rule is weak and vulnerable. I hereby order you, my son, to take good care of strangers and treat them respectfully so that they will prefer to stay with you than go elsewhere." For a thousand years, the Hungarian kingdom adhered to this principle. Here below are just a few examples which illustrate this.

During the course of their history, the Hungarians have assimilated many cultures and peoples. The Turkic (Pechenegs and Cumans) and Iranian (Jazygians), for instance, horsemen who invaded the Carpathian Basin after the Hungarians had settled there, but who eventually decided to unite with the Hungarians after a time. That was also the case with the Slavic speaking peoples, especially later with the Slovaks known in the Hungarian kingdom as *Tót* and with the Germans who emigrated to Hungary in waves at different times. In the 13th century, Slavic Ruthenians also filtered into Hungary and settled in Subcarpathia. From the 13th century onwards, there were also the Saxons who emigrated at the invitation of successive

Hungarian kings. These emigrations also served a specific Hungarian interest. In 1241-1242 Hungary had been flattened by the Tatars led by Batu Khan. The Tatars had managed to eradicate approximately 50% of the Hungarian population. King Béla IV, who wanted to rebuild the country, therefore, decided to attract immigrants. Such a decision in no way contradicted the principles that St. Stephen had once laid down for his people.

The Saxons settled in the south of Transylvania, at the foot of the Carpathians on the Hungarian border, so that they could defend the country and work the land there. In his *Andreanum* of 1224, King Andreas II gave the Saxons complete autonomy. In return they were only required to remain loyal to the Hungarian Crown which is what they did until the First World War. Living under Hungarian rule for more than 700 years the Saxons managed to function as a successful community and to contribute to Hungary's economic and cultural prosperity. After Trianon the Rumanian authorities ruthlessly obliterated this community. Before the Second World War, there were some 850,000 Saxons, but now there are only around 50,000 left. This is all thanks to the deportations and human trading practices of the Ceausescu regime when Saxons were sold to West Germany for 10,000 DM a head. The land of the Saxons, once a prosperous region of Transylvania, is now a desolate sight. Since the Saxons have left, the area has gone to rack and ruin. The Saxons who were forced to emigrate have assembled in Germany and are waiting until the time is ripe for them to return to their Saxon homeland in Transylvania.

The Turkish invasion was followed by further waves of immigration which ultimately led to much destruction and loss of life. The defeat that the Hungarians suffered at Mohács (1526) was particularly devastating. In this battle, the Hungarian army, led by the young king Ludwig II, then only 20 years of age, suffered a dreadful defeat at the hand of the armies of the Turkish Sultan, Sulijman I. The battle against the Turks led to the loss of about half of the Hungarian population, thus, shrinking the country's population to the level of some 200 years before. After the Turkish wars, the Habsburg kings invited Germans, particularly Swabians, to help repopulate the country. The Swabians settled mainly in the cities and in the Bánát region where their industriousness and fervour contributed to the region's renewed prosperity.

In the wake of the Turkish conflict many Serbs also moved to Hungary. On 6th April 1690, the Austrian emperor, Leopold I, urged the peoples of the Balkans to band together with the Austrians in a campaign to oust the Turks. In a letter addressed to the Serbian orthodox patriarch of Pec, Arsenije Crnojević III, he appealed to the religious leader to use his influence to inspire the Serbs and Albanians to support this worthy cause. The rising against the Turks was a failure and the rebels were forced to flee. The Serbian refugees, around 36,000 families, were allowed to settle in the southern region of Hungary. Eventually, in 1694, these Serbs decided to remain in Hungary. In exchange for military services the Austrian emperor exempted them from having to pay taxes. Later, at the time of Trianon, the presence of Serbs in the country's southern region would be instrumental in the decision to assign tracts of land in that area to Serbs, Croats and Slovenians.

From the 13th century onwards the Vlachs, ancestors of the Rumanians, gradually left the Balkans and made forays into Hungary. The earliest known document of the Hungarian kingdom to make mention of the Vlachs dates from the year 1222. It was during the reign of King Andreas II that the very first Vlach settlement was established in Transylvania, in the area of Fogaras.[67] Afterwards, more and more Vlachs streamed into Transylvania, because they were being forced out of the Balkans by the Turkic tribes and because they were fleeing from being exploited by their own boyar masters. Around 1700 some 40% of the population of Transylvania consisted of Vlachs. The Rumanian migration to Transylvania may be quite easily documented. With the rise of modern Rumanian nationalism that focused on myth-forming, as explained in the previous chapter, Hungarian hospitality was soon forgotten.

At the end of the 18th century the Rumanians formulated their continuity theory and in 1791 handed over a petition to king Leopold II, the so-called *Supplex Libellus Valachorum*. In this petition, which referred to 'Vlachs' rather than 'Rumanians', the Rumanians requested that on the basis of historic privileges they might be given the same rights as all the other peoples living in Transylvania: the Hungarians, Szeklers and Saxons. "The Rumanian nation is by far the oldest nation of our time. We have historic evidence to prove this, continuity of tradition, language similarities and traditions and habits which stem from the Roman colonists who, at the beginning of the second century of the Christian era were brought here by the Emperor Traianus ..." It should be pointed out that the demands made by the Rumanians were quite unrealistic, because at the time people in Transylvania were not ethnically divided up but lived in a rather feudally structured society. As part of the Hungarian nobility Rumanian aristocrats were politically represented, but not the Rumanian population as such, no more in fact than Hungarian serfs were represented.

Apart from the hospitality and tolerance shown towards foreigners and those who were ethnically non-Magyar the Hungarian culture also showed considerable religious tolerance. In the semi-independent Hungarian principality of Transylvania (1542-1691), complete religious freedom was proclaimed in the *Edict of Torda* pronounced in 1568, during the Diet at Torda. Under the monarch, János Zsigmond, who reigned over Transylvania and the East Hungarian part from 1559 to 1571, many religions were recognized, alongside of Catholicism - the denomination of the oppressor. There were Protestants, Lutherans, Calvinists and Unitarians. Transylvania, thus, became a place of religious toleration and a bastion of Protestantism on the territory ruled by the Hungarian Crown. This declaration of religious tolerance came at a time when the rest of Europe was being divided by devastating sectarian wars, such as the Thirty Years' War.

In the War of Independence of 1848-1849, the Hungarian Jews fought on the Hungarian side, against the Habsburg Court. In 1849, the equal political and civil rights bestowed on the Jews were negated by the Austrians who accused the Jews of having committed high treason. With the *Ausgleich* (1867) the Hungarians also stipulated that the Jews should be fully emancipated. This stipulation was laid down in section XVII of the law of 1867. The law stated that Jews had the same political and civil rights as all the Christian inhabitants of the country and that any laws contravening this stipulation would automatically be made legally void. Furthermore, in 1895 the Wekerle administration passed a law that formally recognized Judaism as a religion. The country's liberal policies towards Jews encouraged a huge migration movement of Jews to Hungary from other Eastern European countries. Many Jews streamed into Hungary from Galicia where they were being persecuted. Before 1848, there were 241,000 Jews in Hungary. After the introduction of the emancipation laws the number of Jews living in Hungary more than doubled, by 1870 there were 550,000 and when World War I broke out in 1914 there were almost 1 million Jews living in Hungary. The vast majority of them settled in Budapest which soon received the rather derisive nickname 'Jewapest'.

Another minority group that has traditionally been the target of much persecution in Europe has been the gypsies but in the kingdom of Hungary they were allowed to live in freedom. They had first appeared in Europe in the 13th century and in Western Europe they were often subjected to persecution. In Prussia, for example, a decree was sent out in 1761 ordering that all gypsies over the age of eighteen must be hanged. Such decrees were completely alien to the Hungarians. Hence, the reason that today there are still so many gypsies living in the Carpathian Basin that once belonged to the Hungarian Crown. It is true that in post-communist Hungary gypsies sometimes suffer social discrimination. Their formal status, however, was satisfactorily regulated in 1993. The Hungarian parliament has adopted the law on national and ethnic minorities providing cultural autonomy and local self-rule for national and ethnic minorities.[68]

The above-mentioned facts pertaining to tolerance towards foreigners and people of different religious denominations contrasts sharply with what anti-Hungarian propaganda alleges to be true about Hungarians. The propaganda slogan of the Entente powers and the upholders of the Little Entente which is currently circulated throughout Bratislava, Bucharest and Belgrade, namely that 'for a thousand years' the Hungarians oppressed their peoples must, therefore, be nonsense. Even today, Hungary opens up its frontiers to many refugees. Though experiencing economic hardship, Hungary has absorbed more than half a million war refugees from ex-Yugoslavia, not only ethnic Hungarians from the Southern Lands, but also Bosnian Muslims, Croats and even Serbian conscientious objectors.

Mental-moral imperatives

It is officially understood that the Hungarian Holy Crown was a gift from Pope Sylvester II to St. Stephen, the first Christian king of Hungary. The truth of the matter is that there is a special relationship between the Hungarian people and the Hungarian Holy Crown. For Hungarians, the Hungarian monarch, as a person, is actually less important than the Holy Crown. In a certain sense, the Holy Crown is seen as a living thing. Official sources claim that the Holy Crown consists of two parts: the upper Christian Western part and the lower Byzantine section. Since the Holy Crown was returned to Hungary from the U.S. in 1976 research has been continuing into its symbolic and mystical significance.

One school of thought agrees with the argument that the crown represents a world-view of deep human knowledge with moral implications that has its origins in early Christianity.[69] These researchers reject the officially held view. Lajos Csomor who has been allowed to make a close study of the crown has discovered that the part depicting the Byzantine emperors was mounted at a later date. The decoration attachments are too big for the holes into which they are mounted. This observation corresponds with early observations such as that of Péter Révai, one-time guardian of the Holy Crown, who recorded in 1613 that there was an image of the Holy Virgin Mary mounted in the place where later the Byzantine emperor Michael Ducas came to be displayed.

According to the art historian Gábor Pap the images of Jesus and the Holy Virgin Mary are extremely important symbols. The depiction of Jesus is to be found on the top of the crown, thus, symbolizing his proximity to God and higher things. Mounted on the upper ring Jesus and Mary serve as intermediaries between God and the angels and the apostles and saints who are mounted on the lower ring. The latter symbolize the fulfilment of practical duties in the world such as defending the country (Saint Demetrius, Saint George) and protecting the health of the people (Saint Damian, Saint Cosmas). The question one is compelled to ask is why Byzantian elements should have taken over the place of the Holy Virgin Mary. It would be more logical to see a combination of the images of Jesus and the Holy Virgin Mary than of Jesus and the Byzantine Emperors because, as mother of Jesus and protectress of the Hungarians the Virgin Mary fits better into the context.

Pap maintains that this is evidence of an attempt to invest the Hungarian Holy Crown with a new significance. In the Habsburg Court and among the Russian tsars, there had been renewed plans to revive the Byzantine Empire and to use the Holy Crown as its new symbol. This idea eventually developed into the formation of the Rumanian and Serbian state. Pap is convinced that as long as the Byzantine elements remain of the Holy Crown the Hungarians run the risk of being integrated into a 'new' Byzantine state. This notion is not as far-fetched as it sounds. During the time of the Rumanian occupation of Hungary, the Rumanians made an attempt to steal the Hungarian Crown from the National Museum. It was thanks to Bandholtz, an American general, that this did not happen. As long as the Holy Crown contains Byzantine elements the Hungarians in the Carpathian Basin will not be safe.

Hungary's constitution, known as the *Aranybulla*, which refers to the Golden Bull of 1222 that was presented to the Hungarian aristocracy by the Hungarian king, Andreas II, is the second oldest in Europe. The Golden Bull is only a few years younger than the English Magna Carta which it resembles in concept. Just as in the Magna Carta, the Golden Bull bestows on the country's nobles the right to rebel against a ruler who does not properly serve the interests of his country. In Hungarian history, the role played by the country's constitution and laws has been important. Through the ages the constitution has proved more reliable than political will. When, between 1904 and 1908 a nationalistic government briefly came into power in Hungary it was unable to push though its Magyarization policies, because the constitution which guaranteed those living in the lands of the Crown of Saint Stephen and the nationalities of the Hungary equal rights stood in the way of such politics. One can still today detect a great respect among Hungarians for the constitution and laws of the country.

Willingness to compromise

In past centuries, the Hungarians have proved to be prepared to compromise on issues with which they agreed but always on the condition that they could determine their own destiny. A series of compromises in recent times commenced with the *Ausgleich* of 1867. In 1867, the Hungarians drew up an agreement with the House of Habsburg, an agreement known as the *Ausgleich*. The Hungarians reconciled themselves to the idea that emperor Franz Joseph who in 1849 had brutally quashed the Hungarian's struggle for independence would ultimately become king of Hungary and they gave up their strive for full independence.

The architect of the *Ausgleich*, the Hungarian politician Ferenc Deák, achieved a resounding diplomatic success when, after the Austrians had been defeated against Prussia in 1866, the Viennese Court proved willing to enter into negotiations. Not only did Hungary and Austria become equal partners, but Hungary was required to finance only 30% of the combined imperial and royal costs. This meant that for the first time in a long while money started to pour into Hungary from Austria. As well as the Ministry of Finance, the Ministries of Defence and Foreign Affairs were communal, but apart from that Hungary was independent.

After the agreement with Austria the Hungarians one year later, in 1868, drew up an *Ausgleich* with Croatian-Slavonia based on their historic rights. In the framework of the Crown of St. Stephen Hungary regarded Croatia-Slavonia as an autonomous area. Croatia-Slavonia that was governed by the Viceroy of Croatia in the name of the king was fully autonomous in the field of domestic affairs, law, religion and education. This corner of the realm was, furthermore, permitted to use its own national emblems and forty of its representatives were allowed to sit in the Hungarian parliament. Members of the Croatian-Slavonic parliament, the *Sabor*, were permitted to correspond with the Hungarian monarch in Croatian. It is true that the Viceroy of Croatia was appointed by Budapest and that the Croats had no direct railroad connection with Vienna but the accusation that the Croats were oppressed for a thousand years is not very convincing. The fact that the Croats broke away from Hungary in 1920 had more to do with their Slavic orientation than with any negative feelings towards the Hungarians. The times are truly changing though. In the new Croatian constitution of 1991 the *Sabor* has recorded that the Croatian parliament never ratified the separation from Hungary and the unity with Serbia.[70]

In the inter-war years, Hungarian domestic politics were totally preoccupied with the matter of revising the Trianon convention. Obviously, it was never the intention of the Hungarians to attempt to reconstruct the kingdom of St. Stephen in the Carpathian Basin. Led by the geographer, count Pál Teleki, the aim of the Hungarian government, after the First World War, was to demand justifiable territorial boundaries. This process involved establishing new borders in the Carpathian Basin that followed the ethnic lines. In comparison with what had been approved by the Entente powers for the newly created nations after World War I, Hungary's demands were really very modest. Hungary very much wanted to include its ethnic Magyars within its borders, but it did not want to dominate the other peoples of the Carpathian Basin. Hungarian willingness to compromise was motivated by the underlying idea of wanting to justify the objective to integrate the peoples of the Carpathian Basin and create unity there. This would only be possible if they worked in co-operation with the other peoples of the Carpathian Basin. The Hungarians were, therefore, satisfied with the fair frontiers proposed under the auspices of the Axis-powers of Hitler's Germany and Italy and agreed to by the Allied Powers of Britain and France during the time of the Vienna Awards.

In the First Vienna Award of 2nd November 1938, it was decided that Hungary should be given back the southern part of what used to be known as the Upper Lands, an area of 12,103 square kilometres with approximately 1,030,000 inhabitants, 830,000 of whom were Hungarian. Some 66,000 Hungarians remained in Czechoslovakia and 140,000 Slovaks ended up in Hungary.[71] András Rónai, a colleague of count Teleki wrote in his memoirs about the negotiations with the Slovaks; about how there had been an atmosphere of mutual trust and he commented that the newly created border was ethnically the most fair and accurate one in Europe.[72]

Endeavours were also made to reach a compromise with Rumania. In what was known as the Second Vienna Award which was signed on 20th August 1940 the areas of Transylvania that were populated predominantly by Hungarians were given back to Hungary. The Hungarian government responded to a request made by the Rumanians who were afraid that Hungary might try to win back Transylvania by military means to negotiate on the status of Transylvania. The Hungarian claims were also supported by the Soviet-Russian minister of Foreign Affairs. On 23rd June 1940, Molotov told the Hungarian ambassador in Moscow that "the Soviet Union would not mind if Hungary's claims were realized at Rumania's expense, nor would it object in the future." The Transylvania problem was closely allied to the Bessarabia question. In June 1940, the Soviet Union had won back Bessarabia from Rumania. This issue will be returned to in part three.

It was in Transylvania that Hungary's biggest Trianon sacrifice was made. In Trianon, Rumania had requested and received a far bigger portion of Transylvania, inhabited by a mere three million Rumanians, than the area of the Hungarian kingdom left for the eight million Hungarians who lived there. In the next part of this book, we shall discuss the lot of the 1.7 million Hungarians who ended up in Rumania and were treated as second class citizens in detail. The Hungarians were not simply interested in Transylvania because of the numbers of Hungarians living there or because of the economic opportunities the area offered, but also because it was the region where they had their cultural roots, where the Hungarian state had its cradle. During the period of Turkish occupation, Transylvania had for a long time ensured the continuity of the Hungarian state and enabled the Hungarian culture to survive. At the time of the Second Vienna Award, Transylvania was divided down the middle. The northern region again fell under Hungarian control whilst the southern part remained the domain of Rumania. Northern Transylvania that covered an area of 43,104 square kilometres had a population of 3,011,000 inhabitants of which 1,867,000 were Hungarian and 1,036,000 Rumanian, a ratio of 62% to 34.4%. In Southern Transylvania there were 404,188 Hungarians. The Second Vienna Award had provided much better ethnically balanced demarcations than those laid down in the Trianon Treaty. It enabled more Hungarians to live in Hungary and, thus, fewer to be left in Rumania. Furthermore, the balance between the numbers of

Rumanians in Hungary and the numbers of Hungarians in Rumania was also better.

Today, we again see instances of Hungarian willingness to establish compromises with neighbouring countries. The Hungarians do not want to practice irredentist or revisionist politics at the expense of other nations in the Carpathian Basin. All the Hungarian national communities in Hungary's neighbouring countries have formulated concepts for autonomy that are firmly rooted in the notion that peace must be maintained between the various peoples of the Carpathian Basin. Any negative conclusions drawn from Hungarian endeavours to stand up for autonomy using peaceful means and democratic, parliamentary channels must be seen in the context of malicious negative image-forming. Indeed, it is a problem that has assailed Hungarians since the time of the Treaty of Trianon. Such misconceptions should now be forcefully decried once and for all.

The drive for freedom

At different times in their history, the Hungarians have been known to make enormous sacrifices for freedom. When the Hungarian kingdom was divided into three after the battle at Mohács, the Hungarians fought various wars of independence to reunite their country and to free parts of it from alien Habsburg or Ottoman tyranny. Relying heavily on the semi-independent principality of Transylvania and backed by the Protestantism alive in Eastern Hungary and in Transylvania, the Hungarians initiated a series of wars of independence against Viennese absolutism which were variously led by István Bocskai (1557-1606), Gábor Bethlen (1580-1629) and Ferenc Rákóczi II (1676-1735). These wars of independence had the unanimous support of the Hungarian population. In 1848/1849, the Hungarians once again rebelled against Austrian absolutism and centralism in the wake of the revolution that had commenced in Paris on 15th March.

In 1848, it had been the poem, *Talpra Magyar* 'Stand up Hungary', recited by its young author Sándor Petőfi to a crowd gathered in front of Hungary's National Museum that had inspired the Hungarians to take up their arms once again. There also a proclamation had been read out listing the Hungarians twelve demands relating to gaining more freedom. The Viennese Court proved unwilling to meet these demands and this in turn led to armed combat. The Hungarians immediately formed an army, the *honvéd*, which was commanded by Lajos Kossuth. After managing to hold out for a year the Hungarians were eventually defeated by the armies of the Russian tsar Nicholas I when they were defeated in Transylvania. After the War of Independence had finally been quashed, the Hungarians were heavily punished by the Habsburgs. Thirteen of their leading generals were executed at Arad and martial law was imposed on the country. Hungary was ruled by the Austrian governor, Alexander Bach, the union with Transylvania was rescinded and in Southern Hungary - in order to weaken the country - a separate administrative region was created, the Vajdaság (Vojvodina), that fell directly under Viennese control.

In 1956, the Hungarians revolted against communist oppression. The Hungarians had never been able to reconcile themselves to the Soviet-Russian presence in their country. Communism was an ideology that was alien to the Hungarians. They objected especially to the terrorism that communism brought with it and to the unlawful way in which the system operated. This was even too much for the Hungarian communists. Hence, in the autumn of 1956 the Hungarian yearning for freedom once again rose to the surface. The leader of the Hungarian uprising, Imre Nagy - once a firm communist - rebelled against the absolutist character of the Communist Party and objected to the fact that Hungary had joined the Warsaw Pact countries. The decisive moment came when the Hungarian army, led by colonel Pál Maléter, took the side of the insurgents, a move that did not pay off, because Hungary was left to defend itself alone. The West rigidly stuck to the East-West divide agreed to at Yalta (1945). After the uprising had been quashed, the Hungarians were left to reconcile themselves to the fact that for a long time to come they would have to remain part of the Eastern Bloc.

What the Hungarians had failed to achieve in 1956 finally became possible in the latter part of the eighties. Soviet-Russian dominance in Central Europe slackened and the approach adopted by party leader Gorbachev opened up new possibilities to reform communism, also in Hungary, in a movement that ultimately would lead to the collapse of the whole system. The reforms were supported and pushed through by sympathizers within the Hungarian Socialist Workers' Party, Hungary's young technocrats. It was the four-man strong group of: Miklós Németh, Imre Pozsgay, Rezső Nyers and Mátyás Szűrös that really created the driving force behind the fall of communism. The Hungarians were the first to open up the iron curtain by letting East German refugees pass over the Austrian-Hungarian border.

Not only Hungarians in Hungary contributed much to the fall of communism in Central Europe, but also Hungarians living in neighbouring countries. They, too, were instrumental in bringing down the communist regime and building up democracy. In Rumania, the young Reformed Protestant minister László Tőkés was 'the spark that blew up the powder keg', the individual who shook up the Rumanian *mamaliga* 'maize porridge'. In December 1989, Tőkés entrenched himself in his parish in Temesvár (Timisoara) and refused to the command of the Securitate, the loathsome Rumanian security forces, to leave his parish. The members of his parish supported him and this gave rise to a masssive demonstration in the city of Temesvár which in turn induced the fall of the Ceausescu regime. In Czechoslovakia, the human rights movement Charta '77 actively opposed communism.

The Hungarian language

Before going on to examine certain aspects of the Hungarian language, I would like to reiterate that having a knowledge of

Hungarian is not necessarily synonymous with having Hungarian identity. Count Széchényi, for instance, spoke little Hungarian and regarded German as his native language. This, however, did not diminish his significance on the matter of Hungarian identity. The Csango-Hungarians, a group of ethnic Hungarians of around 200,000 living on the other side of the Carpathians in Rumanian Moldavia near to the city of Bacau (Bákó) have partly lost their knowledge of the Hungarian language. In one area, the Csango-Hungarians speak a kind of Hungarian that is archaic and has many Rumanian loan-words. Yet these people are regarded by others and themselves as Hungarians. The same applies to the many Hungarian descendants of the Western diaspora who no longer learn Hungarian as a mother-tongue. This does not correspond to the Hederian theory that sees language as the salient characteristic of a nation. The Hederian definition might be widely accepted in Indo-Germanic culture, but it is less important to the Hungarians.

The Hungarian language does have a number of unique characteristics into which until now, however, little research has been done. In the previous chapter, I explained how it has come about that in the past 150 years studies into the origin and structure of the Hungarian language have primarily been governed by the Finno-Ugric language theory. I further explained how the field was chiefly investigated by German philologists, such as Josef Budenz and Pál Hunfalvy, who were planted in Budapest to force the origins of the Hungarian language to fit into a German Indo-German mould. The German experts stuck to the framework established by Herder and even extended it to make it apply to the Hungarian people. To Herder's mind, language and origins were synonymous. Hence, the emergence of the theory about the Finno-Ugric origins of the Hungarians.

The research programme of the German Indo-Germanic researchers into Hungarian and the Hungarians was launched by Pál Hunfalvy in 1851 during a speech held at the Hungarian Academy of Sciences that was already under German control.[73] The lines of research postulated by Hunfalvy were strange to say the very least. In his opinion, carrying out word analyses would not be a good way of isolating Hungarian lexical roots. Hungarian lexical roots could only be analyzed if they were compared with cognate languages. Nowhere in his discourse does Hunfalvy explain how one may determine exactly which langauges are related to Hungarian. If the relationship was established by way of lexical roots then what we have here is a classic example of circular reasoning, which means that the scientific paradigm must, therefore, be rejected.

The programme that had a better theoretical basis for research into the Hungarian lexicon based on the structure of the Hungarian language, was the one developed by the Hungarian linguists János Fogarasi and Gergely Czuczor who, prior to 1848, had been invited by the Hungarian Academy of Sciences to compile an explaining and etymological dictionary. Already in 1851, Hunfalvy had levelled heavy criticism against the dictionary that had come to be known as the Czuczor-Fogarasi (CzF) dictionary. In that dictionary, it is presumed that Hungarian root words are one syllabic words with no suffixes. Hungarian is known as an agglutinative language, which means that new words, grammatical functions and meanings are created by affixing suffixes to roots or derivates. For instance, one can express continuity of action by adding the suffix *-get* to the verb *beszél* 'talk'. The resultant word *beszélget*, therefore, means 'to have a chat'. The principle of adding suffixes to words, of agglutinization, is not peculiar to Finno-Ugric languages, but occurs in languages throughout Asia.[74]

Hungarian roots are determined by the consonant combinations. Vowels may be freely interchanged within what is known as a consonant grid, thus producing new meanings of the same basic concepts as is demonstrated by the following example. The consonant grid *kVr* in which *V* represents a vowel produces the following roots: *kar* "arm", *ker* "root", *kor* "time", *kör* "circle" and *kur* "root". A number of these root words exist only in agglutinated form, as derivatives, as we shall see later. What all these roots have in common is that their basic meaning includes the concept of *round* and that is what makes them belong together. With the help of the agglutination principle it becomes possible to form huge organic word groups in which the original root *kVr*, meaning *round*, remains recognizable. This gives the Hungarian lexicon explosive-generative force and cohesion. In a metaphorical sense, one can spring from one Hungarian word to another via the vowels. Doubtless all languages have at some time in their history explored this principle but in many languages this capacity has been lost, thus making such languages analytic and static, i.e. left with a residue of separate words for separate meanings with no correlational cohesion.

As Czuczor and Fogarasi explained in an article written in 1861, they used these same principles when compiling their dictionary.[75] Language research carried out in Hungary has not generally followed the principles of Czuczor and Fogarasi but has, for 150 years, kept to the lines first laid down in the programme presented by Hunfalvy which does not specify which words are Hungarian roots and which ignores the existing cohesion of Hungarian words. From an Indo-Germanic point of view, this approach is understandable, because Indo-Germanic words code every meaning in a different word. Indo-Germanic words have become static-registratory, while Hungarian words have retained their original word-generating power.

In the Hungarian Historical-Etymological Dictionary (TESZ) compiled according to the Hunfalvy, Indo-Germanic tradition, the elements of the organic word groups that form an unmistakable entity are completely unravelled and found to derive from other languages. The structural and semantic cohesion of words is distorted beyond recognition in the TESZ as this list demonstrates:

	CzF	TESZ
kar 'arm'	Hungarian root	Old Turkish
karika 'ring'	Hungarian derivative	possibly Hungarian
karima 'edge'	Hungarian derivative	North Slavic
karám 'corral'	Hungarian derivative	unknown

		Hungarian
karing 'surplice' derivative	not mentioned	
ker 'root'	Hungarian root	not mentioned
kerek 'circular'	Hungarian derivative	derives from ker-
kerül 'attainment'	Hungarian derivative	Finno-Ugric
kerít 'provide'	Hungarian derivative	Finno-Ugric
kering 'turn'	Hungarian derivative	deríves from ker-
kéreg 'bark'	Hungarian derivative	derivative
kor 'time'	Hungarian root	Old Turkic
korong 'disc'	Hungarian derivative	Slavic
korc 'round belt for female clothing'	Hungarian derivative	Old French
korlát 'enclosure'	Hungarian derivative	origin unknown
kör 'circle'	Hungarian root	analogy
körös 'around'	Hungarian derivative	Hungarian adaption
köröz 'orbit'	Hungarian derivative	derivative
körny 'vicinity'	Hungarian derivative	neologism
környez 'approach'	Hungarian derivative	neologism
körül 'roundabout' derivative	Finno-Ugric	Hungarian
kur 'root'	Hungarian root	not mentioned
kuritol 'loiter'	Hungarian derivative	origin unknown
kurkál 'search'	Hungarian derivative	origin uncertain

Research into the Hungarian lexicon that is based on the principles of the Hungarian language has finally got off the ground.[76] The organic word groups give insight into ancient cultural coding systems. As exemplified in the list above, the concept *time* is linked to *round* via the root *kor*. Time is a circular concept conforming with the sun's rotation and with sundials, the instruments that register this movement. What makes Hungarian so interesting is the fact that old concepts, such as the notion about time, are conveyed through the language. Clearly we may expect spectacular breakthroughs in this particular area in the near future.

It is not only research into the Hungarian lexicon that has stood still for a long time, but also research into Hungarian grammatical rules, notably in the field of sentence structure, that is syntax. It is only since the eighties that study into the subject of syntax has really flourished. All the making of inventories and analyzing of Hungarian grammatical structures is not yet complete, but in this area we also may expect to see interesting breakthroughs. The Hungarian linguist, Imre Pacsai, has demonstrated that the phenomenon of reduplication is one that occurs in a number of languages in Eurasian areas and it cuts right across established language family barriers. The phenomenon of reduplication and word twinning is something that occurs often in Hungarian. For example *szánt-vet* is a compound created from the verbs 'plough-sow' and it means 'to till the ground' while *csere-bere*, 'exchange-non existent word' means 'batering'. Pacsai has demonstrated that in this respect Hungarian, Zyryans, Uiguric, Chuvash and Russian are members of one family group. It is highly probable that these languages developed reduplication by being in contact with each other. In the coming decades, much linguistic research will be devoted to examining the phenomena arising from contact between languages of the Eurasian continent.[77]

Mental and material cultural heritage

The roots of Hungarian culture extend throughout the entire Eurasian area. Early Hungarian art strongly resembles that of the Scythians, Huns and Avars, peoples who inhabited the Carpathian Basin before the Hungarians arrived there. The archaeologist, Gyula László, has provided convincing evidence to prove that where the mental and material culture of what he calls the 'steppe peoples' is concerned, there is definitely continuity.[78] László has managed to establish similarities between the wrought ironwork and the ornamentation of the steppe peoples and that of the Hungarians by comparing objects that date from the time of the Arpád dynasty.

Splendid samples of such handiwork can be seen amongst the artifacts of the Nagyszentmiklós Treasure trove (Sînnicolau Mare) that was discovered in 1799 in the Transylvania place of Nagyszentmiklós that lies to the south of the river Maros. The hoard which consists of 23 pieces includes: goblets, chalices, plates, drinking horns and jugs, all of which are made of pure gold. The treasure currently forms part of Vienna's Art History Museum collection. According to László the gold artefacts come from two dinner services, one of which belonged to the sovereign, probably Ajtony, who reigned over the southern region of Hungary at the beginning of the 11th century. These pieces belonging to the Hungarian king's service have runic characters on them and decorative patterns that are reminiscent of decorations found on objects such as coins and coronation attributes dating from the early Arpád dynasty period. The remaining artefacts belonged to the Hungarian queen and pre-date those of the king. The gold objects belonging to this part of the collection are embellished with representations of people and animals. The depictions tell stories that are also familiar from Hungarian mythology, such as the one of the eagle with outspread wings that holds a naked woman in its claws. The woman is either shown offering the bird something to drink or holding a leafy twig in her hand.[79] The eagle with outspread wings is a familiar decoration on Hungarian coats of arms. László presumes that the scene depicts the legend of Emese, the progenitress of the Hungarians or that it pertains to the legend of the Turul, the totemic eagle of the Hungarians. In the legend the birth of Álmos the king is described as follows: "Ügyek, the distinguished and noble king of Scythia married Emese, daughter of Onedbelia, the tribal chief from the river Don area in Hungary. He gave her a son whom she called *Álmos* (the one who had been dreamed of). The child was given this name because of a divine vision of his mother's in which God had come to her in the shape of an eagle and had made her pregnant ..." For the archaeologist László, the most persuasive evidence that the Treasure of Nagyszentmiklós is of Hungarian origin is the recurrence of the sun symbol seen in other early Hungarian artefacts. The Hungarians, too, regarded themselves as *Sons of the Sun*, a myth with a common source, namely, that of the struggle between Light and Darkness. This same theme recurs in medieval murals depicting scenes from the Legend of the Holy King, László (1077-1095).

105

The figure central to these church murals is the national saint of medieval Hungary, King László, protector of the country's frontiers, the frontiers of historic Hungary. Saint László was particularly revered in border areas. Because of Trianon and the changing of the historic borders many of these old Hungarian churches and frescoes fell into foreign hands, when the land they were on went to the neighbouring countries of Austria, Slovakia, Serbia, Rumania, Slovenia, Croatia and the Ukraine. Within Hungary's existing territory few church frescoes of the Legend of Saint László remain.[80] Apart from having to do with Trianon this also has to do with the fact that the area now covered by Hungary corresponds roughly to the area that was ruled by the Turks when they occupied Hungary during the time of Ottoman occupation. The Turks who stormed Vienna every year anew destroyed virtually everything in their path. In this way, the Hungarian cultural heritage from the Arpád period came to be virtually wiped out in what is now Hungary. It was only in outlying areas that Hungarian culture survived, notably in semi-independent Transylvania that was left undisturbed by the marching Turks.

The frescoes of the Legend of Saint László provide a variation on the old theme of the struggle between Light and Darkness, a theme that is repeated everywhere from the Far East to Hungary. So far, endeavours to invest the frescoes with Western interpretation have been rather unsuccessful. The designs and the symbols take us back to distant places in time and space. St. László was an important royal saint of the Arpád dynasty. The royal Hungarian dynasty has produced quite a number of saints. Saint László is buried in the cathedral at Nagyvárad (Oradea, Großwardein), the cathedral that he built. His tomb is a place of pilgrimage for Hungarians. In Nagyvárad, there also used to be a huge bronze statue of him dating from the latter half of the 14th century. In the church where he lays buried, murals have been painted to glorify his life and his wondrous deeds. Numerous legends have been created around him most of which have as their theme the battle of Kerlés-Cserhalom against the Cumans, the Turkic horsemen who invaded Hungary on different occasions during the course of the 11th and 12th centuries.

Both the shorter and longer mural scenes depict the Hungarian army marching out of Nagyvárad followed by the battle against the Cumans. One Cuman is seen escaping from the scene of the battle on horseback taking a kidnapped Hungarian girl with him. The arrows shot by the Cuman cannot injure Saint László, who follows in hot pursuit, but likewise Saint László is unable to wound the Cuman with his lance. In the next scene, the girl is seen dragging the Cuman from his horse, then the two heroes are seen locked in unarmed combat. The two figures stamp on each other's feet, grasp each other by the belt and shoulders, but neither is able to get the upper hand. Finally, the girl who has been freed slashes the Cumans Achilles tendon with an axe. The king and the girl then behead the Cuman who by now has lost all his strength. Having beaten the Cuman, Saint László hangs up his weapons on a tree and lies down to rest with his head in the girl's lap. The girl then cleanses the hero's hair by delousing it.

In Europe, such fresco scene sequences are only to be found in churches situated in the border regions of the former Hungarian kingdom. By 1913, it had already been established that these frescoes were not unlike certain Scythian depictions on view in the Hermitage in Saint Petersburg. The images present ancient traditions and symbols which pre-date the Western Christian culture of the Hungarians. For instance, the gesture of 'delousing hair' - also recurrent in traditional folk ballads - though uncommon is recognized as symbolizing love-making. The girl delouses her lover's hair. There are other scenes, too, that transport one into the distant past. The sight of the two heroes standing up to fight alongside their horses is reminiscent of depictions found on bronze belt decorations unearthed in the Ordos region in a meander of the river Huangho. The theme of the *holy battle* is one that occurs often in Persian art. The frescoes of the Legend of Saint László should be seen as fitting into this tradition and occurring on its western-most periphery.

Certain elements of the mural described above convey that what is really being shown here is a duel of cosmic proportions. Saint László's horse is painted white and the king himself is also flooded in light. The Cuman, by contrast, is portrayed in dark colours, as is his horse. The heroes are seemingly indestructable until the moment when the Achilles tendon of the Cuman is slashed and he loses all his strength. This indestructability of the two heroes reminds one of Eurasian heroes, they, too, were seemingly unbeatable. Clearly, the fight is more than a struggle between two mortals: it is a battle between the cosmic powers of Light and Dark. The Legend of Saint László is essentially Eastern mythology presented in a Christian guise. The stature of the girl in the story rises to unparalleled heights when in one representation of this legend, created in the Vatican Legendarium (around 1340) the saved girl turns out to be no one less than the Holy Virgin Mary, patroness of Hungary!

It goes without saying that for the Hungarians such extensive losing to other countries of so significant a part of their cultural heritage stemming from the earliest days of the Hungarian kingdom, is extremely painful. The churches with the murals described above are almost all situated outside the country's present borders. The Hungarians not only attach much importance to the former areas of the Hungarian kingdom because of the large Hungarian communities living there but also because of such precious monuments, such valuable parts of Hungarian cultural heritage in those areas. This also explains why the plans of the Rumanian dictator, Ceausescu, to raze to the ground Hungarian villages at the foot of the Carpathians in Translyvania were so detrimental: such monuments were also destroyed in the process. Another less radical method employed by Rumanian and Slovak authorities in recent years is that of simply failing to renovate such Hungarian monuments their excuse being shortage of funds. This is why many of the churches and their frescoes are becoming ruined, sometimes beyond repair.

The churches in Transylvania do not just contain frescoes. In other respects too, they are Hungarian cultural goldmines. Hungarian runic writing has been found in a number of the churches, living proof that this kind of writing was used well into the Middle Ages. A further feature of the churches in Transylvania and in the Partium is that they have ceilings with painted wooden coffers. Such ceilings are virtually unique to Hungarian Protestant churches and the decoration dates from the time of the Reformation. The coffers are painted with symbols and motives deriving from the astro-mythological beliefs that permeate Hungarian culture. The responsibility resting on the local Hungarian population and, ultimately, on European people in general to preserve these Hungarian treasures for future generations is enormous.

Not only all that is precious, such as the treasure of Nagyszentmiklós, the Holy Crown and monuments like all the churches with their frescoes, runic inscriptions and painted wooden ceilings bearing motives and symbols of Hungarian culture, but also the written Hungarian culture is important creating as it does a fund of knowledge and mental-moral imperatives. Here one thinks of all the existing myths, sagas, legends, fairy tales, ballads and chronicles. During the time of communism this rich legacy was ridiculed - regarded as naive folklore and as being completely divorced from reality. To demonstrate that the old Hungarian ballads certainly do have a mental-moral content here is a free translation of the folk ballad of *The Wife of Kelemen the Mason.*[81]

> *Twelve masons where are you going to?*
> *"We're leaving when we find work!"*
>
> *"Come, come, I'll take you on,*
> *to build the big fortress of Déva,*
>
> *For a bushel of gold, two bushels of silver,*
> *Two bushels of silver, three bushels of bronze."*

*They started to build the big fortress of Déva.
What they built in the morning fell down in the afternoon,*

*What they built in the afternoon fell down at night
What they built in the afternoon fell down at night,*

*The twelve masons sat down to talk:
"The first man's wife to come here
Will be taken and burnt,
Will be taken and burnt.*

*Her beautiful white ash will be mixed in the cement
That we'll use to build the high fortress of Déva!"*

*"My God, my God, give me a black forest
so that my wife can turn back!"*

*God took care of it, yet she doesn't turn back,
God took care of it, yet she doesn't turn back.*

*"Hello, hello, Kelemen the Mason!"
"Welcome, welcome dear wife!"*

*"I've come to visit you!"
"You have come to be beheaded."*

*"I know you are capable
of murdering people to earn money!"*

*They took her and broke her neck in two
Then she was burnt, then she was burnt.*

*Her beautiful white ash was mixed in the cement,
Her beautiful white ash was mixed in the cement.*

*That was used to build the big fortress of Déva
That was used to build the big fortress of Déva.*

*The price was paid with a bushel of gold,
with a bushel of gold, with two bushels of silver*

*With two bushels of silver, with three bushels of bronze
With two bushels of silver, with three bushels of bronze.*

*Kelemen the Mason left for home
His daughter asked: "Father, my dear father,*

*Father, my dear father, where is my dear mother?"
"She is far away, this evening she'll come home!"*

*The evening came, but she didn't return,
The evening came, but she didn't return.*

*His other daughter asked: "Father, my dear father,
Father, my dear father, where is my dear mother?"*

*"Your dear mother is in the big stone wall,
Your dear mother is in the big stone wall."*

Building such a fortress on a vulcanic mountain in the Southern Transylvanian city of Déva was of course a colossal project, of megalomanic proportions. The Ballad of *The Wife of Kelemen the Mason* warns us about the destructive effects of such a megalomaniacal project. In his fervour to help build the fortress of Déva Kelemen the Mason is even prepared to sacrifice his personal happiness, his wife and his family. Kelemen the Mason symbolizes the person whose stakes are too high. Hungarians know that the price paid for megalomania can be high, too high, and they are reminded again of this in the ballad of *The Wife of Kelemen the Mason*.

PART II

Trianon and its consequences for the Hungarians

Hungary before the First World War

After the First World War and the Treaty of Trianon (1920) Hungary, as it had historically been known, ceased to exist. Like the Carpathian Basin Hungary had been a natural geographic entity in the heart of Europe. Historically, it had been a multinational state composed of different peoples living with ethnic Hungarians (Magyars). There were Slovaks in the Upper Lands, Germans dispersed throughout the country, but living mainly in the cities, Serbs in the southern part of Hungary, Ruthenians in Subcarpathia and Rumanians in Transylvania. After the liberal republican movement led by Lajos Kossuth had been defeated during the anti-Habsburg struggle for independence of 1848/1849 Hungary's democratizing process again came to a standstill. The Hungarians were alone in their fight for independence. The West sympathized with Hungary and its aspirations but failed to support its cause because of a firm conviction that the Habsburg Empire was crucial in the process of maintaining the balance of power in Europe. Even the different Hungarian nationalities turned against the revolutionary movement because Vienna had offered them greater political freedom if they pledged to help quash the Hungarian struggle for independence. In 1849, the Tsar of Russia, Nicholas I, sent in 200,000 fresh Cossack troops to swell the Habsburg ranks of the emperor Frans Joseph, thus forcing the Hungarians to lay down their arms. With the crushing of the Hungarian struggle for independence, which had very much been modelled on the ideals underlying the French Revolution, also came the postponement of plans to thoroughly revise the socio-economic structure of the Habsburg Empire.

Though the Hungarian nobility was made up of all nationalities within the Dual Monarchy it was essentially and traditionally *Magyar* in character. After failing to secure freedom for themselves in 1848, the Hungarians had put up passive resistance to Austrian rule. When in 1866 the Austrians were defeated by the Prussians at Königratz the Hungarians, seized their chance to make their status, within the Habsburg Empire, equal to that of the Austrians. The Hungarian nobility then drew up an agreement with the Viennese Court that came to be known as the *Ausgleich* (1867). Many of the conflicts arising between the various nationalities of the Dual Monarchy that were later given a nationalistic slant by the various nationalist movements with slogans like 'oppressed by the Hungarians for a thousand years' basically arose from social and economic problems. These problems gained an ethnic dimension because the Hungarian nobility was largely composed of *Magyars*, but even the Magyar peasantry was repressed by the Hungarian aristocracy. In addition, since 1867 Hungary had been enjoying a period of peace for the first time in a long while. Between 1867 and the outbreak of World War I, Hungary experienced unprecedented economic expansion. The industrial sector saw spectacular growth. The cities, notably Budapest, developed rapidly as did infrastructure and the railway network. The conservative-liberal faction of the Hungarian nobilty saw national diversity as an obstacle to the process of turning Hungary into a modern state. In 1868, the liberal politician, Baron Jozef von Eötvös, wanted the nationality law to do no more than ascribe cultural rights to the different nationalities. For the various nationalist movements seeking territorial autonomy this was not enough. Offering cultural rights for the different nationalities was not something that was peculiar to Hungarian liberals and their approach to the nationality problem. It was a general political point on the agenda of all European liberals.[82]

The 'Magyarization' politics of the end of the last century should be viewed in this context. For the Hungarians there was nothing racial about being Magyar; that way of looking at matters was strange to them. What the Hungarian state did try to do was to establish Hungarian as a means of communication so that direct contacts between central government and regional authorities might become more efficient. The regional elites, like the Rumanian Orthodox Church in Transylvania, were opposed to introducing Hungarian into the education system completely as this would weaken their position as intermediaries between central government in Budapest and their own clientele, the

Rumanian population, on whom their power depended.[83] Introducing Hungarian into state school education was labelled an act of 'racialism' by those opposed to Hungary, such as the British historian R.W. Seton-Watson. Church schools, for instance, did not comply with the rule of enforcing Hungarian. In such schools education was optional in Rumanian and Slovak areas. In the years leading up to the First World War, two basic power conflicts were, therefore, giving rise to tension. There was the problem of leaving a feudal era which, for political reasons, was going more slowly than it had in Western Europe and the ambition of building up a centralized modern state clashed with the linguistic interests of the people situated on the periphery of the Hungarian kingdom. This only intensified nationalistic opposition from Slovaks, Serbs and Rumanians, all of whom were able to rely on the support of their respective ethnic fellows across the border. For political reasons all these movements were supported by the Western Allies.

The background to the First World War

On the eve of the First World War, various continental powers were busy competing for power in Europe. After the Franco-Prussian War of 1871, the German Union was established in Versailles. This was something that was humiliating for the French. After 1871, Bismarck's Germany wanted to establish a place for itself amongst the recognized colonial world powers of France and Great Britain. Germany was now also on its way to becoming a world power. France sought revenge for her defeat against Germany in 1871 and wanted to win back Alsace-Lorraine that had been lost in the 1871 war with Prussia. France was, furthermore, worried that Germany might manage to establish permanent hegemony on the continent. Germany's power had to be reduced. The French were depending on Russia and Pan-Slavism to neutralize Pan-Germanism. As a world naval power Great Britain was starting to feel threatened by Germany. Traditionally, Britain's foreign policy has always relied on their being a *balance of power* between Germany and France. As far as Britain was concerned, the two continental powers of Germany and France had to remain in equilibrium, so that neither could dominate the continent and ultimately turn against Britain. On 8th August, 1915 *The Times* reported the following about England's entering into the war: "England would certainly have joined France and Russia even though Germany would have repected the neutrality of Belgium [...], because it was in her interest to defeat Germany, as England had defeated Philippe II, Louis XIV and Napoleon I." Russia was striving to gain more of a hold in the Balkans and in the Adriatic coast region and was interested in the Straits of the Dardanelles. In this expansionistic plan, the Serbs functioned as an advance guard and they were used by the Russians as a battering-ram. In Central and Eastern Europe, Russia was particularly seeking to compensate the losses incurred in Asia during the war against Japan in 1905.

France initiated an anti-German alliance by forming ties with Great Britain and Russia. In 1892, France and Russia signed a military pact and in 1904 France and Great Britain settled an agreement known collectively as the *Entente Cordiale*. Germany managed to bind together the Central European states with what was known as the *Triple Alliance*. In 1872, the German Empire established a military pact with Austria-Hungary and with Italy that came to be known as the *alliance of the Central Powers*. On the eve of the First World War, two big European military power blocks, therefore, stood on opposing sides: the Entente and the Central Powers backed by all their respective allies. The Entente's allies were Serbia and Rumania, countries which had evolved during the second half of the 19th century at the expense of the decaying Ottoman Empire. The Balkan states boosted the Entente Powers and offered them a good strategic position behind the Central Powers. Bulgaria, a third Balkan country, and the Ottoman Empire felt threatened by Russia and its two Balkan allies, Serbia and Rumania, joined forces with the Central Powers.[84]

Whether or not Austria-Hungary could be seen as being a part of the European great powers before the First World War remains a moot point. In his book *The Rise and Fall of Great Powers* (p.215-216), Paul Kennedy argues that the Dual Monarchy could not really be placed in that category even though he concedes that it did at the time constitute a strong economic entity. According to him, internal ethnic strife undermined the Dual Monarchy rendering it less effective. There is a school of historians though, such as István Deák of Columbia University, which maintains that Austria-Hungary did constitute a stable power with good economic prospects. Austria-Hungary was, however, leaning ever more heavily on Germany in order to counteract Slavic Orthodox pressure that was building up on the southern flank that was supported by Russia.

In 1908, Bosnia-Herzegovina was annexed by Austria-Hungary. The Dual Monarchy chose to implement a preventative Balkans policy in the hope of obviating Greater-Serbian aspirations which revolved around the desire to establish a Slavic state on the Adriatic coast that would envelop the south Slavic peoples and the Slavic speaking groups in the southern parts of the Austro-Hungarian Empire. Franz Joseph's successor to the throne, Franz Ferdinand, had his own plans for the southern Slavic peoples. Franz Ferdinand had worked out the concept of Austro-Slavism, a plan which postulated that next to Austria and Hungary the Slavic peoples of the Dual Monarchy could also be given autonomy within the Habsburg Empire. Austro-Slavism clashed with Greater-Serbian nationalism. It was, therefore, not surprising that the man who assassinated archduke Franz Ferdinand on 28th June 1914 in Sarajevo came from extreme nationalist Serbian circles. The assassination plot had been the work of the secret society *The Black Hand* which operated under the cover of the Serbian government and Russia. It was this murder of Austria's crown prince, Franz Ferdinand, that precipitated the First World War that was to last four years, a war that was to claim the lives of millions of people and radically changed the map of Europe.

In the First World War, the great powers were basically motivated by imperialistic objectives: they wanted to expand their territories and spheres of influence or obtain more raw materials to fuel their economies. From that point of view, the Austro-Hungarian Monarchy was a rich source. Geographically it occupied a strategically good position in the heart of Europe and its population was on the whole reasonably well educated. Around the turn of the century, its economy had enjoyed a real boom. Cities like Prague, Budapest and Vienna had rapidly become centres of European civilization. Through its alliance with Germany Austria-Hungary became part of the German sphere of influence after having functioned as France's counterpart in the continental balance of power for a long time. In this constellation it was in the interests of the Entente and Russia to weaken the power of the Dual Monarchy.

The First World War was not just an imperialistic war, there was also an ideological side to it. Germany and Austria-Hungary were authoritarian-clergical, semi-feudal states with no interest in the liberal and democratic systems of the West. In France and Great Britain, efforts were made to introduce civil democracy to Central and Eastern Europe. It would have been better if the German Empire and the Austro-Hungarian Monarchy had, at an early stage, become middle class liberal democracies. Little research has been done into the question of why the middle classes emerged so slowly in this part of Europe. In Hungary, this social group had not been able to fully develop because large landownership had been so dominant in the economy. Furthermore, the quashing of the anti-Habsburg liberal uprising and War of Independence of 1848/1849 had temporarily halted the democratization process in Hungary, though it did help to finally abolish serfdom. Nevertheless, the Austro-Hungarian Dual Monarchy continued to be seen as a last bastion of a backward type of Catholicism in Europe. The question one has to ask is whether this impression was true. The Dual Monarchy might have been conservative, but it did at least form a constitutional state that enjoyed reasonable prosperity. Something that the inhabitants of that particular part of Europe have not been able to enjoy since the end of the First World War. There were, therefore, ideological differences between the Protestant naval power of Great Britain and anti-clergical France on the one side and the Catholic Austro-Hungarian Empire on the other side.[85]

The Hungarians were concerned about Pan-Slavism, an ideology aimed at making Europe Slavic that was being embraced with increasing enthusiasm by the Slavic peoples of Hungary and which could rely on Serbian and Russian support. When the armies of Napoleon had been defeated, Tsarist Russia had gained the status of a world power and this had only stimulated Russian ambitions in the direction of world-wide hegemony. The Russians felt called to free the Slavic peoples who were 'suffering' under the yoke of Austrian and Turkish oppression. On top of this, the Russians had long harboured an overriding desire to expand. At that time, Pan-Slavism was employed as an instrument by the Russian rulers to pave the way to penetrating into the Balkans.

Where Hungarian territorial integrity was concerned, the prospect of Russian autocrats masquerading as 'Slavic and Orthodox overlords' amounted to a threat and a danger. They had couched their aims in the same terminology as that previously used to describe monarchs who also sought to rule over the Catholic Slovaks and Croats next to the Orthodox Rumanians and Serbs. As baron Miklós Wesselényi, the 19th century Hungarian liberal put it: "Thanks to Russian indoctrination and Slavic revolutionary propaganda the greater part of the Slavic, Greek and Rumanian peoples now honour the Russian Tsar as their emperor."[86] Not only authoritarian Russians wanted the Slavic region of Central Europe to come under Russian rule, but also Russian liberals. The Pan-Slavic congress of 2nd June 1848 in Prague gives a good impression of what kind of attitude the Slavs had towards the Hungarians. Serbs and Croats saw in the Hungarians their biggest mutual enemy. The Czechs, Slovaks and Slovenes, by contrast, wanted to preserve the Habsburg State. It was only the Poles, the old allies of the Hungarians, who supported Hungary. The conclusions drawn in the final communiqué aptly summed up the atmosphere of the congress; it denounced Hungarian 'tyranny', but made no mention whatsoever of the oppressed Poles and

Ukrainians. Probably, Tsarist propaganda had been wielded to manipulate the opinions of people at the congress.

The Hungarians were opposed to the annexation of Bosnia-Herzegovina in 1908 which would increase the proportion of Slavic speaking peoples within the Dual Monarchy and give rise to internal tensions. It was for this same reason that the Hungarian prime minister, István Tisza, opposed propositions made within the crown council to send out a military expedition to punish Serbia in the wake of the murder of Franz Ferdinand. In the summer of 1914, Tisza tried to convince Franz Joseph, the emperor and king, that the Dual Monarchy might well disintegrate, if war was to break out in Europe. The advice of the moderate Hungarian premier was blatantly ignored, but his assessment of the situation had been correct.

For a long time, the countries of the Little Entente, Czechoslovakia and Rumania, saw Tisza as one of the biggest supporters of the military expedition to punish Serbia and of the First World War. Worse still, for a long while the Czech, Benes, spread the rumour that Tisza was the person most responsible for the outbreak of the First World War. It was easy to understand why Tisza was blamed for starting the war. After all, the successor states of Czechoslovakia, Rumania and Yugoslavia had been either entirely created or had extended their territory at Hungary's expense. The minutes of the Austro-Hungarian crown council published in 1919, the memos and writings of the Russian Ministry of Foreign Affairs made public in 1918 and the British *Blue Book* specified the exact reasons for the visit of the French Minister of Foreign Affairs, Raymond Poincaré, to St. Petersburg. All this written evidence served to effectively eradicate the myth that the Hungarian Tisza had been some kind of a jingoist.[87]

The French consciously worked towards bringing about a war and the outbreak of the First World War was a consequence of the obscure machinations of the Russian-Serbian alliance. France lent huge sums of money to Russia to help the country recover after its defeat in the 1904-1905 war against Japan.[88] In 1909 and from then onwards, Iswolski, the Russian ambassador in Paris, paid out substantial sums of money to systematically bribe the French press to create anti-German and Austro-Hungarian feeling. Poincaré, the French Foreign Affairs Minister, knew what was going on. The only thing that he requested was that Iswolski keep him informed of his activities. Bruno Naarden informs me that these activities to bribe the French press by the Russian authorities actually had already started in the nineties.[89] In this way, French public opinion was prepared for war. After the assassination of Franz Ferdinand, the Russians also were the first to mobilize their armies. The scheming plan of 1914 had been to corner Germany and Austria-Hungary, so that they would eventually declare war which was what France in particular very much wanted. The notion that Hungary was guilty of instigating the war is, therefore, pure fabrication. In fact, as far as Hungary was concerned, when Russia was defeated in 1915 all their war objectives had been satisfied. As an ally Hungary did not want to pull out of the war and it was convinced that continuing the war would be a bad thing. The only way to avoid being surrounded by the Slavs was by depending on Germany and Hungary knew exactly where it stood.

Propaganda had been crucial in destroying the AustroHungarian Empire. Notably, British and French propagandists had managed to successfully 'demonize' Austria-Hungary. The Dual Monarchy was construed as constituting a threat to European peace and as being a bastion of militarism, authoritarian-clergyism and backwardness. In his publications, the British historian R.W. Seton-Watson spearheaded his attack especially at the Hungarians. It was clear that with the Ausgleich of 1867 the Hungarians had chosen the German side and the Entente countries certainly did not appreciate this. The 'thousand year long' period of oppression of various nationalities at the hands of the Hungarians was, therefore, seized upon and grossly exaggerated. What had come to be known as Magyarization policy was only effective at the end of the last century. This policy was detrimental to the different nationalities but, for its time, it was relatively mild.

Otherwise, it was precisely this thousand year long Hungarian history based on principles of tolerance, integration and a desire for freedom that was positive about Hungary. The propaganda of Seton-Watson and his friends was fuelled by lobbyists from circles in the later successor states of Czechoslovakia, Rumania and Yugoslavia. These people had quite a big influence on the war and on the outcome of the peace agreements in Paris that were to establish a new order in Europe. It was T.G. Masaryk in particular, the man who was later to become president of the First Czechoslovakian Republic and his younger assistant master, E. Benes, who were successful in conveying their concepts of a new Europe. Virulent anti-German and anti-Hungarian sentiments were central to the propaganda programme of both these lobbyists. Masaryk and Benes gave people the impression that a Central Europe governed by Czechoslovakia, Rumania and Yugoslavia would effectively counterbalance German power in Central Europe, encircle Hungary to neutralize it and would lead to the establishment of liberal-civilian democracies in the region. The events of the thirties in this present century have demonstrated clearly enough that the alliance of the Little Entente, the alliance of the successor states, was not strong enough to carry off such a plan. The Czechoslovakian concept of Central Europe left the door wide open to Nazi German expansionist politics. Neither were stable, liberal middle class democracies that could possibly survive in this part of Europe.

At the beginning of 1918, it was not clear who was going to win the First World War. The successes of the Central Powers early in 1918 opened up the opportunity for new alternatives concerning the map of Europe. Poland would be put back on the map and loosely linked to Austria-Hungary. Greater Bulgaria would dominate the Balkans. Serbia would be kept under control by Austria-Hungary. In 1916, Italy and Rumania had left the camp of the Central Powers to which they had been affiliated in exchange for the promise of territorial reward by the Entente after the winning of the war. On 17th August the Entente Powers had signed a secret agreement with Rumania in Bucharest. With the shifting of sides it had been promised that the Rumanians would receive Transylvania, which was Hungarian, and a substantial portion of Eastern Hungary as well. According to article 4 of the pact that was published on 3rd February 1919 in the French newspaper *Le Temps* - obviously with the aim of reminding the Entente of its promise - the Hungarian-Rumanian border would follow the river Tisza just to the west of the city of Debrecen.[90]

After Russia had withdrawn from the war in 1917, the Entente was left with one last big trump card in the form of the United States of America where the academic, Woodrow Wilson, had become president. The United States entered the war on the side of the Entente powers. Wilson believed that the US should become involved in the war in order to ensure just peace. The First World War was to be the war to end all wars.[91] With the objective of making the world a just and peaceful place after the First World War Wilson worked on a 14 point programme, aided by a team of advisors, that was to reorder the world. Wilson wanted to introduce a supranational consultation body that would regulate the perpetual struggle for power between rival nations. One of the most important principles of Wilson's New World Order was that of the right to self-determination for all peoples.

Since then this same principle has frequently been criticized as it is believed that it would ultimately lead to ethnic chaos in the world. I believe, however, that the problems in Central Europe mainly derived from, and still do derive from, applying this principle one-sidedly and undemocratically. The problem in Central Europe is that big national communities are forced to live in countries that are national tyrannies. The satisfactory solution to this problem can only lie in a regulated application of the self-determination principle. I shall return to this point in part three of this book. For the nationalities of Austria-Hungary Wilson's plan guaranteed autonomy, but not the right to form a state (article X). Wilson's autonomy concept opened the door to separatism and state forming. It meant that if the Entente side won, a number of new small states would evolve in Central Europe.

The road to Trianon

When the Tsarist army in Gorlice was utterly defeated in 1915, the Hungarians regarded the war as over. With the defeat of Russia and the occupation of Serbia the main preventative defensive objective had been realized, namely that of neutralizing aggressive, expansionistic Russian politics in the Balkans. During the war, the Hungarians had remained loyal to their allies. Tisza's attitude might perhaps even be seen as symbolic. Even though Tisza had openly opposed the war he had not failed to fulfil his military duty. Tisza had made a promise and he was not going to break it. Hungary remained loyal to her allies. Italy and Rumania, by contrast, had changed allegiance during the course of the war by going over to the Entente camp. It had not, however, been a war aim of the Entente Powers to disrupt the Dual Monarchy which, during the war years, had remained stable. Only the Czech soldiers had gone over to the Russian side. Hungary was simply conquered by politics of accomplished facts.

The Allies proposed an armistice with Austria-Hungary, which was agreed to and signed on 4th November 1918 in Padua. The Austro-Hungarian army then laid down their weapons and Hungary withdrew itself from the war. In fact the armistice of 1918 turned out to be a trap. During the war, hardly anyone from the enemy camp had set foot on Hungarian soil. During the course of 1918 the social democrats, led by count Mihály Károlyi, had seized power in Budapest and declared Hungary to be independent. The Red Count, as he was mockingly called, turned out to be no realist.

Count Károlyi had blind trust in the Entente and the peace that Wilson offered. Károlyi opened his inaugural speech with the exclamation *Vive la France* at a time when Rumanian troops led by French generals were charging through Transylvania. The Hungarians, by nature a loyal folk, were puzzled by the French guile. The sympathy that the French received from Hungary was derived from mixing genres. For centuries, literary Hungarians had looked to Paris for their inspiration and the same people often also played a role in Hungarian politics. This was why French prestige did such wonders, so much, in fact that Károlyi allowed his Minister of Defence, Béla Linder, to disband the Hungarian army with the words: "I don't want to see another soldier". This turned out to be a great miscalculation, because in breaching the armistice agreed to at Padua the armies of the Entente and their allies, the Czechs and Serbs, were given free access to Hungarian territory. Hungary was no longer able to defend itself. A country that renounces its army also gives up an important way of exerting pressure. The Hungarian army should, therefore, never have been disbanded not only in connection with the defence of its own territory, but also because in the peace talks that were to follow the Hungarians were, thus unable to exert any military pressure. Hungary was, therefore, no longer able to win back areas, as the Turks had done under the command of Kemal Ata Turk, that had been lost during the First World War before the definite peace agreement was signed. Wilson's 14 point programme and the worshipping of French prestige and culture had been as effective as the Trojan horse.

In fact, it would seem that the Hungarians have not learnt much from history. Even today, with war being waged in former Yugoslavia at Hungary's southern border and with the Hungarian minority in North Vojvodina like caged rats, there are politicians arguing that the Hungarian army, which is already depleted and poorly armed, should be substantially reduced. In Hungary, there is a deep-rooted sort of confidence that the West will step in and lend a helping hand, if Serbia decides to attack Hungary.

Count Károlyi and his Minister of Foreign Affairs, Oszkár Jászi, were unable to satisfy the high expectations of the Hungarians themselves on the matter of maintaining the country's territorial integrity. Attempts made by Jászi, who was in favour of a federal restructuring of the Dual Monarchy, to come to an agreement with the nationalities of Hungary, the Slovaks and the Rumanians in Transylvania, failed. The autonomy that Jászi offered the Rumanians and Slovaks was rejected. At the beginning of 1919,

Czech and Rumanian troops had occupied parts of Hungary and the representative for the Allied Powers, the French lieutenant-colonel Vyx, forced the Hungarians to part with more land than had been agreed to at the time of the armistice at Padua. In connection with the aftermath of the war, there was also great socio-economic tension making count Károlyi's position impossible. The communists led by Béla Kun and other front soldiers who had formerly been imprisoned in Russia and who had subsequently joined the Bolshevik movement revolted and proclaimed a Soviet-style Republic in Hungary in March 1919.

The Hungarian Soviet Republic that had been set up in Hungary was to be an imitation of the Soviet Republic that Lenin had managed to establish in Russia after the successful Bolshevik coup d'état of 1917. (See Richard Pipes, *The Russian Revolution*, New York, 1990). As this Hungarian Republic was based on violence, it formed a rupture in Hungarian history. Though the Hungarians might have been exposed to authoritarian power structures in the past, their state had seldom used violence against its own people. It was a law-abiding state with a long constitutional tradition. The Hungarian communists immediately abolished the constitution and introduced crude ways of achieving their ends. This was one of the main reasons why the Hungarian Soviet Republic was unable to steal the hearts of the Hungarian people. By 1919, there were Bolshevik death squads operating in the country that at random picked up 'opponents' of the regime to eliminate them. The most disreputable of all these was Tibor Szamuely who used to travel around Hungary by train seeking out people who were 'guilty' and executing them in the train. Even today, people outside the communist circles still recall the dreadful deeds committed by the Hungarian Bolsheviks with horror.

To stay in power the Hungarian Soviet Republic played the card that had so often been played in Hungary: the national card. The Republic tried to win the support of the Hungarian people by using the Hungarian red army to push back the Czech armies that had invaded the Upper Lands and the Rumanian armies that were in Transylvania. The Hungarian red army was mobilized under the guise of national symbols and in the name of preserving the country's territorial integrity. The Hungarian Soviet Republic had a bad influence on the peace negotiations that were continuing in Paris at the time. In Paris, the Allies were afraid that the red danger that had taken hold in Hungary might easily sweep across the whole of Central Europe where the disintegration of the Habsburg Empire had left a power vacuum. At any rate, it was true that the communist presence in Hungary did not improve Hungary's chances in Paris. Clemenceau, the French president, who instead of president Wilson chaired the peace conference secretly gave the Rumanians the backing and the go-ahead to precipitate the fall of the Hungarian Soviet Republic. They then invaded Hungary, plundered the countryside and occupied the capital of Budapest. The Rumanians even tried to steal the Hungarian Holy Crown and the Crown Jewels from the National Museum. It was thanks to the interception of the head of the Entente mission, the American general Harry Hill Bandholtz, that these precious possessions were not stolen. Details of this incident are recorded in the general's diary.[92] At the end of November 1919, the Rumanian armies were ordered to withdraw from Budapest which meant that the Rumanians were able to strengthen their hold in East Hungary. They did not leave Hungary until the end of March 1920.

The British, who did not want the French to have absolute power in Central Europe, gave their approval for a national Hungarian army to be formed in Szeged. It was to be commanded by admiral Miklós Horthy, commander-in-chief of the Austro-Hungarian navy and a close confidant of the King, Franz Joseph. On 16th November 1919, the national army restored law and order in Budapest. It was not until 4th June 1920 that the peace treaty, viewed by the Hungarians as a dictate, was ready to be signed by all parties in Trianon. The Hungarian delegation, led by count Albert Apponyi was held under arrest in Trianon, a suburb of Paris, and only allowed out for an hour each day for a little fresh air.[93] The Trianon Treaty was to have dreadful consequences for Hungary. It can probably be termed one of the most violent peace treaties of recent history.

The Treaty of Trianon took 72% of Hungarian territory away and 64% of its inhabitants. One in three ethnic Magyars ended up in one or other of the neighbouring states. Of the 232,000 square kilometres of land that Hungary was forced to renounce, Czechoslovakia was given 63,000 square kilometres and Yugoslavia and Rumania respectively 63,000 and 102,000. Even Austria, that had been on the same side as Hungary, was given an area of land of 4,000 square kilometres, the so-called Burgenland of West Hungary. Hungary was reduced from 325,000 square kilometres to 93,000. The area that Rumania annexed from Hungary that is to say, the eastern part of East Hungary and Transylvania, was, therefore, larger than what remained of Hungary itself after Trianon.

Under the pretext of the right to self-determination Hungarian statehood, as it had existed for a thousand years, was undermined and Hungary was chopped into pieces. Clearly, the right to self-determination did not apply to the losers, only to the winners and their allies. This then was what had come of the just peace that Wilson, the American president and winner of the First World War, had envisaged for the peoples of Europe. The seed had been sown for renewed conflicts in Europe. In Trianon, it had not been a case of what the actual facts and ethnic relations were, but rather whose arguments most closely corresponded to the interests of the winners of the war, notably the French and British. No referendums were held. Later Masaryk, the Czechoslovak president, was to admit that in 1918 it had been necessary to make a choice between holding referendums and creating new states. It had, therefore, been by no means certain that the Slovaks, for instance, would unanimously opt to break away from Hungary. The fact that in this century alone Czechoslovakia has already been divided twice and looks unlikely to ever reunite would seem to be proof enough that Masaryk's fears were justified. It was only in the case of Burgenland which had been allocated to Austria, another loser in the war, that a referendum was held after Italy had arbitrated. In the West Hungarian city of Sopron (Ödenburg) and thirteen surrounding towns, the majority of the people opted for Hungary.

Western statesmen, such as the British prime minister Lloyd George and the French president Clemenceau knew desperately little about ethnic and cultural affairs in Central Europe. Politicians lower down the ladder and civil servants were subsequently allowed to make decisions that were to have far-reaching consequences for millions of people and for the relationships between the peoples of the region. In Paris, Wilson's principles had not been adhered to, because the American president had failed to make an impact and so Clemenceau had dominated the scene during the peace conference. In the US presidential re-election campaign Wilson's position was weak. On top of all this, he was exhausted and a sick man. Clemenceau, therefore, became the celebrated champion of the Paris peace conference. Only interested in weakening the position of the Germans and strengthening the position of the French in Europe, Clemenceau was a typical product of continental power politics. The Hungarians who were thought of as being hand in glove with the Germans were, therefore, destined to suffer. The people who had put their trust in the French, such as the Czechs, Rumanians and Serbs were treated like favourite children and given everything they desired.

Since the right to self-determination was obviously something that was not reserved for the Hungarians, the Allies had clearly not lived up to their professed war objectives. Trusting that peace would be established by fair means the Central Powers had laid down their weapons believing that the agreement would be honoured. In Europe, probably the only thing remotely comparable to the Treaty of Trianon was the way in which Poland had been divided up in 1772 and 1795. In the Treaty of Frankfurt, of 1871, the Prussians had been extremely fair towards the French if we compare their fate to that of the Hungarians at Trianon. In an endeavour to justify the decisions taken at Trianon propaganda mongering began. The aim was to convince the world that the Austro-Hungarian Empire had been responsible for the outbreak of the war in the first place. In fact article 161 of the Treaty of Trianon explicitly states that Hungary was guilty of starting the war. As has been explained, this was nonsense. Tisza, the Hungarian prime minister had functioned rather as a moderator.

For the most part the boundaries introduced by Trianon cut right across ethnic Hungarian territory. They were drawn next to the railway lines in such a way that the whole network came to lie outside of truncated Hungary. The total length of the Trianon boundaries following railway lines amounts to approximately 1000 kilometres which is some 43% of the complete extent of the Trianon boundaries. According to the Hungarian geographer Zoltán Palotás this is a fairly unique state of affairs in political geography. The railway lines that created the new boundaries simultaneously formed an infrastructure network of almost 900 kilometres to the north and east of Hungary and almost 100 kilometres to the south. This vital rail route ran straight through ethnic Hungarian territory. The argument presented in favour of drawing the boundaries thus at the time of the peace congress in Paris was that the new states needed rail connections. Alternatives were not entertained during the conference.[94]

Only 40% of all the newly formed frontiers followed ethnic lines and 60% made deep inroads into ethnic Hungarian territory. Furthermore, it was not only for reasons of communication that the newly established frontiers were distinctly disadvantageous to Hungary. Economic and strategic considerations played a part too. For instance, the city of Budapest came to lie within cannon shooting range of Czechoslovakia. In other words, Hungary's capital and most important city could easily be bombarded from Czech territory. The new borders cut right through towns or cities that were inhabited by Hungarians who, thus, suddenly became detached from their own community. The victims of Trianon were the Hungarian people who were made 'minority' groups in neighbouring countries overnight. The Trianon Treaty did contain statutes pertaining to minorities which ascribed cultural autonomy to Hungarians who found themselves in new states, but unfortunately these statutes were not respected.

It has sometimes been said that the Hungarians could have been hit even harder by Trianon, which is no great consolation. It is true though that things could easily have turned out much worse for Hungary. Benes not only claimed more land for Czechoslovakia from the north of Hungary, including, for instance, the mining region in the Miskolc area, but he really also wanted to surround the Hungarians completely. Benes wanted to sever Hungary's lifeline with the West. It had been via the Austrian-Hungarian border that Hungary had managed to maintain its contact with the West. This was, therefore, the reason why Benes proposed creating a corridor that would link Czechoslovakia with Yugoslavia and pass through West Hungary. The Serbs also demanded more land. They were interested in the area around the city of Pécs where there are uranium mines. After the end of the First World War, Serbian troops moved into this area on the assumption that they would be able to stay there. The Rumanians claimed the river Tisza, which lies just south of the East Hungarian city of Debrecen, to be made their western border. They reminded the Hungarians that in the secret treaty of 1916 the Entente Powers had agreed to this boundary line. It would seem that all the demands made by these new states finally went too far for the Allies. The fact that these imperialistic claims were not honoured probably had more to do with rivalry between the Allies than anything else. It was quite clear that the US and Great Britain were not happy about a too strong French dominance on the continent. The US refused to sign the Treaty of Trianon and instead drew up its own peace treaty with Hungary. This means that where Trianon problems are concerned the US has its hands free and may act as an intermediary in Central Europe.

The Trianon secrets

Here above, I have briefly sketched how the Austro-Hungarian Empire came to an end and how Hungary was divided up by the

Treaty of Trianon. The self-determination principle of which the Entente Powers had boasted during the war in order to convince the Central Powers that peace would be established in a just and fair way had been flouted. To what extent one wonders was Wilson, the American president, aware that continental European politics was not founded on high ideals, but revolved rather around power political considerations and the national interests of separate states. What is in any case certain is that France was the country to have profited most from having won the First World War. The French defeat of 1871 had been adequately avenged and France had won back Alsace-Lorraine, an area inhabited by speakers of French and German that had only belonged to France since the time of the French Revolution. In the Treaty of Versailles, the Germans were ordered to contribute huge sums of money towards all the rebuilding work that needed to be done in Europe and after the war the French put the Germans under further pressure by moving in and occupying the Rhineland region. The new Central European states, the revised Polish state, Czechoslovakia, Rumania and Yugoslavia, which had come into being partly thanks to French intervention, oriented themselves towards France which in turn was interested in surrounding Germany and blockading Soviet Russian expansion in the direction of Central Europe. The states in the heart of Europe: Czechoslovakia, Rumania and Yugoslavia formed an alliance which came to be known as the Little Entente and which aim it was to surround and weaken Hungary. Truncated Hungary had already been pretty weakened, because it had lost a substantial portion of its natural resources and vital industries like, for instance, its Transylvanian oilfields and its minefields in the Upper Lands. The Treaty of Trianon, furthermore, stated that the Hungarians must plough massive sums of money into post-war recovery projects and they were allowed only to have a small army. In broad outline these then were the main outcomes of the war.

Much research still needs to be done into the whole question of the background to the Trianon Treaty. Many matters remain unexplained and shrouded in mystery. For instance, how was it possible for German Austria to receive a portion of West Hungary, the area known as Burgenland? Was there not something very paradoxical about all this? If indeed the French did want to combat Pan-Germanism in Europe by pursuing Pan-Slavism why then did this area voluntarily pass over to German jurisdiction. Did it have something to do with compensating for the loss of South Tirol in Austria to Italy? It goes without saying that the motives underlying the decisions taken at Trianon are of interest to historians, political scientists and academics in other fields, but for the Hungarians there is also another dimension to it. They need to find out what was contained in the secret agendas of the concerned great powers and their neighbouring peoples. How was anti-Hungarian propaganda instigated and how did the anti-Hungarian lobby operate in the West? When it comes to the propaganda and stereotypes described in the first part of this book, one has to ask whether they still have an effect today? How can the Hungarians escape from the difficult position that Trianon has put them in? What geostrategic programmes should be adopted? I shall put forward some suggestions in the third part of this book. All countries and peoples involved in fighting for their freedom must apply themselves to such questions.

Since Trianon little concrete research has been done in this field, mainly because in the inter-war years Hungary was in an awkward position. As has been explained above, Hungary had come out of the First World War badly weakened. It then also had to cope with a stream of refugees; Hungarian soldiers and civil servants who, in the new states, were not permitted to work for the government or who were only allowed to remain if they completely changed their allegiances. Hungarian civil servants were required to make an oath of allegiance to the Rumanian, Czechoslovak or Yugoslav constitution and take on the Rumanian, Yugoslav or Czechoslovak nationality. In Hungary, research into the secrets of Trianon had already commenced during the inter-war years, under the inspired leadership of count Pál Teleki, the man who was later to become prime minister of Hungary. The work was left uncompleted, because the country was pulled into the vortex of the Second World War. Hence, the reason also why the Hungarian negotiating delegation was ill-prepared for the Paris peace talks of 1947. The Hungarians lacked a clear negotiation strategy in Paris and so stuck to the border revisions that had been sanctioned by Hitler and Mussolini.

When the communists came into power in 1948, research into Trianon related issues came to a complete standstill, for a number of different reasons. By that time, the Soviet Union itself had become a successor state as well. In order to thank Stalin for all Soviet Russia's efforts, Benes gave the Soviet leader Ruthenia, the most easterly part of the First Czechoslovakian Republic or, as the Hungarians call it, Subcarpathia. According to the Allies, plans to revise the Trianon agreements at the time of the 1947 Paris peace congress were rejected by Stalin himself. From the peace negotiation reports it may be deduced that the Allies had agreed to a limited number of proposed frontier changes in Hungary's favour. It was notably the American delegation that was pushing for these changes. During the communist period any matters likely to give rise to unrest within the communist camp became taboo, especially where national or ethnic questions were involved that ultimately challenged basic communist ideology. In communist Hungary only a small group of specially selected researchers who had proved themselves loyal to the communist party were allowed to carry out any research into Trianon related issues.

Until now the only serious studies to have been carried out into the Trianon stipulations and their consequences have been those of a number of Hungarians living in the diaspora and the British academic C.A. Macartney who, during the inter-war years, criticized the Trianon Treaty, because he found it both unjust and impractical.[95] After the fall of communism, it was the Hungarian historian Ernő Raffay who finally broke the taboo surrounding Trianon research with the publication of his book *The Secrets of Trianon*.[96] Within a very short time 200,000 copies had been sold in Hungary. However, Hungary still has not managed to set up an academic institute for studies into Trianon and its consequences.

Those to benefit most from Trianon were the Czech emigrants who had turned their backs on the Austria-Hungarian, like Thomas Masaryk and Eduard Benes who managed to sway French and British policy makers and other people in influential positions. In his memoirs, Benes claims that during his time in Paris he maintained contacts with three organizations: the Masonic Lodge, the Human Rights League and the French Socialist Party.[97] Serb and Croat emigrants exiled in Paris also occupied themselves with lobbying activities. The underlying aim of all the campaigning was to convince the Entente Powers that the Austro-Hungarian Monarchy must be destroyed and nation states created in its place. During the First World War, in 1916, Benes had published the pamphlet *Destroy Austria-Hungary!* which outlined this programme in no uncertain terms. The ideas first launched by Benes were taken up by certain French academics, such as the historians Ernest Denis and Louis Eisenmann, influential journalists like Andre Tardieu and the above-mentioned influential pressure groups. Through his contacts Benes managed to win over to his side powerful diplomats like Philippe Berthelot, Jules Laroche and Pierre de Margerie at the Quai d'Orsay, the French Ministry of Foreign Affairs. After the war, the same group of men was responsible for drawing up the new boundaries and laying down the peace treaty stipulations. While Benes was busy lobbying in Paris, Masaryk took care of the Anglo-Saxon regions. Masaryk was in close contact with the chief editor of *The Times*, Henry Wickham-Steed and with R.W. Seton-Watson. With their help he managed to start up the periodical *New Europe*, a forum for those interested in restructuring Europe in accordance with considerations of "nationality, minority rights and geographical and economic realities" to guarantee that war would not break out again. Masaryk was also in touch with influential groups of Czech, Slovak and Ruthenian emigrants domiciled in the US.

The ordinary Hungarians were hardly aware of all the lobbying and propaganda activities that were going on at the time. After the war, Count Apponyi who had headed the Hungarian delegation in Paris declared that politically the Hungarians were really oriented towards Vienna. After the Ausgleich of 1867 Hungary had been forced to look to Austria. The diplomatic service of the Dual Monarchy had contained few diplomats promoting Hungarian interests. This explains why the Hungarians were unprepared for events when Austro-Hungarian nationality representatives commenced their lobbying and propaganda offensives in the various capitals of the West. When it came to Hungarian matters, French political moves were carefully worked out as the following quotation from Count Apponyi's memoirs illustrates:[98]

> "No words need be wasted in explaining why the French press was hostile to our mission, for this hostility was a natural consequence of the situation. How carefully this hostile attitude had been worked up may be seen from the following almost incredible details. Thirteen years earlier, in 1907, on the occasion of an Inter-Parliamentary meeting held in Berlin, I had delivered a humorous speech at a dinner-party. In the course of this, I remarked that, if the man in the moon came down for a short time to the earth and asked me which of our so-called world languages he should learn for the sake of his general education, I would unquestionable recommend German, because the assimilative power of the German intellect would open the way for him through excellent translations to the greatest number of cultural achievements in other lands. This was brought up against me in the Paris press - I repeat, after thirteen years - as a proof of excessive pro-German feeling! Still more amazing was a reference in the Paris press to an equally humorous after-dinner speech which I had made in Budapest many years before the outbreak of the war, in honour of dr. Gyula Vargha, then head of the Bureau of Statistics. On the occasion of some jubilee or other, his friends arranged an agreeable little dinner-party, at which I remarked that Vargha, who was also a lyrical poet of some standing, would be capable of transfiguring even the driest figures into petry by the ardour of his patriotism. I had completely forgotten about this speech, and was

astounded to see it reprinted by the Paris press in 1920 as evidence that Hungarian statistics were no more than poetical falsification."

To what degree the Western greater powers were perhaps seeking bridgeheads in Central Europe for economic reasons has not been properly researched. Was it possibly the case that Central Europe became more important to the British, and in their wake the French, when colonial expansion in Africa and Asia started to wane and the Germans, who they had managed to keep away from obtaining colonies, were showing interest in Central and Eastern Europe as well? Is it conceivable that this economic rivalry between the greater continental powers was instrumental in causing this imperialistic war to break out? The notion that the whole colonial mentality certainly played a part was reinforced by a telegram from the French general, Berthelot, who was in charge of the Rumanian troops in Transylvania in 1919. The telegram that was sent on 2nd January 1919 to the French War Office went as follows: "Si nous dennons aux Roumains les satisfactions auxquelles ils ont droit et si nous tenons nos engagements, nous aurons dans la Roumaine une véritable colonie française de plus de 15 millions d'habitants où nous pourrons développer notre commerce et notre industrie et où nous nous trouverons comme chez nous." The French general dreamt of establishing a French colony on the Danube at the expense of the Hungarians.

The intertwining between French politics and the military-industrial complex warrants more attention that it has received up until now. For instance, Raymond Poincaré, prime minister from 1912 to 1913 and afterwards president from 1913 till 1920, maintained intensive and fruitful contacts with the Saint-Gobain Society to which he was legal adviser. Alexandre Millerand (1859-1943), Minister of Defence from 1914 to 1915 and prime minister in 1920 was legal adviser at the Schneider munitions factory.[99] These were the politicians who told Count Albert Apponyi, the Hungarian League of Nations representative, several months after the signing of the Trianon Treaty that any revisions of the treaty were impossible. Count Apponyi wrote the following on the matter in his memoirs:[100]

"The most interesting conversations I had were with the new President of the Republic, Alexandre Millerand, and with Monsieur Poincaré, who was then looked upon as the head of the extreme nationalists. I also called on Paléologue's successor, Berthelot, who was the actual head of French foreign policy, and not so well disposed towards us as his predecessor. The welcome I received from him was most courteous, but the conversations which I had with him calculated to destroy any illusions I might still cherish. He was always stressing the fact that the peace treaties which had just been signed must never be altered, and that Hungary would have to reconcile herself to this situation. This was no surprise to me, and for that reason I was not greatly impressed. It was Raymond Poincaré who spoke out more clearly than any..." The whole question comes to this: Is Hungary definitely prepared to accept the situation made for her by the Treaty, without any intention of bringing about a change? If so, we can get on very well together."

As far as the matter of the Treaty of Trianon was concerned the main guilt must firmly lie with the French who had sought contact with the Czechs, Rumanians, Serbs and Tsarist Russia even before the war started. Apparently, the French had no difficulty co-operating with Tsarist Russia which could not exactly be described as a progressive country. The main objective of the Russians was to free all Slavs, a move which would automatically have led to the demise of the Austro-Hungarian Empire. Before the war, the French had supported this Russian goal and even before the Great War began parts of the Austro-Hungarian Empire had been promised to the Russian allies.

The Russian plans involved turning Serbia into a Slav bridgehead in the Balkans so that in this way areas of the Dual Monarchy could be annexed from the Balkan side. The French supported this Russian initiative. André Tardieu, head of the *Agence des Balkans,* a press agency that functioned as a mouthpiece for Athens, Belgrade and Bucharest and was seen by the French Foreign Affairs Ministry as normative when it came to the matter of issuing information from the Balkans, made a provocative speech in Bucharest on 11th April, 1914. The title of his speech alone was very bold, 'Transylvania: the Alsace-Lorraine of Rumania.' The comparison was, however, false. Whilst the French could draw on some historical claims to Alsace-Lorraine, an area that had been French from the French Revolution until the Franco-Prussian war of 1870-1, Transylvania had never been a part of Rumania. The fact that the address was heard by the entire French corps diplomatique and enthusiastically applauded at the end only encouraged Rumanian irredentism. A French state loan to the tune of twelve milliard golden francs was even paid out to Tsarist Russia, so that it could expand and modernize its army and extend its railway connections in a westward direction, that is to say, behind the Central Power countries. When it came to the outbreak of the war, the part played by the Russians and the French was dubious. The Russians and Serbs backed up by the French political leadership, supported extreme nationalistic terror organizations were responsible for the outbreak of war. According to the French journalist, Henri Pozzi, Russian diplomats were involved in preparations for the Sarajevo attack. British endeavours to mediate were torpedoed by Russia. Furthermore, long before the Austro-Hungarian troops had been mobilized the Russian army's units were all lined up and ready for battle. Finally, Poincaré, the French president, spurred the Serbs and Russians on to go to war.[101]

France sacrified 1.5 million people to win back Alsace-Lorraine, which had a population of 1.5 million people, 1.5 million Frenchmen lost their lives. It is strange that in his book *A Diplomatic History of Europe, since the Congress of Vienna* the French historian René Albrecht-Carrié perpetuates the myth of justified peace:"France had no quarrel with Hungary, being, in fact, to some extent sympathetically inclined towards that country at the time of peace-making..."[102] The part played by Serbia was not exactly appreciated by everyone in the Entente countries either. On 3rd August 1914, the following was written in the English newspaper, *The Manchester Guardian:* "If Serbia could be pushed out to sea and sunk then the atmosphere in Europe would improve considerably" and on 8th August John Bull wrote in the same paper: "Serbia must go. Let it be wiped off the map!"

The fact alone that in the ten years leading up to World War I Russia, France and Great Britain had spent some 46 thousand milliard French francs on defence compared to the 23 thousand milliard French francs budgeted by the Central Powers would indicate that the Entente Powers were seriously preparing for war.[103] The exact role of Wilson, the US president, remains obscure. Was Wilson's 14 point programme a tactic aimed at demobilizing the Central Powers or was he really interested in the right to self-determination. What is curious is that it would seem that he started to believe in his own myth. He called the Treaty of Versailles: "an uplifting objective of mankind" and "the first treaty signed by the greater powers that did not serve their own ends."[104] In Irene Willis' book *England's Holy War* which examines the part played by English pacifists in the war, reference is made of the fact that the Americans remained neutral for three years of the war. During that time, they only sold weapons and ammunition to the Allies. It was only when the Allied Powers were faced with the threat of defeat that the US became involved in the war on the side of their customers. As usual, the reason given for this involvement was, that it was done in the interests of 'upholding democracy'.

The losses of Trianon

After the Great War, Hungary found itself in a difficult position, the Magyars had suffered heavy losses. Between 1914 and 1918, two million Magyars had been killed and 2.8 million soldiers of other nationalities from the Dual Monarchy had either died, gone missing or had been made prisoners of war.[105] The Hungarian losses were considerably higher than those suffered by other nationalities within the Dual Monarchy and the country had been drastically reduced in size. On the continent, Hungary had been effectively isolated because it had lost its only seaport, the royal free city of Fiume (Rijeka) and its access to the Adriatic coast. Since the time of Trianon, Hungary has been made really continental. The country's economic losses were extortionate. Hungary had, for instance, lost all its forest area. Its woods had gone to the countries around Hungary, chiefly in Slovak, Subcarpathian and Transylvanian parts. As a result, the entire Hungarian forestry and timber industry simply disappeared overnight. The successor states did not take away everything though. The mountainous Carpathian area is not suitable for arable farming, whereas the fertile river area of the Hungarian lowlands is. So, there was always grain and bread enough in Hungary. The successor states, by contrast, had to put up with grain shortages. The new borders created because of Trianon also disrupted the country's infrastructure.

In 1913, the total length of the Hungarian railway network was 22,081 kilometres. By the time Hungary had been truncated, it was only left with 8,364 kilometres of track. Because of the geographical and economic unity existing in the Carpathian Basin before the First World War a logical network had evolved in which railway lines naturally converged on Budapest. Trianon had utterly disrupted the whole system making transport, trade and communication between the parts of the former Dual Monarchy extremely difficult. The already poor links were further hampered by the inordinately long waiting times created at the border crossing zones of the new 'national' states with their autarkical economic policy.[106]

Hungarian losses were not only great in human, territorial and financial-economic terms, but also in cultural respects. The extent of the loss may best be illustrated by looking at the history of the two old holy cities of *Kassa* (Kosice) and *Kolozsvár* (Cluj) that were respectively absorbed into Czechoslovakia and Rumania.

In 1910, Kassa had 44,210 inhabitants of whom 33,350 (75.4%) were Hungarian. For centuries, it had been the cultural centre of the Hungarian Upper Lands. Many important events and personalities in Hungarian history and culture are closely linked to this particular city. It was under the rule of the last king of the Arpád dynasty that the city really flourished. That was when the foundations were laid for Kassa's cathedral, one of the most beautiful Gothic structures in historic Hungary. King Matthias supervised the completion of the building of the cathedral. It was during the reign of the Transylvanian-Hungarian King János Zápolyai that the city began to form its Hungarian character and in medieval times many Germans lived there. The city's annals, which had originally been written in German started to be written in Latin during this period. Streets, vineyards and gardens were given Hungarian names. The fact that many Hungarians lived in the city is illustrated by the nationality of the city's judges nominated for election as High Court judges. Of the 100 names of the candidates put forward 50 were Hungarian, 25 German and 25 Slovak.

Kassa played a prominent part in the Wars of Independence waged by Transylvanian-Hungarian kings in their struggle against Habsburg absolutism. Kassa was a place of retreat for István Bocskai and Ferenc Rákoczi II. During Bocskai's reign the Hungarian parliament assembled twice in Kassa. While Bocskai's struggle for independence continued, the Holy Crown was kept in Kassa. It is known as a holy city, because the great freedom fighter, Ferenc Rákoczi II and his mother, Ilona Zrínyi, who defended the castle of Munkács (Munkacevo) for a long time are both buried in the cathedral's crypt. In present Slovakia, a strange atmosphere surrounds the crypt. The Slovaks feel uneasy if they hear Hungarian being spoken there and the vault itself is barricaded. In fact there is nothing to indicate that Ferenc Rákoczi II is actually buried there and it is certainly not easy to gain access to the crypt. It is easiest to enter when one does not show that one is Hungarian.

The city of Kassa also enjoyed prominence during the struggles of the Hungarian Reformation and Counter-Reformation movements. It was in Kassa that Hungarian was first ever spoken in church services. The city also produced its fair share of martyrs, of both the Catholic and Protestant faiths. In this city, Catholic Hungarians were to go down in church history as the 'martyrs of Kassa' because they had been murdered by Protestants. Hungarian Protestants living in Kassa had been murdered at the command of Gob, an Austrian general. It was not only through its religious and political history that Kassa became important, but also because it was a city where Hungarian literature and art flourished.

Hungary's most renowned lute player, Tinódi Sebestyén, composed much of his music in Kassa. It was also the place where Bálint Balassa, an early lyric poet wrote many beautiful love poems. It was in Kassa that cardinal Péter Pázmány, leader of the Hungarian Contra-Reformation, introduced a new literary style with the writing of his first prayers. Furthermore, it was the city where the Hungarian press was born. A paper published by the monarch, Ferenc Rákóczi II *Mercurius Verdicus ex Hungaria* was printed in Kassa. The language innovator, Ferenc Kazinczy, lived and worked in Kassa. His work of the beginning of the 19th century contributed to forming the modern Hungarian language. Together with other poets Kazinczy began publishing *Kassai Magyar Muzeum,* Hungary's first academic and literary journal. Kassa was a city of artisans and craftsmen and a national centre for Hungarian goldsmiths. Hungary's first theatre was in Kassa where, in 1816, the very first play in the Hungarian language was staged, long before theatres and plays were performed in the capital of Pozsony.[107]

The second city which is perhaps even more important to Hungarian history and culture is Kolozsvár. In 1910, on the eve of the First World War, the city had 60,808 inhabitants of whom 50,704 (83.4%) were Hungarian. In 1910 a small proportion of the city's inhabitants were Rumanian. Kolozsvár is connected to the Hungarian Hunyadi national dynasty. Matthias Hunyadi, who later became the Renaissance King, Corvinus, was born in Kolozsvár in 1440. The house where he was born still stands today in the city centre where there is also a statue of him.

The imposing statue of King Matthias on horseback has in recent years been the target of repeated attacks mounted by Funar, the city's extreme nationalist Rumanian mayor. On more than one occasion he has threatened to have the statue removed to enable excavations to be carried out in the central square to prove that there was once a Dacian settlement in the heart of Kolozsvár. In accordance with Rumanian state doctrine, the Daco-Roman ancestry myth of the Rumanian people, this would then provide conclusive evidence that Kolozsvár was first and foremost a Rumanian city. Probably Funar also realizes that there are no Dacian settlement remains beneath the statue, but that is immaterial. In the first, place he, of course, intends to show the Hungarian people of the city who is all-powerful in Kolozsvár and which people, as far as the Rumanians are concerned, do not belong there. The statue which is decorated with Rumanian flags to symbolize Rumanian rule can be removed by Funar at any given time. Living under such constant threat makes the city's Hungarians feel uncomfortable. They naturally enough presume that the aggression is really directed towards them and not towards the statue of King Matthias. In this way, pressure is easily exerted on the Hungarians of Transylvania while the statue of Matthias, which is in fact a UNESCO listed protected European monument, is turned into a chess piece in the anti-Hungarian psychological warfare game.

Kolozsvár has also played an important part in Hungary's church history. Ferenc Dávid, one of the moving spirits behind Hungary's Reformation and founder of the Transylvanian Unitarian Church hailed from Kolozsvár. Even today the city is still an important centre for Hungarian Protestantism. The diocesan seats of the bishops of the Transylvanian Reformed and Unitarian churches are in Kolozsvár. Ethnicity and religious denomination are one and the same in Transylvania, the Hungarians are both Reformed and Unitarian. The vast majority of Saxon Transylvanians are Lutheran. The Rumanians are either Greek Orthodox or Greek Uniate, that is to say, Catholic. So, any attack in Transylvania directed at the Reformed or Unitarian denominations automatically causes a charged anti-Hungarian atmosphere.

Just like Kassa, Kolozsvár has close links with the emergence of Hungarian culture and art. János Apáczai Csere, an education reformer who studied at Dutch universities and published the first Hungarian encyclopedia in Utrecht in 1653 lived in Kolozsvár with his Dutch wife, Aletta van der Maet, until the time of his death. The most famous Hungarian politician and political writer of the 17th century, count Miklós Bethlen, lived and worked in Kolozsvár. It was also the city where Kelemen Mikes was educated, the man who later became personal secretary to King Ferenc Rákoczi II. After quashing the struggle for independence in 1711, Mikes accompanied Rákoczi II to Rodosto in Turkey where Rákoczi and his freedom fighters were given asylum. The letters written by Mikes during his time in exile which were addressed to a fictitious person in Transylvania have become part of Hungary's great literary heritage. Kolozsvár is one of the most important cities in the history of the printing press. The best known Hungarian printer, Miklós Kis de Misztótfalu, who had learnt his trade in Amsterdam later returned to Kolozsvár where he spent the last years of his life.

Kolozsvár was, therefore, also a centre for the Hungarian printing press. The country's first journalist, Sándor Szacsvay spent most of his life there and is buried in Kolozsvár. Of the 163 different

Hungarian newspapers to be published after the time of the Ausgleich (1867) no less than thirteen of them were printed in Kolozsvár. When Transylvania was annexed by the Rumanians in 1920, Kolozsvár continued to be important in the press world in what was now occupied territory. The two leading Hungarian newspapers outside Hungary of the inter-war years, *Ellenzék* 'Oppostion' and *Keleti Ujság* 'The Eastern Newspaper', were both published in Kolozsvár. Once again today the city has become a centre in the Transylvanian Hungarian press world.

In the field of art history Kolozsvár is probably the one Hungarian city that has contributed most to Hungarian and Central European art. The statue of Saint George that stands at the castle in Prague is the work of the two most famous medieval sculptors, the brothers Márton and György Kolozsvári, both of whom hailed from the city from which their surname derived. King Sigismund was responsible for the construction of Kolozsvár's St. Michael's cathedral, a structure which, together with the cathedral of Kassa constitutes one of the high points of medieval architecture.

Kolozsvár was a cultural centre par excellence. It was the place where, in 1792, Hungary's first theatre was built, 45 years before any theatre in Budapest opened its doors to the public. The grand historic drama *Bánk Bán* 'Viceroy Bánk' by the playwright József Katona that tells of the murder of the wife of King Andreas II, the German consort Getrud, who wanted to Germanize Hungary in the 13th century was first staged in Kolozsvár. On 15th March, the day when Hungarians commemorate the anti-Habsburg Revolution of 1848 Bánk Bán is always performed at Budapest's National Opera House. In Kolozsvár, a city now dominated by Rumanian extreme nationalists that abhor everything that is remotely Magyar and where the play was performed for the first time, it is now banned. Transylvania's oldest scientific society, The Transylvanian Museum Association (EME), was established in Kolozsvár.

In honour of the fact that Kolozsvár has contributed so richly and in so many ways to Hungary's cultural history, the city has been given the epitheton ornans *city of treasures*. Sadly, Rumanian rule in Transylvania has done much to overshadow this cultural glory. The city briefly had the chance to recover when, after the Second Vienna Award of 1940, it returned to Hungary for a while. This was, however, nothing more than the calm before the storm. The 'modernization' of the city at the time when the anti-Hungarian, Rumanian dictator Ceausescu was in power did much to destroy whole quarters of the old historic inner city. Here also the few Hungarian treasures that do still exist are under perpetual threat of being lost should Funar and his extreme nationalist henchmen have another of their anti-Hungary destructive purges.

Hungary during the interbellum

After Trianon, Hungary was left with a much reduced territorial area, what came to be known as truncated Hungary. Over three million Hungarians found themselves living in successor states. Seven out of every twenty ethnic Magyars ended up in one or other of the successor states where they were subject to foreign rule. It was not long before these Hungarian 'minorities' were treated with animosity in these new states. These problems will be discussed at length below.

New Central European states

The Treaty of Trianon turned Hungary into a homogeneous nation state with 7,600,000 inhabitants, more than 90% of whom were ethnic Magyars. The country's two ethnic minorities, its 400,000 Germans and its 100,000 Slovaks were dispersed throughout the country. As a result of the decisions made at Trianon, more than three million Hungarians ended up living outside the new boundaries in the successor states of Czechoslovakia, Rumania and Yugoslavia. These were artificial states that had not been created in a democratic way. No referendums were held and requests, like the one lodged by the Hungarians in Transylvania, to be allowed to remain a part of Hungary were not entertained by the Entente Powers. The countries that had lost the war, Germany and Hungary, wanted to revise the peace stipulations as quickly as possible while the winners of the war and their allies did everything to hold on to the agreements. The national minorities - mainly Hungarians and Germans - the people who did not belong to the states of their nationality and who had become the victims of the peace agreements did not feel happy or at home in the national tyrannies of the new successor states.

Since Trianon, there has been continual anti-Hungarian oppression in the Carpathian Basin regardless of the ruling political system of the day, whether it was authoritarian-nationalistic, fascist, communist or democratic. If the successor states of Austria-Hungary are able to lose 'their' Hungarians in one way or another then it is no longer necessary to let the right to self-determination apply also to Hungarians. Hence, the reason why now, and in the past, these countries have done everything in their power to get rid of their Hungarian inhabitants. In the remainder of this part of the book we shall explore the whole gamut of tactics employed over the years. It should be noted that since the fall of communism in 1989 efforts to obliterate Magyar identity have gone on uninhibited. It would be naive to believe that just because the country's political climate has become more democratic such practices have automatically ceased altogether. The demagyarization constitutes the most consistent policy of these states. I shall call this the politics of *ethnic engineering* where the goal is to reduce the numbers of Hungarians to satisfy the purposes of the nation states in which they live.

Czechoslovakia

Czechoslovakia evolved as a completely artificial creation made up of three entirely different regions. In the west there was the kingdom of Bohemia and the Great Duchy of Moravia. Here the population was two-thirds Czech and one-third German. The

Germans who were concentrated in the German-Austrian border area, the part known as Sudetenland, had tried to break away in 1919. At the Paris peace conference, Benes had opted for historical unity of Bohemia so as to include Czechoslovakia's sizable German community. The second region of the Czech state was Slovakia, an area which since the 10th century had been part of the Hungarian kingdom. Until 1920 Slovakia did not exist. Historically the area was known as the Upper Lands and Slovaks who lived there were hardly conscious of their ethnic identity. If one asked a Slovak about his ancestry he would allude to the district from where he came. Benes claimed for Czechoslovakia a much larger area than that inhabited by Slovaks. In this case, his argument could not have been based on historical considerations, because Slovakia had never been a part of the Bohemian kingdom. His concerns now were based on strategic and economic factors. The new state had to extend as far as the Danube and Foch, the French Marshal, saw the Danube as a natural defence line. Supported by Foch, Benes succeeded in convincing the congress of the correctness of this decision. Czechoslovakia annexed the city of Pozsony (Bratislava, Preßburg), a city which had for a long time been the capital of the kingdom of Hungary and which, in 1920, was chiefly inhabited by Hungarians and Germans. Czechoslovakia also annexed the left bank of the Danube which again was chiefly populated by Hungarians: The third Czechoslovakian region was Carpathian Ruthenia, Hungary's Subcarpathian area, which had been a part of the Hungarian kingdom since 895. Nothing came of the autonomy that Masaryk and Benes had promised the Ruthenians.

The First Czechoslovakian Republic was, therefore, built on quicksand. Czechoslovakia was in fact a multinational state. Of its fourteen million inhabitants only 64.3% of them were either Czech or Slovak. The country included the following nationalities:[108]

Czechs	6,661,000	48.9%
Slovaks	2,100,000	15.4%
Germans	3,124,000	22.9%

Magyars	745,000	5.5%
Ruthenians	462,000	3.4%
Poles	76,000	0.6%
Other	445,000	3.3%

The First Czechoslovakian Republic was seen as a Slavic state despite the fact that it had more Germans than Slovaks living in it. The Germans and Hungarians who should rightfully have been equal constitutional entities were given dubious national 'minority' status. The Slovaks and Ruthenians who had expected to be autonomous were not given that kind of freedom by Prague. It was obvious that the tensions that had caused the downfall of the Austro-Hungarian Monarchy would one day come back with as much avengence in the new country of Czechoslovakia.

Greater Rumania

Together the Treaty of Saint-Germain, which ordered that the Dual Monarchy be dissolved and the Treaty of Trianon saw to it that Rumania was doubled in size. In 1920, the country covered an area of 295,000 square kilometres but later it was given the following additional regions: Bessarabia from Russia, Bukovina from Austria, Transylvania, part of East Hungary and a portion of the Bánát region, also in Hungary. The same applied to Rumania as to Czechoslovakia. All the newly gained territories had completely different histories from that of the core Rumanian state, the kingdom on the other side of the Carpathians. Furthermore, Rumania was not a homogeneous nation state, even though it liked to think of itself as that. Roughly one-third (28.1%) of the approximately eighteen million inhabitants of Greater Rumania were non-ethnic Rumanians. It was particularly the Hungarians who did not feel at home in Rumania. The country consisted of the following ethnic groups:[109]

Rumanians	12,981,000	71.9%
Magyars	1,425,000	7.8%
Germans	745,000	4.0%

Jews	728,000	3.9%
Ruthenians	582,000	3.2%
Russians	409,000	2.2%
Bulgarians	366,000	2.1%
gypsies	262,000	1.4%
Turks	154,000	0.8%
total Rumanians		71.9%
total national minorities		28.1%

The kingdom of the Serbs, Croats and Slovenes: Yugoslavia

The old kingdom of Serbia was also richly rewarded by the peace treaties. First known as the kingdom of the Serbs, Croats and Slovenes what later came to be known as Yugoslavia grew to a size of 248,665 square kilometres. Yugoslavia gained part of Bulgaria, the Vojvodina region of Hungary, the Bácska area of Hungary, the autonomous lands of the Hungarian Crown, Croatia-Slavonia and from Austria: Slovenia, Dalmatia and Bosnia-Herzegovina. Broken down as follows the country eventually had 11,245,000 inhabitants of which 15% belonged to a national minority:[110]

Serbs	5,365,000	47.7%
Croats	2,834,000	25.2%
Slovenes	1,024,000	9.1%
Germans	513,000	4.7%
Magyars	472,000	4.0%
Albanians	441,000	3.7%
Bulgarians	274,000	2.7%
Turks	236,000	2.3%
Rumanians	72,000	2.3%
Italians	14,000	0.6%

As long as Hungarians remained in successor states, there was concern that one day Hungary would demand back the various occupied territories with their fellow nationals. Hence, the reason that the many Hungarians living in the successor states have been given such a hard time since Trianon. The Hungarians were confronted with policies that were designed to firmly repress their national and cultural identity. To achieve this common end of theirs, the successor states introduced a whole range of discriminatory governmental measures aimed directly and unremittingly at their Hungarian minorities. Such politics, in which no means are too drastic, may rightfully be termed *ethnic engineering*.

Ethnic engineering

In the new states it was not long before authoritarian regimes developed where, by means of centralism and internal nationalistic expansion, every effort was made to alter the ethnic balance within the successor states. To effect these changes the respective authorities employed a politics of *ethnic engineering*. The main objective was to form homogeneous nation states. According to insiders Czechoslovakia was the only exception to the rule. Even today, the First Czechoslovakian Republic still has the reputation of being a model democratic Central European state. It is a difficult myth to abolish and one that is certainly not subscribed to by the Slovaks, Hungarians and Germans. The Czechs regarded the Slovaks as backward Catholic farmers who, to their way of thinking, obviously had no right to seek autonomy. Prague looked upon Slovakia more as occupied territory than as a partner nation. In Slovakia itself, tension only mounted because of the pressure that the Slovaks were bringing to bear on the Hungarians. During elections for the federal parliament in Prague, the manipulation in the constituencies of Southern Slovakia caused the Hungarian candidates to win more votes than their Slovak counterparts in districts where Slovaks were in the majority. This manipulating of statistics was brought to light by various censuses. A census was held in the East Slovak city of Kassa (Kosice) on 2nd December, 1930. At the time, Hungarians were up in arms about the way the census was being conducted. The census officials were instructed that people who had been born in Kassa and were citizens of that city could not be regarded as Hungarian. Ironic when one thinks that in

1910 the city was almost exclusively inhabited by Hungarians.[111] It was, therefore, obviously common practice to manipulate election results and census statistics in the 'democratic' land of president Masaryk.

In Rumania, it was not long before the Hungarians were exposed to a ruthless Rumanization. Nationalistic Rumanian historiographers, historians and propaganda mongers of the Western Entente countries characterized Hungarian rule over the Transylvania Rumanians as a process of Magyarization. According to them Hungarian authorities had used crude oppressive methods to strip the Rumanians of their national identity. Now, 75 years on we should start to recognize this for what it was: anti-Hungarian propaganda aimed at increasing the power of the Entente countries, notably France, in Central Europe and thus in Europe as a whole. We should separate this from the real facts.

In his book, *As a minority and as a majority: Rumanians and Hungarians (1867-1940)*, based on *Rumanian* sources, Sándor Bíró has demonstrated that in the Hungary of the Dual Monarchy Transylvanian Rumanians were in many respects no worse off than their fellow nationals who were being ruled by Russia in Bessarabia or for that matter, Rumanians in the Rumanian kingdom itself or Rumanians living in the Balkans.[112] With all these comparisons the following facts are relevant.

Rumanians in Hungary (1867-1914)

- The financial position of Transylvanian Rumanians, many of whom were farmers, improved continually, partly because they were able to buy more agricultural land.
- The Hungarian authorities gave people complete freedom to organize meetings as they wished, hardly imposing any restrictions. During the time of the double monarchy, anti-government demonstrations could be held up and down the country, there were absolutely no restrictions imposed.
- There was freedom of the press and no censorship. Rumanian newspapers and publications were allowed to print whatever they

liked. Even publications openly calling for Transylvania to be united with Old Rumania could be published.
- Transylvanian Rumanians and Rumanians from the kingdom were able to have contact with each other without any difficulty.
- The Rumanian language could be used freely, in court hearings, regional meetings, churches, schools, in the villages and in private and public life.
- On the grounds of equality in the eyes of the law Rumanians were able to defend their rights against Hungarians. A high court ruling stated that Rumanians were permitted to sing their anti-Hungarian national anthem and to distribute photographs of the Rumanian monarch in Transylvania.

Rumanians in Rumania and elsewhere (1867-1914)

- The standard of living amongst Rumanian farmers was continually lowered. During the Peasants' Uprising of 1907 11,000 Rumanian farmers were murdered by their own government.
- Opposition parties were unable to convene meetings. Secret police agents and prefects made these meetings impossible.
- In Bukovina, the Austrians exercised preventive censure for the Rumanian press.
- The Russians saw to it that the Rumanians living in Bessarabia were isolated from their fellow nationals in Rumania. Iorga, the Rumanian historian wrote: "The two worlds are separated from each other by solid steel frontiers."
- In Bessarabia and in the Balkans, the Rumanian language was banned from churches, schools, public life, the press and even from private life.
- In Bessarabia and in the Balkans, violence was rife. The Russian authorities deported Rumanians. Without warning, Rumanians who held on to their national identity were murdered by Greek gangs that were not tried.

With Bíró I would conclude that Rumanian community living in the state of Hungarian between 1867 and 1914 became financially stronger, their national consciousness was raised and they grew more resolute in their dealings with the outer world. They were able to enjoy their national and cultural identity without having to live in fear. The Rumanians living in Bessarabia and in the Balkans had been deprived of their human rights. Their destiny and their perspectives for the future were uncertain. Political representation was lacking. Bíró, therefore, concludes that on the basis of a comparison of the facts drawn from Rumanian sources there is no reason to presume that the Rumanians in Hungary could only survive if the Hungarian state, recognized their claims for political independence. It was not so much a matter of having to free the Rumanian community from the threatening grasp of the Hungarian state but more a matter of claims being laid on East Hungarian territory and the territorial integrity of the Hungarian state being broken down. Above we have seen how, with the help of the Entente countries, the Rumanians were able to realize this strategic objective.

It was quite a different matter, though, for the Hungarians left behind in Transylvania after the Treaty of Trianon who were forced to submit to Rumanian rule. In the space of 22 years between 1918 and 1941 when Northern Transylvania was liberated life had become impossible for the Transylvanian Hungarians. Through his research into five areas of social life Bíró has been able to give a good general impression of the wellbeing of the Hungarian minority in that period. He examined the following aspects: the Hungarian's financial-economic position, the use of the Hungarian language, the position of the Hungarian churches, the situation of the Hungarian culture and identity and the human and civil rights situation for members of the Hungarian national community. These five aspects will be discussed in detail below.

The financial-economic position of the Hungarians in Greater Rumania
The financial-economic political principles of Greater Rumania were nationalistic and chauvinistic and based on the principle that "Rumanian labour and initiatives should be supported in all areas. All jobs should be reserved for Rumanians who were lagging

behind economically and financially due to unfortunate historic circumstances." The Rumanian state intervened in a nationalistic kind of way. The Rumanians received proportionately 24% more governmental support and the Hungarians proportionately 16.4% less support. As a result, the Hungarian agrarian sector became systematically undermined. All the state-owned property that had been leased to Hungarian farmers was taken away from them after Trianon. The Rumanian border guards and their descendants who had defended the Hungarian-Rumanian border were allowed to keep their property that had come to them during the Austria-Hungary era. The Szekler-Hungarians who had likewise been border guards were forced to give up their property to the Rumanian state which meant that 100,000 Szekler-Hungarian farmers were left completely without land.

The Rumanian state initiated a series of measures aimed at seriously weakening the financial-economic position of the Transylvanian Hungarians. The state was given first option when it came to the compulsory purchase of land and other property in the border area with Hungary. The underlying political objective was to break Hungarian continuity which crossed Hungarian-Rumanian border by introducing settlements. The Rumanian state was given exclusive rights to exploit lucrative health resorts and spas in the Szekler region. The Hungarians were given no access to the real estates in the King's Land in Szeklerland. The Rumanian state linked colonization policy to land reforms. Agricultural land that belonged to Hungarians or to the Hungarian state was dispossessed and then reallocated to Rumanians who then moved to Hungarian territory. After Trianon, 111 Rumanian settlements were set up along the Hungarian-Rumanian border. The Rumanian Ministry of Agriculture saw to it that pasture land that the Rumanian courts had ordered should be given back to Hungarians was not rightfully returned.

Hungarian labourers were not in a much better position. The Hungarian federation of labourers was Rumanized. Hungarian labourers employed by the Rumanian government lost their jobs. Rumanian employment laws that were founded on racist criteria were enforced. Hungarians in Transylvania who ran small businesses and who constituted 18% of all the Hungarians in Rumania were required to pay ever higher taxes, until inevitably many of them went bankrupt. Traditional Hungarian cooperatives were closed down and the property used for Rumanian purposes. Hungarians were required to pay eight times as much tax for their notices and signboards and commercial establishments were Rumanized. In its loaning policies the National Rumanian Bank was unmistakably anti-Hungarian. It was always harder for Hungarian businesses or enterprises to obtain money loans. The property, houses and estates of Hungarian aristocrats was divided up between Rumanian intellectuals. Hungarians employed in the civil service were either sacked outright or given a state examination in the Rumanian language that was so tough they would almost certainly fail and, thus, instantly lose their jobs.

The Hungarian language in Greater Rumania
The Rumanians proclaimed in a declaration of 1st December 1918 made at Gyulafehérvár (Alba Julia) that Transylvania was to join Old Rumania. The declaration recognized that all nationalities have a right to speak their own native language freely. The Paris agreement on minorities of 9th December 1919 also recognized the right to use Hungarian, but in the inter-war years the Rumanian crown council adopted a completely different policy. In 1922, Hungarians were forbidden by the Rumanian authorities to submit documents that were written in Hungarian. Their slogan was "Speak only Rumanian." Speaking Hungarian in public was also subject to restrictions. The Rumanian constitution of 1923 only made reference to Rumanian language usage which elicited heavy protest from German Saxons. In 1930, the different nationalities were prohibited from speaking their own language. Only the prefect of the Bihar district allowed Hungarian to be spoken locally. According to the new government law of 1936 severe penalties would be imposed on Hungarians who did not adopt Rumanian as the language to be spoken either locally or regionally. Hungarians were forbidden to speak Hungarian during court sittings and in town halls. In 1938, the

Rumanian commandant of the sixth Kolozsvár (Cluj) army issued a decree stating that people who used any language other than the officially recognized one in government offices could be given a two-year prison sentence. Petitions submitted to the legal authorities could only be drawn up in Rumanian after 1922. Censorship banned the use of Hungarian place names. In the end, Hungarian could only be used in trading, in the cinemas and in the market places.

Hungarian churches in Greater Rumania

Under Rumanian rule Hungarian church communities were broken up. The Reformed church parish 'Along the King's path', a church community situated on the Rumanian-Hungarian border, was not officially recognized by the Rumanian authorities until twenty years after Trianon. In 1927, the Transylvanian-Hungarian Roman Catholic archbishopric was made subordinate to the Bucharest archdiocese by a concordat drawn up between the Vatican and the Rumanian state. The possessions of the Hungarian Catholic Church were handed over to the leaders of the Rumanian Uniate Church. The Rumanian state and the Vatican negotiated on the possessions of the Hungarian Catholic archbishopric. The edict agreed to in Rome abolished the archbishopric and instructed that its possessions be passed on to Hungarian Catholic churches and schools. The agreement was effected by the Rumanian state some eight years later, after much wrangling. The Rumanian authorities also stood in the way of the Hungarian Evangelical community, when it endeavoured to establish a religious community. The Hungarian Evangelical church was not recognized by the Rumanian state until 1940.

Hungarian churches had no official written legal status. The Rumanian constitution of 1923 gave Rumanian churches a more privileged position than non-Rumanian churches. The Orthodox Church became the established church and the Uniate Church was made superior to the other denominations which received the status of 'cults'. The stipends of Orthodox priests were paid out by the state and the holy days of the Orthodox Church were turned into national holidays since theirs was now the established church. The bill on religions of 1928 guaranteed no equality in the eyes of the law for churches in general. The financial situation of the Hungarian churches grew worse. Hungarian denominations were stripped of all their possessions. Any relevant favourable legal stipulations on land reformation were implicated to the benefit only of Rumanian religious communities and not allowed to apply to the Hungarian ones.

In 1924, an American commission observed that there had been 43 legal transgressions against various Hungarian churches. The possessions of the Hungarian churches were donated to Rumanian churches which sometimes did not even exist yet. When it came to the Rumanian Uniate Church it was automatically given back all its possessions. The Hungarian monastic orders were forced to relinquish all that they owned to the Roman Catholic archbishopric in Bucharest. After 1932, the salaries of Hungarian priests were reduced while their Rumanian counterparts started to receive remuneration that was three times as high. There was great violation of religious freedom during the course of the thirties. Priests were arrested, tortured and imprisoned without reason. After 1934, Hungarians living in the Szeklerland region were forcefully converted to Rumanian orthodoxy. Five Rumanian government ministries pressed for forceful conversion to the Orthodox faith. Any Szekler-Hungarians who clung to their Reformed beliefs were tortured. Reformed Protestant children right across the board were forced to attend Orthodox Rumanian church services against their will. Hungarian religious gatherings were forbidden. A statement of an official church authority read as follows: "The police dictates the rules to be observed during church services. The heads of state schools have the right to determine the nationality and denomination of their pupils. The police determines what fundamentals are to be imparted in religious education." Religious persecution reached its peak between 1938 and 1940. By the end of the thirties, it was common practice for Hungarian church services to be perpetually disrupted. Hungarians were by then virtually prohibited from observing any events in their religious calendar. The people appointed by the Rumanian Ministry to sort out the Hungarian's grievances were those who had perpetrated crimes of violence against Hungarians.

Hungarian culture in Greater Rumania
During the inter-war years, things deteriorated rapidly for the social web responsible for transmitting Hungarian cultural values: the schools, cultural organizations and the press and theatre. In 1920, educational policies changed course. In the new scheme of the aim was to assimilate non-Rumanians and suppress their education systems. Many Hungarian schools were closed down. Anghelescu, the Minister of Education, stuck to an anti-Hungarian policy. A ban on the freedom to give or follow lessons in one's own language meant that Hungarians were prevented in an artificial way from sending their children to Hungarian schools. The directors of state schools could at any time prevent Hungarian children from registering in Hungarian religious schools. The objective throughout was to see to it that Hungarian education died out. Rumanian court outcomes that recognized Hungarian complaints were not respected and followed up. Even the names of Hungarian children were scrutinized. Those who had no Hungarian sounding names were automatically considered to be Rumanian and obliged to attend Rumanian schools. In the end, 75% of all Hungarian children of compulsory school age were forced to attend Rumanian schools. Hungarian teachers were discriminated against under Rumanian educational policy. Minister Anghelescu made Hungarian teachers ineligible for fare reductions on public transport, for state subsidies and their diplomas were not recognized as valid. They were, furthermore, obliged to sit an examination in the Rumanian language so that history, geography and social studies could be taught in Rumanian. Those left teaching at Hungarian religious schools lived in poverty and their prospects for the future were uncertain.

A legal stop was put to educational autonomy. Hungarian, Bulgarian and Russian areas were turned into Rumanian cultural zones. The ultimate goal was to speed up the process of cultural Rumanization. A statement on the objective of the cultural zone claimed: "There are no Szekler-Hungarians." There was a rapid decline in the number of schools providing secondary education. In the 1919-1937 period more than 50% of all Hungarian schools closed down. The premises of Hungarian Catholic secondary convent schools were expropriated by the Rumanian state. Once their property had been taken away by compulsory purchase order, the Hungarian schools were no longer able to survive.

Living under the chauvinistic policies of Anghelescu, Hungarian teachers were finding themselves in increasingly difficult positions. Increasing numbers of Rumanian teachers were being appointed to positions in Hungarian schools. It was compulsory to teach four subjects in Rumanian. The chauvinistic Rumanian educational campaign was at its zenith between 1933 and 1937, when Anghelescu was minister of education. In 1936, the Rumanian teachers' union declared: "If the children of minority groups want to live in Rumania then they will have to be taught by Rumanian teachers and brought up in the language and spirit of Rumanian culture."

After 1925, Hungarian school children were forced to sit their final examinations in Rumanian. In 1925, 75% of the candidates failed and in 1934 85% of school leavers failed their final examinations. As a consequence, the numbers of children attending Hungarian schools was even further reduced. Subjects relating to Rumanian national matters had to be taught in the Rumanian langauge and the Rumanian teachers decided which children would be placed in the highest four grammar school classes. It had become very difficult for teachers in Hungarian schools to teach their own language and their own history. In Hungarian schools, there was no trace of irredentism. The Rumanian 'Militia' and civil army was brought into Hungarian schools. There were few Hungarian schools that taught skills and crafts and Hungarian pupils tended to be rejected when they applied for courses in business studies, economics and commerce at Rumanian institutions.

The Hungarian university at Kolozsvár was Rumanized. The Rumanian state simply did not tolerate Hungarian universities.

There were proportionately fewer Hungarian students than Rumanian students in universities and higher education institutions. In university and higher education, it became necessary to sit entrance examinations. After 1930, it became very difficult to perpetuate the Hungarian intelligentsia. Kolozsvár University's medical faculty was transferred to Bucharest. All the Hungarian student unions were banned.

During the inter-war years, it became increasingly difficult for important Hungarian cultural societies to operate. The Rumanian university made free use of the Transylvanian Museum Association's (EME's) scientific collection and facilities. When the university had been Hungarian, any items loaned from the association had been payed for, but the Rumanian university did not pay the association anything for the collection items it borrowed. The Rumanian university simply tried to take over the entire EME collection. Until 1930, the Transylvanian Museum Association found it difficult to arrange meetings, but later the society started organizing short meetings. The censoring body still found a way, though, to put its stamp on these meetings. For fifteen years, Transylvania's Hungarian Cultural Society (the EMKE) was just not recognized. The society was hampered by censorship and by the country's martial law system.

After Trianon, Hungarian daily and weekly newspapers were printed again and Hungarian journalists organized themselves in unions. After 1929, with the rise of censorship in Rumania, the quality of the Transylvanian Hungarian press started to deteriorate but the Hungarian press was vital to the survival of Hungarian hope for the future. The Hungarian papers contained absolutely no trace of irredentist sentiment.

In the dramatic arts acting standards had been high in Transylvania up until the time of Trianon. On 30th September 1919, the Hungarians staged their last play performance in Kolozsvár's Hungarian National Theatre. The theatre was then taken over by the Rumanian state. Hungarian plays were only allowed to be performed very sporadically. Because taxes were so high it was hard for Hungarian theatres to stay open. The Rumanian theatres paid 13% taxes whilst the Hungarian theatres were required to pay 25%.

The rights and civil freedom of Hungarians living in Greater Rumania
Hungarians' most important human and civil rights were curtailed by the following restrictions:

Individual freedom. Private and personal freedom was heavily restricted because of the fifteen year long situation of martial law. House searches, unlawful arrests and police led terrorism were normal occurrences in Rumania during the early twenties. In 1926, the Rumanian university lecturer Ghiulea declared: "There is no country anywhere else in the world where people have been so badly robbed of their personal freedom as in our country."

Private ownership. Because of the perpetual expropriation of property the right to own property became something that only existed in theory in Greater Rumania. The property of Hungarian monastic orders was taken away from them by the state. As one journalist of the time commented in a French language newspaper that appeared in Geneva: "The fact that the above-mentioned laws can be violated is surely proof enough that the Rumanian authorities miss no chance to pauperize their Hungarian population."

Press freedom. Apart from the period between 1928 and 1933 censorship was in full swing in Greater Rumania. Sometimes, Hungarian papers were scrutinized by three different government censoring bodies. Not infrequently papers that had already been censored were still prevented from going on sale or were taken out of circulation. The Rumanian prefect of Arad said on the subject: "I prohibit it and that's it. I need not further justify my actions." Famous lawsuits were brought against Hungarian journalists and provoking anti-Hungarian feeling was not seen as something that was punishable. A Rumanian summons to hold a Saint Bartholomew's night (a pogrom) against Hungarians was not taken to court. Authors of scientific books and other publications were brought before a military tribunal. A Hungarian ABC book was removed from the bookshelves after it had been censored and an indictment had subsequently been filed against the editors. The basic objectives of Rumanian censorship were: to break down solidarity among Hungarians, to reduce Hungarian national consciousness, to prevent criticism of the Rumanian state, national pride and history and finally, to abolish praise of anything Hungarian. Hungarian newspapers were regularly required to publish articles that served Rumanian national interests.

The freedom to hold meetings and assemblies. Because of the fifteen year long martial law situation there was no freedom to organize meetings. The Transylvanian Museum Association had to ask for permission six to eight days prior to holding any of its academic meetings. After 1938, such meetings were banned altogether. Engagements, weddings and Christenings could only be celebrated after permission had been received from the authorities.

Religious freedom. Great restrictions were placed on the holding of church services. The Baptists were treated like sect members and were prosecuted. When it came to celebrating national Rumanian religious holidays, the country's authorities laid down instructions for the order of service concerning its form and content and dictated which prayers were to be said.

Prohibition on the use of Hungarian national symbols. There was always a heavy ban on the use of the Hungarian national colours of red, white and green, even in connection with folklore matters or when it came to the compiling of booklets. There was heavy opposition to the honouring of Hungarian national heroes. Everywhere in Transylvania statues of István Széchenyi, Lajos Kossuth and Sándor Petőfi were destroyed. In Szatmár (Satu Mare) the statues of Saint Stephen and Saint László were smashed to smithereens.

Contact with Hungarians from Hungary. For Transylvanian Hungarians it was difficult to obtain a visa to enter Hungary. Hungarians from Hungary who were active in intellectual circles were simply refused entry into Rumania altogether.

Hungarians' political rights. At election times, the Rumanian authorities intervened violently in all the proceedings. The Rumanian member of parliament, Vaida-Voevod's statement, "under the Hungarians there was more political freedom" needs no further comment. Or the statement once made by the Rumanian people's representative, Stefan Pop-Cicio: "If, under Hungarian rule, a policeman beat up a Rumanian voter then this would be reported. In such cases the policeman in question would be sentenced to three years in prison. Now Rumanian judges falsify the election results." In 1937, Hungarian voters in the province of Maros (Mures) were given a burst of fire when they went to the polling station.

Equality in the eyes of the law. During the inter-war years, the Hungarians were perpetually discriminated against. The very occasional court acquittals made by Rumanian judges in favor of Hungarians or Hungarian institutions were not acknowledged in practice. Equality in the eyes of the law was, therefore, only something that existed on paper.

The freeing of the Hungarians

Life for Hungarians living in the successor states was extremely difficult. The successor states used every possible way they could devise to influence the ethnic balance in the Hungarian populated areas of their states. Above we have explained in detail how this actually worked in Rumania, but in the other successor states of Czechoslovakia and Yugoslavia the system was not basically any different. These countries had, furthermore, banded together to form an anti-Hungary front, the so-called Little Entente, that had as its aim, to keep Hungary weak and prevent it from possibly trying to revise the Treaty of Trianon or demand territorial restructuring on the basis of the right to self-determination. This latter aim was the main issue at stake in the Hungarian foreign policy of the inter-war period.

In the West there was little enthusiasm for revising the Treaty of Trianon. On 6th May 1920, before the treaty had been signed, the French president, Millerand, wrote to the Hungarian delegation to let them know that "all border agreements that could possibly be protested against on well argued grounds" would be investigated and adjusted accordingly.[113] When French references were made about revising the Treaty of Trianon they always involved one tactical manoeuvre or another. Such letters as the one above sent by Millerand were accompanied by secret messages addressed to the associated powers assuring them that they were not to take the content of the letter too seriously. The Hungarians received some understanding from British Conservatives who were sympathetic to Hungary and its plight because of, as Earl Curzon of Keddleston put it during a debate on the Treaty of Trianon in the House of Lords, "the character of her people, the nature of her institutions and the spirit of her aristocracy."[114] The British Upper House felt that Trianon had been far too harsh on the Hungarians. As Viscount Bryce commented: "Hungary was surely entitled to some more respectful and sympathetic treatment. Hungary is one of the oldest kingdoms in Europe; far older not only than such mushroom states as Prussia and Bavaria, not to speak of Austria, which only came into existence quite lately, but older than old kingdoms like Portugal and Norway, one of the real old great kingdoms of Europe. She had been inhabited by an exceptionally high-spirited and liberty-loving people. She has played a great part in the world, and has striven for many centuries, and on many occasions, for her liberties against the Hapsburgs... Great Britain has always had the warmest feelings for this country."[115] The House of Lords pleaded for the treaty to be revised. Viscount Bryce asked embarrassing questions:"What reason was there why the frontier should not have been so drawn as to bring the Magyar parts of Transylvania up to the Szekler country, for that region of Transylvania is very largely Magyar. If there were difficulties in doing that, why was not something in the nature of a corridor made which would have enabled them to be in communication with the Magyar population of Northern Transylvania? Or why were not autonomous institutions given to them instead of subjecting this purely Magyar community to the alien and unwelcome rule of the Rumans, who have already shown how they are going to use the power unfortunately given to them?"[116]

It was from British Conservative circles that the only international plea was heard for a revision of the Treaty of Trianon. Lord Rothermere, the owner of *The Daily Mail* called for the Trianon Treaty to be revised in an article written on 21st June 1927. He pointed out how unfair the treaty was and he supported the view that the areas along the Hungarian border that were chiefly populated by Hungarians should be given back to Hungary. So Lord Rothermere launched a campaign which he called *Justice for Hungary*. The article that appeared in *The Daily Mail* was attacked by a furious barrage of counterpropaganda generated by France and the Little Entente countries. The whole issue blew up into a media war and did not subside until 1929.[117] Apart from the protest initiated by Lord Rothermere, the Hungarians were very much left to fend for themselves.

The League of Nations which had been set up after the First World War and which was controlled by the Entente countries heard all the grievances of the various Hungarian minority groups but did absolutely nothing to resolve the problems. Hence, the reason that the First and Second Vienna Awards were welcomed by Hungarians domiciled in the successor states of Czechoslovakia, Yugoslavia and Rumania as a liberation. For the Subcarpathian Hungarians their time of liberation came after 14th March 1939, the date when Slovakia declared its independence. One day later, on 15th March, Hungarian armies entered Subcarpathia. As a result, 12,061 square kilometres of land and 694,000 people, notably Hungarians and Hungarophile Ruthenians returned to the Hungarian mother country. The Southern Lands were liberated by the Hungarian army at the end of April 1941. The Southern Lands covered an area of 11,475 square kilometres and had 1,030,027 inhabitants.

It had not been the wish of the Hungarian political leaders to see the Southern Lands liberated. In December 1940, Hungary's prime minister, Pál Teleki, had drawn up a friendship and non-agression pact with Yugoslavia. The main aim had been to play off the countries of the Little Entente on the southern flank (Rumania, Yugoslavia) against each other and provide a counterbalance for the expansionistic politics of Nazi Germany which were directed at Central Europe. After Austria's *Anschluß*, Hungary had come to share a border with Nazi Germany. Through this pact Teleki, furthermore, wanted to show the Allies, notably Great Britain, that it was possible to negotiate with the Hungarians. A military coup d'état initiated by the Serbs precipitated a different anti-Axis course in Yugoslavia which in turn led Hitler to decide to effect his invasion of Yugoslavia, partly by going through Hungarian territory. Admiral Horthy and the Hungarian government refused to give the German armies permission to pass through Hungary. At the beginning of April the Germans marched through Hungarian territory and proceeded to invade Yugoslavia. In true Hungarian style Teleki was very affected by the fact that the pact with Yugoslavia had been broken. He gathered that the Hungarian army which had liberated the Southern Lands on 11th April 1941 was under Nazi control.[118] This last true aristocrat of the Hungarian political scene then saw no alternative than to take his life. Because of the defeat suffered by the Hungarians in the Second World War, the Hungarians living in the liberated areas went through some very hard times just after the war. After the Hungarian armies had been pushed back out of these areas at the end of 1944, the Hungarians who were left behind became the victims of a systematic ethnic cleansing designed to alter the ethnic balance in Hungarian populated areas.

Ethnic cleansing

The Southern Lands, the Bácska-Baranya-Mura region, was liberated in April, 1941. The men active in the Southern Lands were communist partizans who operated under Serbian command and managed to cause considerable personal and material damage to the Hungarian troops. On 20th January 1942, raids carried out in Ujvidék (Novi Sad) that were led by local commandants degenerated into the mass killing of the local civilian population. Around 3,300 people were killed, 2,200 of whom were Serbs.[119] After the Second World War the Hungarian government offered its apologies to the Yugoslavian government and handed over the commandants who had been responsible for these killings: Ferenc Szombathelyi, Ferenc Feketehalmy-Czeydner and József Grassy. The commandants were tried in Novi Sad and later executed.

These Hungarian military actions were nothing compared to the mass slaughterings carried on by Serbian partizans in the Southern Lands under the leadership of Josip Broz Tito. At the end of 1944, when a military administration had been established in Vojvodina, the Serbs moved from village to village and systematically killed off the Hungarian population. The Hungarian publisher from Ujvidék, Márton Matuska, who made a study of the mass murdering of Hungarians in the Southern Lands estimates that within the Hungarian civilian population 40,000 to 50,000 people were killed.[120]

Naturally, this had nothing to do with wreaking revenge for the events of January 1942 in Ujvidék (Novi Sad) when the Hungarians had been the perpetrators of violence. The Second World War was over by then and the Hungarian and German armies had withdrawn from the Southern Lands by the end of 1944. After this huge scale slaughter of Hungarian people had taken place the ethnic balance in South Vojvodina was changed in favour of the Serbs for all time. It was only after communism had fallen that it became possible to publish facts about these mass slaughter actions. Because of the present political situation in Vojvodina that is dominated by the terrorist regime of Milosevic it is really very dangerous to air one's views on this matter.

At the end of the Second World War, in the autumn of 1944, similar atrocities were committed against Hungarian civilians living in North Transylvania. These attacks were carried out by Rumanian fascist Maniu guards in the wake of the Soviet Russian army presence. These fascist guardists were press-ganged by the Rumanian peasant leader Iuliu Maniu to 'liberate' Transylvania. The guardists assembled at Brassó (Brasov) station where they were blessed by Rumanian Orthodox priests before going on to carry out killings in Hungarian villages in Szeklerland, notably in Szárazajta (Aita Seaca) and Csíkszentdomokos (Sindominic). These atrocities which claimed the lives of dozens of victims had a sadistic side to them. Villagers were, for instance, forced to watch how members of their family were beheaded by guardists. The aim of these actions was to scare the Hungarian population into fleeing en masse from the area. The Rumanians hoped that, in this way, they would profoundly influence the ethnic balance in the region before the post Second World War peace negotiations got fully underway. Maniu, however, had slightly misjudged the situation. He had overlooked the fact that Rumania was no Slavic state and that the Soviet Russians, therefore, had nothing to gain from atrocities committed against Hungarians. It was the Soviet Russian army leaders who, towards the end of 1944, finally put a stop to all the Maniu guardist acts of violence.[121]

The Hungarians of Subcarpathia were not spared by the Soviet Russian armies. On 13th November 1944, a military decree was sent out ordering that all men aged between 18 and 50 years of age must report to the authorities. According to estimates some 40,000 men were then made 'prisoners of war' and were deported to concentration camps in the Ukraine, White Russia and the Caucasus. Of the 40,000 men who were deported around 10,000 returned. The remainder died in the concentration camps. In contrast to the families of victims in other countries the Subcarpathian Hungarians were allowed to commemorate their dead in a humane way after communism had fallen in 1989. The organization representing the interests of Hungarians in Subcarpathia, the Hungarian Cultural Federation of Subcarpathia (KMKSZ) arranged a scientific symposium on 18th and 19th November 1989 which had as its title 'The victims of Stalinism in Subcarpathia'. The authorities allowed people in Hungarian villages to erect commemoration headstones to their deported and deceased family members.[122]

Eduard Benes had calculated that during the Slovak anti-fascist uprising of 1944 anti-Hungarian pogroms would prompt the Hungarians of the Upper Lands to take to their heels en masse and flee the area. He knew that deporting Hungarians from the Upper Lands would not be as easy as deporting the Sudeten Germans from the Czech area. Benes had hoped that by setting up a series of shocking pogroms the Hungarians would automatically leave the area so that Czechoslovakia would be freed once and for all from the 'Hungarian fascists'. The Soviet Russian army units that had got stuck in Warsaw in 1944 were unable to offer the Slovaks any help. The anti-Hungarian actions planned by Benes were, therefore, unsuccessful. Later, when the Second World War was over, he tried once again to rid the country of Hungarians. This time, Benes arranged for people to be deported and for population exchanges to take place between Hungary and Slovakia.[123]

In the Košice Program of October/November 1944, Benes was given a chance to get rid of the Hungarians. The so-called Benes decrees declared that collectively the Hungarians had been responsible for the outbreak of the Second World War and for the downfall of the First Czechoslovakian Republic. At this point, Benes also proposed that all Hungarians should be deported, to Hungary but this was rejected in Potsdam. The ethnic cleansing of Czechoslovakia which resulted in a higher proportion of Slavic inhabitants living in this particular city was achieved by different means between 1945 and 1949.

After the Second World War, the Hungarians lost their status as Czechoslovak citizens and everything they owned was expropriated. The Hungarian intellectual Kálmán Janics who first dared to write about this in 1982 was placed under house arrest for a long time after the appearance of his book.[124] The Hungarians were deported to the Czech regions where they were taken to houses of banished Germans. These deportations which took place in 1946 were not exactly carried out gently. Hungarian villages were surrounded by Czechoslovak army tanks and people were simply loaded into transport vehicles. Hungarian adults were required to pin on the letter *M* and children had to wear a blue band and around their necks a white band displaying their individual identification number.[125] In 1946, the war was certainly not over. Hungarians were treated as 'Untermenschen'. During the peace talks of 1947, the Czechoslovak government urgently called for a population transfer affecting the Slovakian Hungarians. Eventually, the Benes administration adopted a policy of 're-Slovakization' that forced Slovakian Hungarians to confess that they originally had been Slovaks and had been Magyarized. Hungarians who applied for re-Slovakization would be given back their citizenship.[126]

The Benes administration had thus done its utmost to completely eliminate its Hungarian population from Czechoslovakia. After the Second World War, 32,000 Hungarians were deported from the country and a further 69,000 were deported to Hungary as part of the compulsory population exchange programme, 6,000 fled, 42,000 Hungarians were deported to Czech regions and finally 327,000 Hungarians were 'reslovakized'.

Returning to hell

When the Trianon borders were reaffirmed at the Paris peace congress of 10th February 1947, Hungary's renewed partitioning became concrete. In the case of the Bratislava bridgehead the border was even changed at the expense of Hungary. Under the pretext of urban development Czechoslovakia had seized the chance to increase the size of Bratislava by expanding across the Danube and into Hungarian territory. At the time of the negotiations the Czechoslovak government claimed five Hungarian villages under Bratislava on the Hungarian side of the Danube. Eventually, it was decided at the Paris peace congress that Czechoslovakia should be given the three Hungarian villages of Oroszvár (Rusovce), Horvátjárfalu (Jatovce) and Dunacsún (Cunovo), in total an area of 6157 hectares.[127]

During the Second World War, the US State Department considered revising the Hungarian borders along the ethnic lines.

There were two camps. The pro-Hungarian side including John F. Montgomery, former United States ambassador to Hungary and Archibald Coolidge, the founder of *Foreign Affairs* who supported Hungary's interests and rejected the 'feudal Hungary' myth. The anti-Hungary camp was led by Hamilton F. Armstrong, a civil servant high up in the State Department hierarchy who obtained his information from the red Hungarian Mihály Károlyi and Oszkár Jászi, whose role played at the end of the First World War had been negative. Armstrong's other informants were R.W. Seton-Watson and Benes both of whom were glad to be of service when it came to making life more difficult for the Hungarians.[128] The State Department was prepared to support Hungary when it came to reducing the rebuilding payments demanded by the Soviet Union, Czechoslovakia and Yugoslavia. The US and Great Britain reached a compromise with the Soviet Union. It was agreed that within six years Hungary should pay these countries a total sum of 400 million dollars rather than 300 million dollars. The suggested border changes supported by the State Department that would have been favourable for Hungary were rejected by Prague and Belgrade. The Yugoslavs went as far as to present a list of further claims, all at Hungary's expense. Belgrade wanted to organize a population exchange for 40,000 Hungarians and make frontier corrections in the Drava area on the Slovenian-Hungarian border and in the Baranya region on the Croatian-Hungarian border at the expense of Hungary. Belgrade also asked the Allies for permission to preserve the 'South Slavic' character of the Southern Lands which in effect amounted to approving the deportation of Hungarians to other areas of Yugoslavia and stimulated the perpetuation of the Serbian settlement policy. During the peace talks, the US managed to keep these absurd claims at bay. The only point which the US and the Soviet Union still needed to clear up was the matter of the Hungarian-Rumanian border.

Byrnes, the American Minister of Foreign Affairs, contended that the Hungarian-Rumanian border should be changed so that as few people as possible would fall under foreign rule. In April 1946, the Transylvania question was raised for the last time at a meeting of vice Foreign Affairs Ministers in London. The Soviet Union supported the view that Transylvania as a whole should belong to Rumania. Byrnes, who was left more or less alone in his view, did not particularly want to put extra pressure on Soviet-American relations because of a 'third-rate issue' like Transylvania. The Soviet Union had various reasons for wanting to stick to the border lines agreed to at Trianon. Because of the annexation of Subcarpathia, the present Carpatho-Ukraine, the Soviet Union had become a successor state itself. Furthermore, in June 1940, the Soviet Union had managed to reconquer the strategically important regions of Bessarabia and North Bukovina from Rumania. In exchange for these areas Stalin was able to offer the Rumanians Transylvania. Finally, it would seem that Stalin had more faith in the loyalty of the Rumanian communists than in the loyalty of the Hungarian ones. In retrospect, in view of the uprising of 1956, this fear was realistic.

This then was the third time, since the time of Trianon, that the Carpathian Basin came under foreign control. In the inter-war years, it had been ruled by imperialist France, before and during the Second World War by fascist Germany and after the Second World War by the communist Soviet Union. On all three occasions the smaller nations of Central Europe found themselves played off against each other and the rule of foreign powers brought disaster to the region. The Hungarians had come out of the Second World War worst of all, theirs had been the rawest deal. Once again millions of Hungarians found themselves living outside their country's borders against their will. This time their human and civil rights were trampled under foot by communist ideology which boasted that it would create a homogeneous and uniform 'New Man'. The Hungarians of the Carpathian Basin had yet one more big ordeal ahead of them.

Anti-Hungarian ethnocide

In the communist era, life was difficult for Hungarians in the successor states because they were made the victims of a double kind of oppression. In the first place, just like the population that formed the majority, they were repressed by virtue of the fact that the communist states wished to have absolute power over their people. The most elementary of human rights such as freedom of speech, press freedom, the freedom to choose where to live etc. were violated. The ultimate goal was to gain absolute control over the human mind through widespread indoctrination, manipulation and brainwashing. In part one, I explained that an effective way of realizing these tactics had been by suppressing national identity and obliterating people's common culture. Generally speaking, particular culture and community awareness provide a firm basis for world orientation.

Apart from this the Hungarians living in the Carpathian Basin - also in Hungary - were kept down in another way. Anti-Hungarianism in the successor states that, since Trianon, had been raised to the level of a state doctrine was further perfected under communist rule. From this point of view it is more accurate to speak of nationalist-communist regimes. For the first time since the Treaty of Trianon the regimes had a serious possibility of getting rid of their Hungarians. In these communist states, Hungarian identity was synonymous with fascism. For Hungarians fighting for recognition of their rights was the same as fighting against communist dictatorship. Therefore, a very close eye was kept on Hungarian dissidents during the time of communist rule. Not only were Hungarians in the successor states deprived of their basic human and fundamental cultural civil rights, but the regimes in Czechoslovakia, Yugoslavia, Rumania and the Soviet Union made direct attempts to liquidate their 'Hungarian minorities'. Hundreds of ways were found to destroy the Hungarian communities. From the whole range of anti-Hungarian policy the following main strategies may be singled out.

Altering the ethnic composition in areas that were densely populated by Hungarians. Regions that were densely populated by Hungarians became fragmented because they were subjected to repeated district divisional changes. By manipulating district boundaries it was possible to bring down the numbers of Hungarians and artificially raise the numbers of people belonging to the 'majority' population group. This policy was reinforced by the politics of colonization that had already been introduced during the inter-war years and by the compulsory deportation of Hungarian intellectuals and workers to other, non-Hungarian parts. The inflated communist industrialization drive that affected ethnic composition in the cities also fitted nicely into this general scheme. The new industries set up in urban areas drew many chiefly non-Hungarian workers who were settled in the cities. As a result, the cities which until the sixties had chiefly been populated by Hungarians witnessed an 'internal' colonization process. At a rapid pace sprawling, ugly communist workers' districts sprung up around the old city centres of places like Kassa (Košice) in Slovakia, Kolozsvár (Cluj) in Transylvania and Ujvidék (Novi Sad) in Vojvodina. Hungarian labourers were kept out of these cities, such areas became forbidden territory to Hungarians. Obviously, this was kept secret but in the case of the city of Marosvásárhely (Tîrgu Mures) such practices have been proven. Since 1989, documents have been found containing details of this policy. The Rumanian authorities wanted to achieve a Rumanian majority in this city by 1996. Had the plan to destroy Rumanian villages and to transfer rural populations to 'agro-industrial complexes' - as the Rumanian Conductor Ceausescu had started to do in the eighties - then the Hungarian community in Transylvania would almost certainly have been flattened. Fortunately for the Hungarian population the Conductor was unable to realize his grand plan.

Breaking down the cultural institutions of the Hungarian community. All the cultural institutions that still existed after the Second World War were systematically broken down. When it came to educational institutions, it was common tactics to merge Hungarian schools with Rumanian, Slovak or Serbian schools under the pretext of 'communist fraternization'. The next step was to Rumanize, Slovakize and Serbize education and to dismiss the Hungarian teachers.[129] In this way, for instance the Hungarian Bolyai University in Kolozsvár ceased to exist as such in 1959 when it was merged with the Rumanian Babes University. Libraries and archives were either destroyed or moved which, thus, effectively eliminated the Hungarian community's collective memory as well. Even today, in this post communist era, it is still not clear where all the various surviving library and archive collections are to be found.

The suppression of the Hungarian language and the restrictions placed on Hungarian in public and cultural life and in education. One of the main aims of the anti-Hungarian homogenization politics was to lay restrictions on teaching in the Hungarian language. By manipulating curricula and the numbers of pupils in a class, it became possible to systematically stamp out Hungarian. At technical schools, for instance, teaching in Hungarian was reduced to the minimum, because it was said to be 'better' for the pupils to learn technical subjects in the official state langauge. When it came to registering the number of pupils required for lessons in Hungarian the figures were again faked. The numbers would be manipulated so that there would not be enough pupils to justify forming a Hungarian class. Alongside of the restrictions placed on the visual and symbolic aspects of language, for example, on the displaying of place names in Hungarian, there was one other major aspect of language that was crippled, namely the expressive and creative side. By the end of the communist era just about everything published in the Hungarian language had been literally translated from Rumanian, Serbian or Slovak publications. Hungarian in Transylvania in particular was virtually void of any creativity. Original Hungarian texts were banned from publication altogether.

Distorting history in education and the culture while at the same time promoting feelings of guilt among Hungarians towards the majority population. All the myths created about Rumanian, Slovak and Serbian history were presented to the Hungarians as dogmas. In these myths, as we explained in part one of this book, the Hungarians were portrayed as barbarians and intruders into Europe. Hungarian history, thereby, came to be viewed as something inferior. There were two particular themes underlying this indoctrination, the Magyarization politics and the supposed 'fascist' past of the Hungarians. The Magyarization politics which was partly increased by propaganda during the First World War has already been discussed in part one. Continually hammering on the Magyarization politics served not only to justify anti-Hungarian policies in these states 'to repay in kind', but also to cultivate feelings of guilt among Hungarians in neighbouring countries. What was drummed into the Hungarians was that the Rumanians, Slovaks and Serbs had suffered 'long and intensely' under Hungarian feudal oppression. It was, therefore, understandable that these nations harboured such strong resentment towards Hungarians. Another favourite theme was, the Second World War and "Hungarian fascism".

The atrocities committed by the Hungarians were exaggerated and those of the Rumanians, Slovaks and Serbs were ignored completely. Hungary was branded as a country of 'fascists' and in the official historiography of the successor states these countries were viewed as victims that had taken on the role of anti-fascist heroes. An anti-Hungarian campaign was launched with the slogan 'Horthy fascism'. In the first part of this book, I briefly touched on admiral Horthy's role in the Second World War. One may wish to characterize his part in the war, however, he was not condemned as a war criminal and during the Nuremberg Nazi war criminal trials he was only called as a witness. The campaign directed at linking Horthy with fascism, therefore, amounted to a gross distortion of the historical facts. Books like *Teroarea Horthysto-fascistâ în nord-vestul României septembrie 1940-octombrie 1944* were written to put psychological pressure on the Hungarians of Transylvania and Hungarians in general.[130] According to Lajos Demény, a Transylvanian Hungarian historian who was affiliated to the Historical Institute of the Rumanian Academy of Sciences, these books were compiled with the help of expatriate Iron Guard members such as Iosif Constantin Dragan who was domiciled in Italy. Books of this genre were based on the propaganda material that had ensued from the Antonescu administration and on the disinformation by the Rumanian intelligence service. These books glorified members of the Rumanian Iron Guard who went before tribunals after the Second World War and were sentenced to death and who have since never been vindicated.[131]

What the Hungarians did in the Second World War was exaggarated while the activities of the Rumanians, Slovaks and Serbs, who served the cause of German Nazi's remain shrouded in mystery. According to Péter Gosztonyi few people realize that on 1st September 1939 independent Slovakia joined up with Nazi German armies to attack Poland. It was not only the case that 'independent' Slovakia allowed German armies to pass through its territory in order to invade Poland but the young Slovak army - Slovakia had declared itself independent on 15th March 1939 - also actively helped with the invasion. Then there were the huge Rumanian pogroms against the Jewish communities in Bessarabia, Bukovina and Moldavia. Matatias Carp described in *Cartea Neagra, Suferintele evreilor din Romania, 1940 1944* (A Black Book on the 1940-1944 Rumanian Holocaust) how the Rumanian army and the Iron Guard together were responsible for the deaths of over 400,000 Jews in these regions, while the Soviet Russian army was being pushed back. Raul Hilberg intimated that "in the Rumanian-administered territory between the Dniester and the Bug (Transnistria), killings were conducted even more expeditiously than in the German military area."[132] The fact is that little is known about the Rumanian mass murders of the Jews, because during the Ceausescu regime the *Cartea Neagra* which appeared in three volumes systematically disappeared from most libraries. Eventually, it was only possible to read it in its entirety by ordering the three volumes separately from different libraries.

Restricting the scope of Hungarian churches. The vast majority of the Hungarian churches in the successor states are either Catholic or Protestant. This created much tension in Rumania, Yugoslavia and the Ukraine where the established church was the

Orthodox Church and where this faith at least went before all others. In Slovakia which is for the greater part Catholic the Hungarian Catholics were and are an integral part of the Slovak church organization. Church organizations proved to be effective vehicles in the process of assimilating Hungarians. Using church organizations as a vehicle to increase power and assimilation was not an unknown strategy in the region. For example, at the end of the seventeenth century the Habsburgs supported by Catholic Hungarian magnates established the Rumanian Greek Catholic (Uniate) church in order to counterbalance Hungarian and German Protestantism and the Rumanian Orthodox church in Transylvania.[133] For the Hungarians their church organizations were something vitally important. The danger of 'mixed' church organizations was that Hungarian Catholics were often unable to follow the mass in their own language, but had to listen to Slovak. Finally, there was always a shortage of Roman Catholic priests.[134] The Hungarian Catholic community in Slovakia still does not have a Hungarian bishop which means that the Hungarian Catholics in the region are perpetually under the pressure of Slovakization.

It was no coincidence that opposition to the reign of terror of the Rumanian Conducator, Ceausescu, which led to his fall, came from within the ranks of the Hungarian Reformed Church. The Hungarian Reformed Church, though heavily infiltrated by the Securitate, was the last Hungarian bastion in Transylvania.[135] At the beginning of December 1989, the young minister, László Tőkés, barricaded himself into his church in Temesvár (Timisoara) after several times having been ordered to leave by the Securitate. On more than one occasion Tőkés and the members of his church had indicated that they were unable to reconcile themselves to Ceausescu's anti-democratic and anti-Hungarian politics. On 24th July 1989, the Hungarian television programme 'Panorama' broadcast an interview with Tőkés in which he expressed how critical the situation of the Hungarian minority in Rumania was and he also criticized plans proposed by the Rumanian government to destroy Hungarian villages. In true Hungarian Protestant style Tőkés firmly believes that in the end it was through a steadfast belief in God that the tyranny was finally overcome.[136] Because of the special role played by the church in Hungarian communities those who served God and believers in general have been extra vulnerable. Tőkés also has found himself under threat more than once. One of his church workers, Ernő Ujvárossy, was found dead in a wood in the Temesvár (Timisoara) area on 16th September 1989. The atrocities committed against presbyters and church workers continue even now that the Conducator has been removed. In the spring of 1990, Árpád Toszó who had played a prominent part in the events of December 1989 was beaten and made an invalid by an unidentified group of attackers.[137]

Psychological warfare targeted at the Hungarian community. The underlying aim was to create a constant atmosphere in which Hungarians perpetually felt intimidated and humiliated and to give them the suggestion that they might well, at any given moment, fall prey to physical violence. In the anti-Hungarian psychological warfare scheme language was crucial. During the communist era in Rumania, Hungarians were officially referred to as 'the nationality cohabiting with the Rumanians'. The objective of this phrasing was to insinuate that Hungarians were merely tolerated on their own native soil. If the official communist way of phrasing was offensive and designed to make the Hungarians feel uncomfortable then the unofficial name given to the Hungarians, *bozgor* 'the homeless' could only possibly make them feel even worse. Encapsulated in this discriminatory metaphor was the message that the Hungarians were not only merely tolerated, but also that they really did not belong in the land of the descendants of the Dacians and Romans. In Slovakia as well, during the period of communism, centrally organized campaigns were launched to make the Hungarians feel tolerated at their native soil only like intruders. In 1967, for instance, the old anti-Hungarian slogan that had been used between 1945 and 1948 "Slovakia for the Slovaks!" was revived. In the spirit of this slogan restraints were laid on Hungarian in the factories and it became compulsory for Hungarian workers to follow Slovak language courses. Between 9th and 11th May 1968, Slovak students in Bratislava organized a 'huge national march' that passed through areas where the population was mixed. The battle-cry of the young guardists was a familiar one "into the Danube with the Hungarians".[138]

The curtailing of personal and cultural contacts with other Hungarians and the viewing of such contacts as a threat to the state. Contacts between members of Hungarian national communities and with Hungarians in the 'mother country' were seriously impeded in the communist era. These contacts could be restricted, because in the socialist countries visas were required for travelling. In this way, it was possible to exercise complete control over contacts between individuals and cultural associations. Official inter-Hungarian contact was only possible between those who belonged to or represented the communist party and its alibi organizations. The Helsinki Agreement that made a bid for the liberalization of travel movements within Europe did help matters a little. Even after this agreement had been signed, though, inter-Hungarian contacts remained troublesome and controlled. Some countries, like the Soviet Union and Rumania, signed the agreement, but in practice the Transylvanian and Subcarphatian Hungarians were given little opportunity to visit Hungary. In the other two countries of Czechoslovakia and Yugoslavia, movement was freer but Hungarian-Hungarian contacts were watched more closely by the security police than other contacts. Contacts between Hungarians in the Western diaspora and members of the various Hungarian national communities were also eyed with suspicion, especially when it came to Hungarians in the West who had political or other kinds of influence.

To summarize, we may, therefore, conclude that under communism Hungarian national communities were exposed to a politics of ethnocide the sole aim of which was to systematically destroy these communities. After having visited Rumania the Dutch journalist Alexander Münninghoff wrote in the Dutch newspaper *Haagsche Courant*, "What is going on in Transylvania today is the most inhumane assault upon the identity of a national minority our world has ever witnessed..."[139] Suppression was severest in Rumania, but in all the communist countries the Hungarians were under heavy pressure. The means used varied in their nature, frequency and intensity but they all remained equally pernicious. Thus, it was that the anti-Hungarian policies initiated in these states in the inter-war years were continued. None of these states was prepared to honour the human rights of Hungarians. Communist ideology provided the perfect cover for anti-Hungarian state nationalism. While realizing that it is truly amazing that any Hungarian community anywhere survived the terrors of communism, one should also realize that the Hungarians were close to total obliteration indeed. Quite soon after communism fell in 1989, anti-Hungarian state nationalism was again rampant, thus proving that it is a real constant factor in Central European politics. So much so in fact that conditions rapidly deteriorated for Hungarian communities. Below I shall focus on the present situation for the various Hungarian communities in Croatia, Lesser Yugoslavia (Serbia), Rumania, the Ukraine and Slovakia and show what the various forms of oppression and ethnocide brought upon these communities look like in the context of the new Europe.

Croatia: the annihiliation of a Hungarian community

In Croatia, there are approximately 40,000 ethnic Hungarians. The place where they live in greatest concentration is in the region known as the Baranya Triangle. This region is a fertile agricultural area that borders on the Danube in the east, on the Drava in the south-west and on the present Hungarian border in the north. The Baranya Triangle covers an area of 1,150 square kilometres and has 55,000 inhabitants. As the region's name would indicate it was once a part of the Hungarian county of Baranya which still exists today under this name on the Hungarian side of the border. At the end of World War I, the ethnic composition of the Baranya Triangle was as follows: 40% Hungarian, 30% German and the remainder either Serb or Croat. The Treaty of Trianon ruled that the Baranya Triangle should

185

become part of the kingdom of the Serbs, Croats and Slovenes. During the Second World War, in 1941, this southern part of the county of Baranya was reunited with the northern part. In 1945, it was once again annexed by Yugoslavia. In the process of federally restructuring communist Yugoslavia, the Baranya Triangle was made part of the Republic of Croatia. After the Second World War, the German people living in the Triangle were eradicated from the area and it was repopulated with southern Slavic people.

According to official population statistics issued in 1991, which should be perused with the necessary caution, there were 19,310 Croats, 12,857 Serbs, 9,920 Hungarians and around 12,000 people of other nationalities living in the Baranya Triangle. A further 2,000 people claimed that Hungarian was their native language. According to estimates issued by the organization representing the interests of Hungarians in Croatia, the Union of Democratic Hungarians in Croatia, some 12,000 of the 40,000 Croatian Hungarians lived in the Baranya Traingle. It was the first area to be attacked by the Serbs during the war between Serbia and Croatia. Between the end of June and 22nd August 1991, the Triangle was taken over by the federal army, in effect a Serbian army. The Serbian army operated according to *the scenario of Belgrade*. The federal army provided the Baranya Serbs with weapons; chetniks and other paramilitary troops attacked non-Serbian villages. The Serbs did this, because they felt 'threatened'. Croatian policemen were murdered, the local inhabitants put up no resistance and the Croatian guard withdrew to the opposite bank of the Drava. Ethnically mixed villages were 'cleansed'. Kórógy (Korod) and Szentlászló (Laslova), two Hungarian villages in East Slavonia were razed to the ground.

After the conquest of the Baranya Triangle on 22nd August 1991, the federal army and the cetnik troops opened up psychological and physical warfare on the civilian population. By the autumn of 1991, the Baranya Triangle had been completely cleansed.

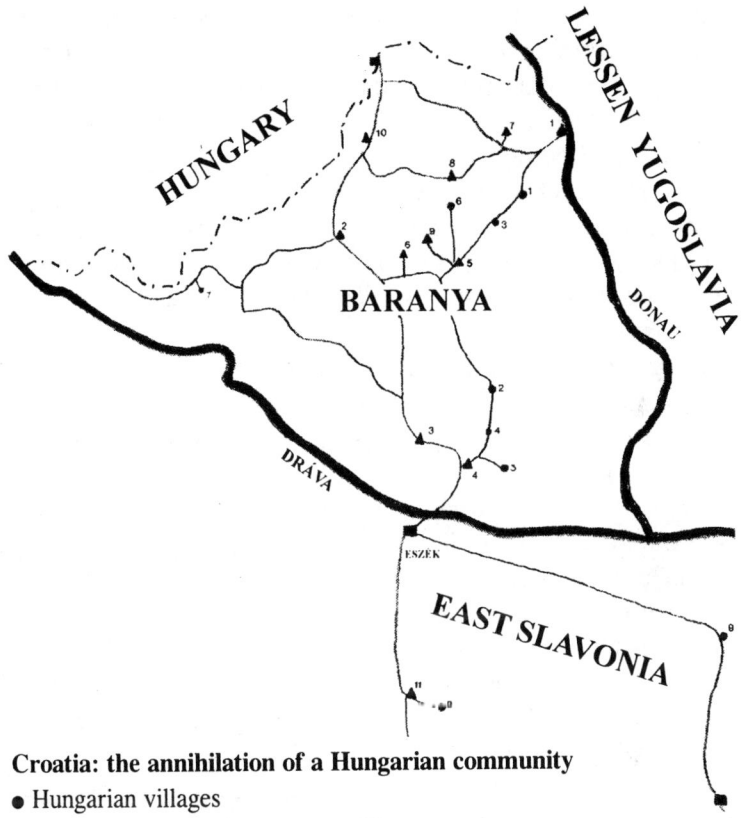

Croatia: the annihilation of a Hungarian community
● Hungarian villages
▼ mixed Croatian and Hungarian villages

Hungarian villages:
1) Vörösmart (Zmajevac)
2) Laskó (Lug)
3) Csúza (Suza)
4) Várdaróc (Vardarac)
5) Kopács (Kopačevo)
6) Sepse (Kotlina)
7) Újbezdán (Novi Bezdan)
8) Kórogy (Korod)
9) Dályhegy (Dalj Planina)

Mixed Croatian and Hungarian villages:
1) Kiskőszeg (Batina)
2) Pélmonostor (Beli Manastir)
3) Dárda (Darda)
4) Bellye (Bilje)
5) Hercegszőlős (Kneževi Vinogradi)
6) Karancs (Karanac)
7) Darázs (Draž)
8) Nagybodolya (Podolje)
9) Kő (Kamenac)
10) Főherceglak (Kneževo)
11) Szentlászló (Laslovo)

- The Baranya Triangle was hermetically closed off. The only access to and from the region was via the Batina bridge over the Danube. To cross this bridge one needed papers and these papers were only issued by the new Serbian authorities. Hardly any permits were handed out.
- All telephone connections were cut off, there was no electricity and mail was censored. There was a ban on listening to Croatian radio and a curfew stating that no one was allowed out after dark.
- The federal army made its presence very much felt, it set up control posts and roadblocks.
- Throughout the Baranya Triangle masked Serbian gangs took to plundering, thieving and murdering.
- Businesses were ethnically cleansed. Non-Serbs were removed from their jobs and sacked.
- Hungarian schools were closed down.
- There were no more medical services.
- Catholic and Protestant clergymen were driven out.
- Non-Serbs received a summons to leave their houses.
- Non-Serbs were made to do forced labour.
- Non-Serbs were forced to serve in the front line.
- Between September and December 1991, 30,000 to 35,000 persons left the region. Some 7,000 of those who left were Hungarian. Virtually all the Hungarian intellectuals and teachers living in the Baranya Triangle fled the area. These refugees are presently in Hungary.

In September 1991, the Serbian army and paramilitary troops immediately began to make ethnic changes in the area by expelling, intimidating and executing people. Serbs were planted in the houses of people who were being forced to flee. Aided by paramilitary troops during the 1991 Christmas vacation period the Serbian army increased its hostile activities. Not only was Eszék (Osijek) bombed but the Serbs found a new way of forcing people to flee the area. All non-Serbs were given the opportunity to leave the region if they agreed to sign a document stating that all their property was handed over to the Yugoslav authorities. In order to get as many people as possible to leave 'voluntarily', the Serbs bombed the houses of ethnic Hungarians at night. After this bout of intimidation, some thirty families fled the region. Those who were Croatian later returned to Croatia via Hungary. Most of the Hungarians went to Austria, Germany or Hungary. In 1991, Hungarians living in the Baranya Triangle suffered the following atrocities (see map):

Kiskőszeg (Batina)
*of the 1,645 people living in this village 821 fled,
*nine persons, seven of them with families, were chased out of Batina (one Slovenian, two Croats and six Hungarians). Their possessions were confiscated and their houses occupied by Serbs,
*five people (one Croat and four Hungarians) were tortured during interrogation,
*four Croats were deported and are now missing.

Darázs (Draz)
*450 out of the 650 inhabitants fled,
*eleven persons (seven of them Croats and three Hungarian) were tortured and driven out of their village,
*one Hungarian policeman who worked on the border was murdered.

Sepse (Kotlina)
*out of the 581 inhabitants 280 fled,
*two Hungarian farmers - one of whom was chairman of the local branch of the Democratic Hungarian Union in Croatia - was tortured during questioning and chased out of his village,
*Ervin Bacsa, mayor of the village, was murdered.

Hercegszőllős (Knezevi Vinogradi)
*1,100 of the 3,580 inhabitants fled,
*three persons - two with their families - (a Croat and two Hungarians) were expelled from their village. Their possessions were confiscated and their houses were occupied by Serbs,
*three Croats were executed.

Pélmonostor (Beli Manastir)
*the town's 3,400 inhabitants all fled,

*four persons (two Hungarians and two Croats) were executed.

Vörösmart (Zmajevac)
*1,100 of the village's original 1,523 inhabitants left,
*eight Hungarian families were chased out of the village, their possessions were confiscated and their houses were occupied by Serbs,
*the Hungarian mayor and the headmaster of the local school were both tortured during interrogation,
*three persons (two Hungarians and a Croat) disappeared,
*a reward of 50,000 DM was offered for the murder of József Csörgits, chairman of the Hungarian Association in Croatia. A reward was also offered for the liquidation of his wife as she chaired the Baranya division of that same association. After the couple had fled the country with their two children mercenaries were sent after them. Their possessions were confiscated and given to the Serbs who now live in their house. The couple's parents are all under house arrest and are not allowed to leave the village.

Laskó (Lug)
*out of the 1,446 inhabitants 650 have fled,
*three Hungarians, two of them with their families, were forced to leave their village,
*the Hungarian priest in the village was tortured.

Bellye (Bilje)
*of the original 2,200 inhabitants only 300 Serbs remain in the village,
*three Hungarian families were violently expelled,
*nine Hungarians were executed.

Dárda (Darda)
*the Serbian population remained,
*five Hungarian families were chased out
*one Hungarian was executed.

Kopács (Kopacevo)

*from the 820 inhabitants 600 fled,
*two Hungarian families were forcefully removed,
*six persons (two of them Croat, four of them Hungarian) were beaten and tortured,
*two Hungarians were questioned, tortured and afterwards deported,
*three persons (two Croats and a Hungarian) were executed.

Baranyavár (Branjin Vrh)
*two Croats were executed by hanging.

Csúza (Suza)
*ten Hungarians and their families were chased out of the village and their houses were plundered,
*a Croat and a Hungarian were deported and are now missing.

These are merely a few of the atrocities committed by Serbs against non-Serbs, notably to Hungarian and Croatian inhabitants of the Baranya Triangle, when they invaded the area in the autumn of 1991. On 25th November 1992, Croatian Hungarians issued an impassioned plea in the form of a memorandum with the following title: *Is the world just going to stand by and watch while Croatia's Hungarian minority is wiped out?* The memorandum was signed by Ferenc Faragó, an independent Hungarian member of the *Sabor* and by the Hungarian cultural society 'Endre Ady' in Zagreb. The memorandum was, furthermore, supported by the following associations: the Vojvodina Croat Association in Zagreb, the Croatian Refugee Community in Vojvodina, German and Austrian Societies (Zagreb division), the Croatian-Hungarian Society, Mothers for Peace (Zagreb) and the Women's Forum (Dubrovnik). The signatories' argument went as follows: "A year ago pro-communist chetniks established the Serbian Republic of Krajina in this area, a state that has never before existed and which is not recognized by anybody. They did this in a region in which, according to demographic figures of the last 110 years, the Serbian population percentage has varied between 12 and 25.5%. The chetniks have been busy eliminating ethnic Croats and Hungarians from this region. These people were forced to flee and leave behind all their possessions and property. At the same time, the chetniks have brought Serbs from elsewhere into the region. According to reports from reliable sources, between 25,000 and 30,000 Serbs were promptly moved into the houses of those who were forced to flee." In the rest of the memorandum, the signatories express their disappointment in the effectivity of the UN peacekeeping forces. Those who signed the document were surprised to see that instead of helping people to return to their houses and to get back all that they possessed the UN forces had actually supported ethnic cleansing by assisting the refugees in their departure. The memorandum further pointed to the dangers of changing the Croatian borders and issued the warning that the chetniks will probably try to extend the unrecognized Serbian Republic of Krajina to cover areas of Croatia and Bosnia seized by the Serbs. The memorandum concludes with the following list of demands: (1) reassess the role of the UN peace mission in Baranja (Baranya) and East Slavonia, (2) see to it that the UN peacekeepers disarm all military and paramilitary troops in the above-mentioned area (3) extend the powers of the UN forces, (4) have the UN security council increase pressure on the Serbian president Milosevic, the person behind all the Serb aggression, and (5) guarantee that Croatian Hungarians will be able to return to their native country and will be given back all their property and that they will receive compensation for all the damage that has been incurred. It has to be noted that desperately few of these demands have yet been met.

Lesser Yugoslavia: Hungarians as cannon fodder for Serbian generals

The region now known as Vojvodina (Hun. Vajdaság) is no natural region, but an artificially constructed region that was created at the end of the First World War after a series of violent conquests that had been carried out in an ethnically homogeneous area almost completely inhabited by Hungarians under the pretext that parts of former Hungary, to be inhabited by Serbs, were to

be linked to what was later to become Yugoslavia. During the course of the 17th and 18th centuries, Serbs, together with peoples of other nationalities, emigrated to the less densely populated areas along the southern borders of what was then the kingdom of Hungary. In 1918, these people only constituted a third of the population in these areas. In 1941, the Southern Lands, with its Hungarian majority, was returned to Hungary. So the following areas once again came under Hungarian rule: Bácska (North Vojvodina), Baranya (now in Croatia) and the Mura region (now Slovenia).

In 1992, when war broke out in former Yugoslavia, the ethnic composition of Vojvodina was very heterogeneous. It is an area inhabited by people of some twenty different nationalities. The Serbs concentrated chiefly south of a line Danube-Timis. The closer one draws to the present Hungarian border the more markedly Hungarian the population becomes, especially in the central and northern parts, in spite of the massive Serb colonization still continuing in the area today. Official Serb statistics, which claim that the population is 20% Hungarian (55% Serb), therefore, give a very misleading picture of the situation. These figures give no real insight into the actual majority ratios, because they do not account for the north-south divide dichotomy. Furthermore, one may definitely question the accuracy of these official statistics when one bears in mind that at the time of the last census it was common practice for people to be openly intimidated. It is a well-known fact that many Hungarians in those parts are afraid to openly admit to being Hungarian. What is also striking is the fact that many people living in areas that were formerly predominantly populated by Hungarians have described themselves as 'Yugoslav'.

At present, 68% of the population in the northern part of Vojvodina (see map) is Hungarian which means that the Hungarians constitute a definite majority there. In the southern region, the Hungarians have not been in the majority for some years, though, they are heavily represented in certain parts. There are now isolated areas within South Vojvodina, extending to as far as just north of Belgrade, where Hungarians sometimes outnumber Serbs.

The Vojvodina map explained
A line running in an east-west direction indicates where the northern area of Vojvodina lies. This area is predominantly inhabited by Hungarians. In making the demarcation, the following principles were borne in mind:
- A certain *majority principle* was observed which means to say that every effort was made to keep Hungarians together in places where their concentrations were highest.
- Because of the so-called *ethnic unravelling* the minority situation on both sides is being minimalized as an alternative way of achieving pacification in the region.

- For Croats living in Vojvodina this solution will give them the chance to escape from Serbian dominance. After the Hungarians, the second biggest national community to come under Serbian threat is that of the Croats. For Croats living side by side with Serbs is no bright prospect for the future and so they cannot really be expected to go on like that. The administrative dividing lines provide the Croats also with their only chance for survival.
- The proportion of the population composed of Hungarians fluctuates between 65 and 70%, i.e. it is around the 500,000 level. Together with the 70,000 Croats they form a majority. The Serbs are, thus, clearly in the minority. The population of North Vojvodina, 750,000 in all, may be divided as follows: 500,000 Hungarians = 66%; 70,000 Croats = 9%; and others, including Serbs, 180,000 = 25%. These figures derive from Serbian statistics that have been adjusted after the way in which the census was carried out. The above figures are estimated and they are the product of a number tried and tested measuring methods. One may, therefore, presume that the statistics quoted here closely approach the real situation. In an unbiased census the results would, therefore, be closer to those quoted above than to those issued by the Serbian authorities.
- There is no longer an overall Hungarian majority in South Vojvodina, but in some areas Hungarians are still in the majority. In contrast to the situation of several years ago, these areas are no longer linked, but often lie isolated within bigger non-Hungarian communities.
- In view of the soundness of the argument presented for establishing the areas of North and South Vojvodina, it has been accepted that where there are doubts as to the certainty of a Hungarian majority (for example, if it is 48%) the area will go to South Vojvodina. As long as the census cannot be freely held, this principle will be adhered to. Hence, a city such as Ujvidék (Novi Sad) does not come under North Vojvodina. On the map, the positioning of North Vojvodina might look like a minimum option but, bearing in mind the present relations, it is at least a realistic option.

The escalation of events in former Yugoslavia led to outright war between Serbia and all the other federal republics. This war which in its first year, by mid 1992, had already claimed the lives of more than 40,000 people and had forced more than two million people to flee the country had been very much at the focus of public attention for some time. Not only the national communities in the most acutely hit areas of Croatia and Bosnia have been affected by the war, but also other national communities who have found themselves in a similar position. Although their basic situation is the same their problems may be seen as less important and acute and less deserving of a satisfactory solution, yet they are still in danger of being forgotten. The national communities concerned are the Hungarians living predominantly in the north of the Vojvodina region and the Albanians who live in Kosovo. In both these areas, the respective Hungarian and Albanian communities are repressed, discriminated against and robbed of their human rights by the Serbs.

The Serbian nationalist oppression to which the Vojvodina Hungarians are exposed is not just something of the last years. Since the war broke out in the summer of 1991, pressure has clearly increased, so much so that the possibilty of mass slaughtering amongst Hungarians cannot be ruled out. Below is a brief review of the repressive measures taken to clarify what the situation and living conditions have been like for Hungarians since Vojvodina was forced to become a part of Yugoslavia:
- During the Second World War, the Vojvodina Hungarians and Germans were subjected to pogroms and mass killings. These massacres which led to the death of around 50,000 Hungarian civilians were organized by Serbian partizans.
- The remainder of the German community domiciled in the south of the Hungarian kingdom, some 400,000 people in all, constituted an important sector of the population were either chased out of Vojvodina altogether by the Serbs or killed.
- After the Second World War, and the signing of a new peace treaty tens of thousands of Hungarians mysteriously disappeared

and have never been seen since. No official judicial investigation was ever set up.

- Vojvodina's constitutional autonomous status was ended in 1988 by Belgrade without the inhabitants of the region even first having been consulted. Since then, the region has fallen directly under Serbian control.
- With the forced assimilation politics of the last years, Hungarian, already a neglected language in Vojvodina, has now been banned altogether as an officially recognized language. The same is true in Kosovo with Albanian. For similar reasons no teaching in Albanian is done in Kosovo and all Albanian teachers have been dismissed.
- In recent years, numerous laws have been introduced which clearly discriminate heavily against the Hungarian people.
- For instance, the decree of 30th January 1992 set out new regional divisions for Vojvodina. It dictated that all areas inhabited by Hungarians should be forcibly divided up and merged with other areas. The basic aim was to undermine all ways of representing Hungarian interests both at collective and regional levels. Since the era of Ceausescu in Rumania, we are all familiar with the consequences of creating false majorities.
- Cyrillic script has been introduced in the region and Latin script has been abolished.
- It is common practice for Hungarian educational establishments to be closed down as well as other Hungarian cultural institutions, such as theatres and museums.
- The Serbian Orthodox Church has been given back the possessions that lawfully belong to it, but had been confiscated by the state during the regime of Tito. A similar procedure does not apply to the Catholic Church to which the Hungarians, Croats and Germans in the area usually belong.
- Hungarian newspapers no longer receive a state subsidy and everything that is written is censored.
- When Hungarians apply for jobs they are systematically discriminated against.
- Members of the political party which represents the interests of Hungarians in the Vojvodina region, the Democratic Community of Vojvodina Hungarians (VMDK, Hun. *Vajdasági Magyarok*

Demokratikus Közössége) and the editorial staff of regional media organizations are frequently arrested without warning or explanation.

- Serbian politicians have called for a ban to be laid on Hungarian political organizations and for the present parliamentary system to be changed. In this way the influence of representatives from non-Serbian groups can be substantially reduced.
- Young Hungarians eligible for military service are compulsorily drafted into the Serbian army in order to support Serbian aggression against Croatia and Bosnia. This practice is distinctly reminiscent of the darkest days of Stalinism when houses were raided at night and men were arrested in their beds. More than 10% of the federal army troops are of Hungarian origin. With insufficient training and ammunition the Hungarians are then deployed in the army's front lines. They are, thus, literally offered up as cannon fodder. In accordance with these practices employed, the Hungarian war casualty numbers are relatively higher than they procentually should be. Every fifth soldier killed in action is Hungarian. Evidence enough surely for the assumption of planned ethnocide against the Hungarians. Not surprisingly this has given rise to a stream of refugees. Thousands of Hungarians have already fled the country.
- The Hungarian deserters who have been arrested can expect lengthy prison sentences. Exactly how many have been arrested is uncertain but the number is definitely high.
- However, it is generally feared that if the outcome of the war between the Serbs and the other nationalities is negative for the Serbs the northern regions of Vojvodina, which are inhabited by Hungarians, will be colonized by huge numbers of Serbs. This will cause a massive exodus and the end of remaining Hungarian life.
- If the federal army is forced to withdraw from Croatia and Bosnia this could have fatal consequences for the Hungarians and Albanians, because the federal army could then be deployed to definitely subject non-Serbs and to secure the new Serbian 'colonies'. Federal army divisions that have been pulled out of Bosnia are being stationed in Kosovo in huge numbers. This is also taking place in the Hungarian city of Kanizsa (Kanijza)

where new barracks have been set up and where artillery directed at Hungary has in the meantime been set up.
- Serb civilians in the Vojvodina region and in Kosovo have already been issued weapons in preparation for the planned mass slaughter.
- In Vojvodina open terrorization is common. The Hungarians are being intimidated and threatened, subjected to assaults on their lives and property and it is quite common for Hungarians to simply disappear. The whole objective is to drive out the Hungarian community. The perpetual smear campaigns in the Serbian media serve only to reinforce this aim. The general level of psychological terror is increasing by the day. By deliberately parading columns of tanks through Hungarian villages and stationing heavy weapons brought in from Baranja and East Slavonia, feelings of anxiety are consciously being cultivated amongst Hungarians. The VMDK has requested UN observers.
- Serbia has two faces. At the end of April 1992, the government of Lesser Yugoslavia established what was known as a Ministry for Minorities. Though the head of the Ministry is an ethnic Hungarian, he does not have the support of the Hungarian population. So far, the ministry has taken no action whatsoever. The Serbian government claims that no soldiers are fighting outside their own territory. At the beginning of June 1992, 5,000 Vojvodina Hungarians were called, or in many cases forced, to take up arms. Many of the Hungarian youths recruited are sent to the front in Bosnia or Croatia. In 1992, many of those buried in Novi Sad who had died in battle in the Dubrovnik (Croatia) area were Hungarians.
- Serbia has double standards. Serbia demands rights for Croatian Serbs, but does not provide the same rights for its own minority groups, the Kosovo Albanians and the Vojvodina Hungarians. The Hungarians are told that they enjoy more rights than any other minority group in the world, but until now absolutely nothing has been settled. The VMDK claims the same rights as those being demanded by Serbia for the Croatian Serbs. The VMDK has put forward a proposal based on the Carrington plan for Hungarian cultural and territorial autonomy in North Vojvodina.

- In August 1992, all the Hungarian mayors of North Vojvodina received letters from the Serbian government ordering them to accommodate Bosnian Serbs within their local communities. What this decree amounted to was a subtle form of ethnic engineering, because ultimately the ethnic balance in the region was going to be radically altered. The decree also included details on how many Serbs should be placed in each respective borough. The quotas lie between 20 and 50% in proportion to the original number of Hungarian inhabitants living within the respective communities. The Hungarian language newspaper *Magyar Szó* of 2nd September 1992 reported the following details:

town or city	number of Serbian colonists	number of inhabitants	number of Hungarians
Topolya (Backa Topola)	2,389	16,681	11,261
Kishegyes (Mali Idjos)	1,745	5,800	5,373
Magyaroscsernye (Nova Crnja)	2,305	2,348	2,022
Ada (Ada)	2,905	12,071	10,057
Csóka (Coka)	2,315	5,234	3,229
Kanizsa (Kanjiza)	2,419	11,551	10,257
Kikinda	2,852	43,043	5,957
Zenta (Senta)	2,800	18,863	18,053
Kula,	2,774	19,310	3,379
Becső,	2,870	26,635	13,597
Szenttamás (Srbobran)	2,485	12,738	4,444
Temerin (Temerin)	1,976	16,922	9,513
Verbász (Titov Vrbas)	3,434	25,838	2,418

- The ethnic cleansing of Vojvodina began in July 1992. Blacklists were made of people who were wanted by the Serbs. At the beginning of July 1992 Hungarian and Croatian inhabitants of the village of Herkóca (Hrtkovci) in South Vojvodina were rounded up and executed or else driven out of the region.[140] Their houses were occupied by Serbs. The whole campaign was organized by the leader of the Serbian Reform Movement, the extreme nationalist, Vojislav Seselj. The name of the village has been changed to Srbslavci 'Serbian Slavia'.[141]

Slovakia: ethnic cleansing with the aid of administrative means

According to the 1991 census, 567,290 Slovak citizens, 10.8% of the total population, claimed to be of Hungarian nationality. At the same time, 608,221 people, approximately 11.5% of the population, claimed that Hungarian was their mother tongue. The total population of Slovakia is 5,274,335, 85.6% of which are ethnic Slovaks. The remaining non-Slovak population amounts to 190,000 persons, 80,000 of which are gypsies, 53,000 Czech and 30,000 Ruthenian and Ukrainian. As these are all official statistics their accuracy has to be queried. Hungarian sources give much higher numbers and put the estimated number of Hungarians living in Slovakia at around 700,000.

The area of Slovakia inhabited by Hungarians forms a continuous line along the whole length of the Hungarian-Slovak border in the south of the country (see map). More than 92% of the Hungarians in Slovakia live in this region where they create a population majority of 61.7%. In 523 of the boroughs in the area where Hungarians are in the majority the percentage of Hungarians is above the 10% level. More than 59% of the Hungarians live in villages where there are less than 5,000 inhabitants. The five towns with more than 10,000 Hungarians are: Komárom (Komárno), Pozsony (Bratislava), Dunaszerdahely (Dunajská Streda), Ersekújvár (Nové Zámsky) and Kassa (Košice). The administrative borders of the districts were established without taking into account the ethnic divisions. As a result, a large number of Hungarians now live in administrative districts that lie outside the areas where Hungarians are in the majority.

On 1st January 1993, Czechoslovakia split up and independent Slovakia came into being. The Hungarian community in Slovakia was basically opposed to breaking up the federal state, because the Hungarians had sometimes been able to rely on support from Prague. Now that Slovak nationalism is being intensified the Hungarians living there have little hope of receiving protection from Slovakia itself. Since communism fell, the Hungarian national community has four different political parties: Coexistence (Hun. *Együttélés*), The Hungarian Christian Democratic Movement (Hun. *Magyar Kereszténydemokrata Mozgalom,* MKDM), the Hungarian People's Party (Hun. *Magyar Néppárt,* MNP) and the Hungarian Citizens' Party (Hun. *Magyar Polgári Párt,* MPP). All four of these parties have expressed their concern about the oppression of the Hungarian community in Slovakia in a memorandum addressed to the Council of Europe. Below is a summary of the main points raised in this memorandum of 4th February 1993.

The legitimacy of Slovakia
The division of Czechoslovakia is a fact, but the local Hungarian community contends that this separation is not legitimate for the following reasons: (1) The division of the Federal Republic was not based on a referendum. Instead of abiding by popular sovereignty the right to self-determination was established through party politics. (2) Proposals to hold a referendum on the splitting up of the Czechoslovakian Ferderation were rejected on the grounds of a federal constitutional law carried on 28th November 1992 with a majority of only two votes (law no. 1992/542). (3) On 19th January 1993, the national council of the Slovak Republic rejected a motion to give Slovak representatives in the federal parliament a place in the council. Article 4 of the above-mentioned law, no. 1992/542 was thereby violated increasing doubts about the legitimacy of the splitting up of the Federal Republic and the establishing of two new states in its place. (4) The Slovak national council had taken unilateral steps towards dividing up the federal state, when it adopted the Slovak constitution on 1st September 1992. The Hungarian political par-

HUNGARIANS IN SLOVAKIA

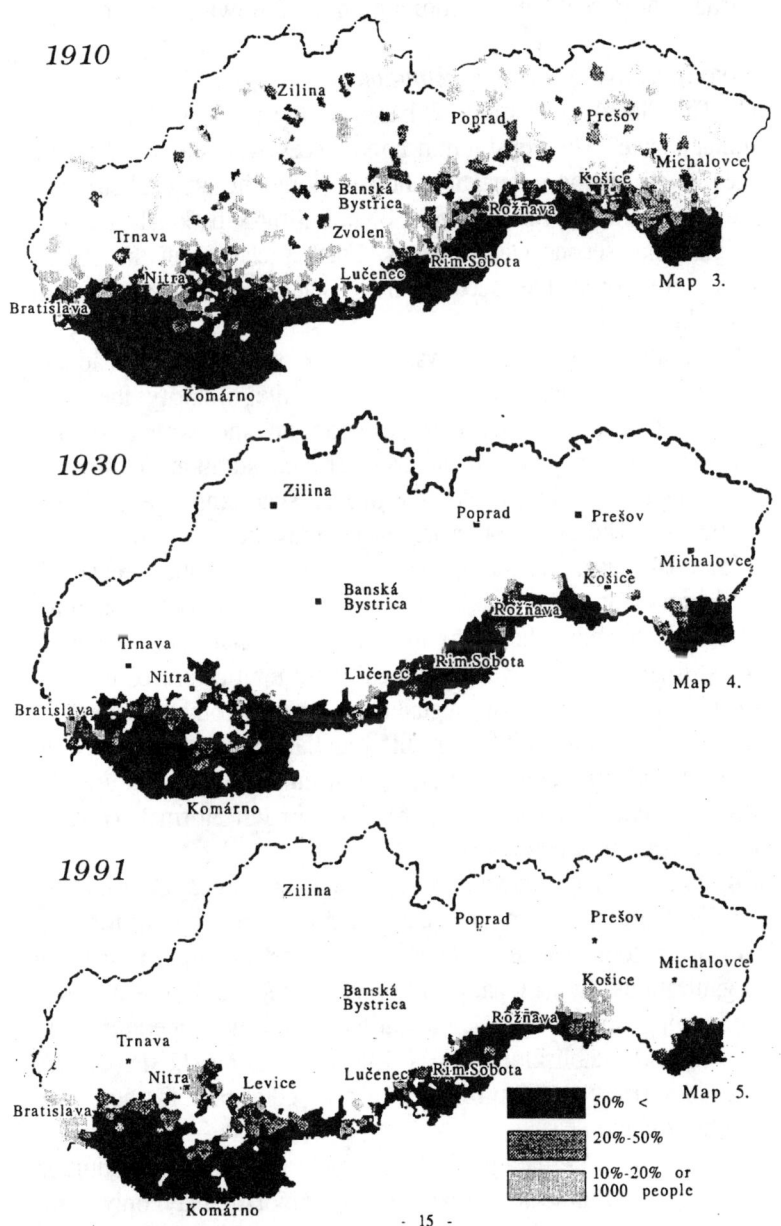

1910

Map 3.

1930

Map 4.

1991

50% <
20%-50%
10%-20% or 1000 people

Map 5.

ties, Coexistence and MKDM, represented in the Slovak parliament rejected the constitution on the following grounds.

Objections to the Slovak constitution
(1) The Slovak constitution is based on the concept of a national unitary state. The constitution commences with the words: 'We the Slovak nation', thus, instantly evoking the atmosphere of a nation state and turning citizens of non-Slovak national or ethnic origins into second class citizens. Further clauses in the constitution reinforce the second class status of non-Slovaks in Slovakia.
(2) As the constitution is vague about the rights of national communities which are numerically in the minority the legal status of these communities depends on the whims of the parliamentary majority of the day. The constitution determines, for instance, that in Slovakia the official state language is Slovak (article 6). The use of other languages must be laid down in new additional laws. At the same time, the constitution makes it obligatory for state and local administrative bodies to publish information about their activities in the official state language. This, therefore, means that national communities are completely unable to use their own languages in official communication. It is, therefore, impossible for different languages to be used in official matters, civil servants are legally obliged to use the official state language, i.e. Slovak, in all formal contacts (paragraph 26, section 5).
(3) The Slovak constitution does not guarantee a right to education in one's own language, nor does it give a right for non-Slovak schools to be established. The setting up of 'cultural organizations' by national communities is tolerated. The concepts underlying such organizations differ from those pertaining to educational establishments as is detailed in article 42. People are not authorized to organize and receive education in their own mother tongue.
(4) According to paragraph 1 of article 34 of the constitution national communities that are in the minority may only form 'nationality associations'. The general right to establish political

parties as outlined in paragraph 2 of article 22 is, therefore, considerably restricted.

(5) The facilities relating to the rights of 'minorities and ethnic groups' are restrictive. Only national communities that form a minority are cited in paragraph 3 of article 34 as possible disintegratory factors. These communities are, furthermore, not allowed to limit the rights of the national majority group in any way. A legal precedent is, thus, created for the future meaning that national communities that are numerically in the minority can be discriminated against.

(6) Though the constitution recognizes the autonomy of small authorities it does not accept the setting up of bigger legal self-governing territorial units.

(7) The constitution does not guarantee that judicial powers remain separate from executive powers (article 145) and that the different types of ownership may enjoy similar rights and status (paragraph 2 of article 20).

(8) The constitution also includes many escape clauses for changing decisions that have been arrived at in a democratic way. The president has the power to rescind a law that has been accepted by parliament. The parliament has the right to reject the results of a referendum.

The objections listed under points (3), (4) and (7) indicate that Slovakia is clearly not intending to abide by the conditions laid down by the Covenant of the Council of Europe pertaining to the protection of human rights and basic liberties.

The violation of rights
Various measures taken by governing bodies and the government would indicate that legal protection has decreased and the intention to discriminate against non-Slovaks has gathered momentum.

(1) Hungarian place names and information boards are angrily removed and replaced with Slovak boards and signposts. The authorities also refuse to enter Hungarian Christian names in their registers of births. In doing so the Slovak authorities refer to the discriminatory language act of 25th October 1990, adopted by the

Slovak parliament in which Slovak is hailed as the country's only official language.
(2) Slovak authorities sabotage the registration of Hungarian names of newborn babies and of persons born in other territorial areas. In doing so they violate a generally accepted principle, laid down in paragraph 1 of article 19 of the Slovak constitution, to the effect that proper names are infrangible.
(3) According to statistics gained from the 1991 census 15.7% of the inhabitants of Slovakia have a mother language that is not Slovak. The state budget for cultural and educational affairs is allocated in such a way that it discriminates against national communities. In 1993, the sum set aside for cultural activities amounted to 2.6 milliard crowns. Only 5% of this, 130 milliard crowns, was spent on the cultural institutions of the country's minorities. It is difficult to assess how much money was budgeted for non-Slovak schools. Statistics from 1991 clearly show that they were in any case discriminated against. In that particular year only 5.4% of the 1.8 thousand million crowns budgeted for education, in other words 800 million crowns was spent on national community schools.
(4) The Slovak government has violated the country's constitution by not appointing judges in accordance with the relevant stipulations.

Retrograde changes in the political and economic system
(1) Privatization has almost come to a standstill on top of which taxing laws limit free enterprise. In the agricultural sector, the negative side-effects of all this hit the Hungarians hardest of all. The government obstructs the development of an independent banking system and stimulates weapon production.
(2) As a result of the governmental changes, many civil servants have lost their jobs. A number of these were ethnic Hungarians who refused to enforce the illegal and discriminatory laws laid down by the government which aim at penalizing minorities.
(3) The state systematically represses people's freedom of speech and the independence of the media. The authorities also endeavoured to restrict academic freedom, when they tried to close down the University of Nagyszombat (Trnava).

Discrimination in conjunction with property rights
(1) The federal parliament in Prague adopted a law on indemnification in 1991 (1991/87). According to this law, subjects and persons who suffered financial or other damages between 25th February 1948 and 1st January 1990 because of the political system may be declared free of damages. This law does, however, not apply to those whose property was confiscated between 1945 and 1948 on ethnic grounds. Under presidential decrees numbers 33 and 108 of 1945 all property owned by ethnic Germans and Hungarians had to be expropriated. Since the presidential decrees of 1945 still apply in Slovakia, and since the new law on indemnification became effective as of 25th February 1948, the ethnic discrimination that began after the Second World War is still perpetuated today. In this way, Hungarians in Slovakia are not eligible for compensation when it comes to matters of expropriation by the state since the Second World War.
(2) On 21st May 1991, the federal parliament passed a law on (agricultural) land (1991/229). This law applies to the same period of time in history as the indemnification law. The only difference lies in the fact that this law reinstates decree no. 26 which was passed by the Slovak national council on 4th November 1948. On this basis the Hungarians who had been given back their Czechoslovak citizenship were able to reclaim, under certain conditions, the land that had been confiscated from them in 1945. The law on (agricultural) land discriminates against Hungarians by setting the compensation limit at fifty hectares in accordance with the decree of 1948. By contrast, other citizens are able to reclaim up to 250 hectares of land. This law was amended on 18th February 1992 (law 1992/93), but the restrictions laid down for Hungarians remain the same.

Not only is new independent Slovakia not interested in respecting the rights of its own Hungarian citizens, but it has also left the international community with no alternative. The obligations agreed to by the Slovak government on 30th June 1993, when it joined the Council of Europe were withdrawn by the Slovak government in December of that same year.[142] According to protocol no. 175 of the Council of Europe, it all had to do with the following obligations.

(1) Slovakia promised that it would tolerate the official spelling of Christian and surnames in languages other than Slovak. Instead of meeting this agreement the Slovak parliament then went on, in law no. 1993/300, to lay down that married Hungarian women should write their names according to Slovak conventions. Hungarian women were, therefore, required to add the suffix - *ova* to their surnames.

(2) Slovakia promised that it would accept bi-lingual place name boards and other public notices. After joining the Council of Europe, the Minister of Transport, Communication and Public Works saw to it that all Hungarian place names and public notice boards were forcibly removed. Furthermore, a bill was proposed which suggested even limiting the use of historical Hungarian place names that had been acceptable to the First Czechoslovakian Republic.

(3) Slovakia promised not to introduce any new administrative or territorial changes that might be detrimental to national communities. In October 1993, the Slovak government appointed seven commissioners and made them responsible for the task of restructuring the country's administrative and territorial divisions. According to the plan of the government, the compact community of Hungarians in southern Slovakia will be broken down into smaller units. The idea is to make the numbers of Hungarians living in the various districts drop to below the 20% level. It is of importance that the Slovak language law states that national minorities may not use their own language in committee situations if in a given administrative district they fall below the 20% level.

(4) According to the Ministry of Education, pupils have the opportunity to follow something known as 'alternative education', which is only available in Hungarian language schools. What this means is that in a Hungarian language school - where lessons are also given in the official language - pupils may have all their lessons in Slovak instead of in Hungarian if the parents so wish. This actually happened in a school in Dunaszerdahely (Danujská Streda) where nine parents of children in a class of 25 asked if the

school could switch to Slovak. Despite the protests of the other sixteen children's parents Slovak became the official teaching language. A petition signed by 46,000 parents has not been able to stop the government from setting aside 100 million crowns for this so-called 'alternative education'.
(5) The Slovak government promised that all discriminatory laws dating from the days of the presidential decrees of Benes would be dropped from the legal system, but so far this has not happened.

Subcarpathia: the obstruction of Hungarian autonomy

According to official figures the total number of inhabitants living in Subcarpathia on 1st January 1990 was 1,258,000, 155,711 of which were Hungarian. Together with the 900,000 or so Ruthenians whose forefathers first settled in Subcarpathia during the course of the 13th century, the Hungarians form the majority of the population in this region. There are also small groups of Ukrainians, Russians, Germans, gypsies etc. in the region. Subcarpathia is surrounded by Slovakia, Hungary, Rumania and the Carpathians (see map). According to various church records there are approximately 100,000 Reformed, 60,000 Roman Catholic and 20,000 Greek Catholic Hungarians living in the region. From this it follows that the number of Hungarians is higher than official statistics indicate. An estimated 200,000 Hungarians live in Subcarpathia, 84% of whom live within a 20 kilometre wide distance of the Hungarian border. This stroke contains 28 authorities in the district of Beregszáz (Beregovo) where Hungarians are in the absolute majority. From times immemorial, Hungarians and Ruthenians have got on well with each other. The Ruthenians of Subcarpathia do not look down upon Hungarian as an inferior language. Since the fall of communism the Hungarian flag flies freely in Subcarpathia and on the streets one can read public notice boards written in Hungarian. For both the Ruthenians and the Hungarians Ukrainian nationalism is now the big threat hanging above their heads.

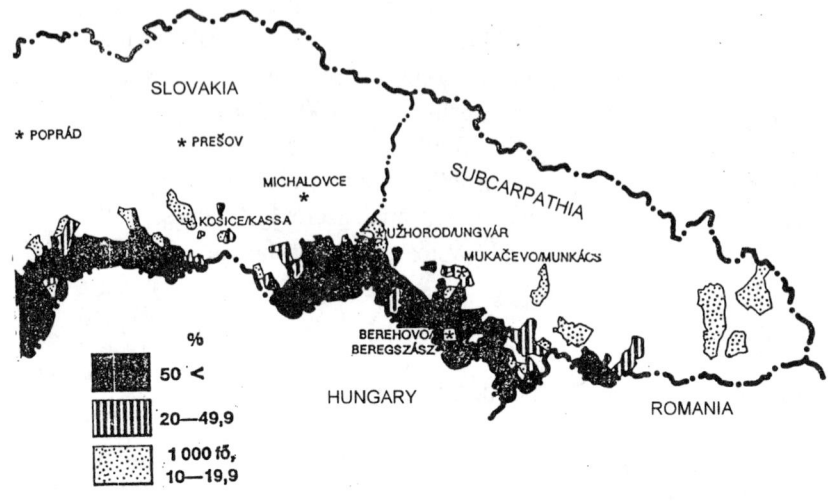

Distribution of Hungarians in Subcarpathia

During the referendum of 1st December 1991, 92.6% of the electorate voted in favour of Ukrainian independence which had been declared on 24th August of that same year. A high percentage of the voters (86%) supported the motion that Subcarpathia should be turned into a 'special administrative self-governing entity'. In the Beregszász district, a region with around 70,000 inhabitants, 81.4% of the electorate (43,482 people) voted for the establishment of an autonomous Hungarian district. In its sitting of 6th May 1992, the Subcarpathian council decided to send the self-government bill for Subcarpathia and the proposition for the introduction of an autonomous Hungarian district to the parliament in Kiev. The Ukrainian government still has not made any decisions on these particular questions.

Before the referendum of 1st December 1991 took place, anti-Hungarian pamphlets were distributed in Subcarpathia by Ukrainian nationalists. Here below is a translation of one such text:

"Dear Subcarpathian-Ukrainian Brothers!

Our Subcarpathia is now in great danger. The former political bigwigs want to sell us out to Hungary. The Hungarian Cultural Federation, together with the leaders of the association of Carpathian Ruthenians who sympathize with the Hungarians, want to force us to become 'autonomous'. They want our area to be separated from the Ukraine.

An extensive propaganda campaign backed by Hungarian funds is currently underway, the point of which is to get Subcarpathians to vote for 'autonomy' on 1st December 1991.

My Brothers! Have you then forgotten the 900 years of Hungarian slavery?

Have you forgotten how they murdered and tortured our people in the spring of 1939?! How they called us 'stinking Ruthenians'?! In all those 900 years our forefathers have not let us become Magyarized. They brought our language, culture and traditions into the twentieth century. And what do we do...?
We must keep our head cool. Let us vote as one man against autonomy. Let us prove to the whole world that we are a self-conscious people and that at the end of the twentieth century it is too late to sell us out.

We declare that Subcarpathia has always belonged to the Ukrainian state. No one can separate us. The unrest and call for autonomy will lead to international animosity and bloodshed. Certain Hungarians say that before very long Ukrainians will be hanged. We will not tolerate this. Remember the terrible years we have been through. The Hungarians are capable of killing us.

We shall make our point clear to the Hungarian extremists and the Ruthenian Hungarophiles. If they do not want to live in the Ukraine then there is another alternative. Let them go to Hungary. That is what we strongly recommend. You are strongly advised not to allow any kind of autonomy to be forced upon us. The Ukrainians will accept no 'autonomy' in Subcarpathia!

You traitors will be cursed by your own people because of your betrayal in these important historic times!... Come to your senses! Just be normal otherwise you will come to a sticky end! Long live the independent and indivisible Ukrainian state. The glorious Ukraine!
Subcarpathian-Ukrainian patriots"

It did not stop at anti-Hungarian propaganda in the form of distributing pamphlets. In January 1992, Hungarian statues were badly defaced. On 7th January, the day when Orthodox Christians celebrate Christmas, the bust of Lajos Kossuth was destroyed in Técső (Tyachev) and in Beregszász (Beregovo) the statue of Sándor Petőfi. Árpád Dalmay, chairman of the Beregszász section of the Hungarian Cultural Federation in Subcarpathia (Hun. *Kárpátaljai Magyar Kultúrális Szövetség*, KMKSZ) in the Beregszász district analyzed the statue defacement as follows.[143] The *Zakarpatszka Pravda* of 18th January 1992 and the *Subcarpathian Youth* of 25th January both published strange reports about the destruction of the Kossuth bust in Técső and the Petőfi statue in Beregszász. Both newspapers gleaned their information from the press bureau of the Subcarpathian Home Affairs Department. In the case of the Técső vandalism, it was reported that one of the criminals was an ethnic Hungarian. The ethnic identity of the other three offenders was not given. In conjunction with the Beregszász crime five different facts were published: (1) the criminal had been identified, (2) it was an inhabitant of Beregszász, (3) it was a gypsy, (4) administrative steps were being taken to prosecute the suspect, (5) the statue had been put back. According to Dalmay, only the first point was correct. The offender was an ethnic Ukrainian by the name of Volodimir Dankavics, an inhabitant of Alsóremete, an electrician employed by the national security service in the Beregszász district. No administrative steps have been taken, but rather a judicial procedure. He has initially been sentenced to two and a half years in prison, but his advocate has appealed. The statue, that has now lost both arms, has not been put back in its place. It is being kept in the KMKSZ's regional district warehouse.

Dalmay wonders if the Home Affairs Department in Subcarpathia and the editorial sections of these two newspapers really are as ignorant of the true facts as they pretend to be. Either they have spread disinformation trying to mislead people or, they have tried to create an anti-gypsy atmosphere.

Transylvania: the anatomy of a pogrom

According to official statistics derived from the Rumanian census of 1992 there are 1.62 million Hungarians living in Rumania or, 7.1% of the population is Hungarian. Church records, however, put this figure at above the two million mark. According to the same census, there are 1,144,820 Roman Catholics, 801,577 people who are Reformed, 76,333 who belong to the Unitarian Church and 449,393 Evangelicals in Rumania. In view of the fact that almost all the members of these denominations are Hungarian, (the Rumanians tend to be Orthodox or Greek Catholic) we can safely conclude that there must indeed be more than two million Hungarians. If we take into account Rumanian demographic developments then an estimate of between 2.1 and 2.5 million Hungarians would be realistic. Of this number 33-35% live in Szeklerland, the so-called Szekler-Hungarians, and along the Hungarian-Rumanian border; 10-12% live in Central Transylvania and 18-20%, like the Csango-Hungarians in enclaves on the other side of the Carpathians in Moldavia. The map below gives an indication of how the Hungarians are dispersed throughout Transylvania.

In a memorandum of 23rd August 1993, the political organization for Hungarians in Rumania, the Democratic Union of Hungarians in Rumania (Hun. *Romániai Magyar Demokrata Szövetség,* RMDSZ), characterized the situation as follows:

(1) Political pluralism goes hand in hand with inequality. When governmental support is lacking even political parties and

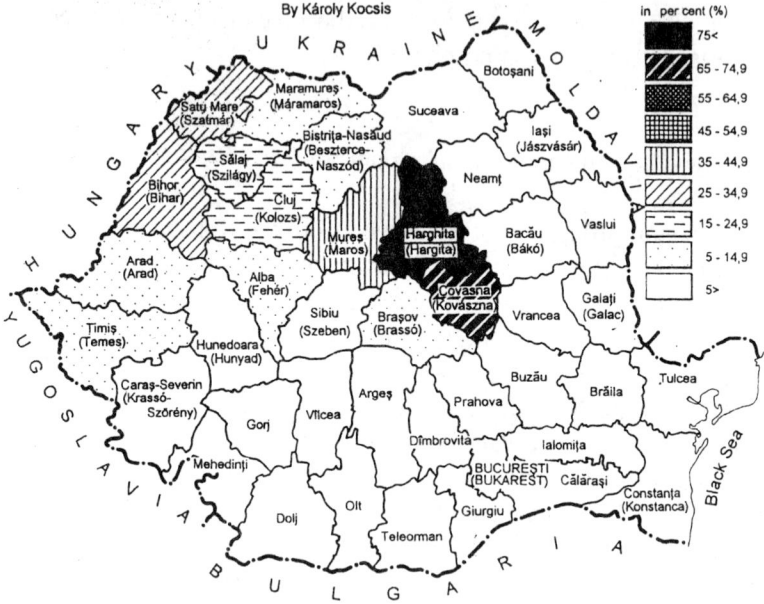

RATIO OF THE VALIDATED VOTES GIVEN FOR THE HUNGARIAN PARTY (UDMR / RMDSZ) ON THE CONGRESS ELECTIONS IN RUMANIA ON 27.09.1992

By Károly Kocsis

associations representing specific interests in parliament are made subordinate to the parties that are in power.

(2) Extreme nationalism has become the salient legitimating factor in Rumanian politics. The authorities sometimes tolerate and encourage extreme nationalistic parties. These extreme nationalistic, semi-fascistic parties like *Vatra Romaneasca* 'Rumanian Hearth', *Romania Mare* 'Greater Rumania' and *PUNR* 'the Party for National Rumanian Unity' constitute a great threat to Rumanian development.

(3) Since 1920, as a consequence of the rule of the Rumanian majority population no representatives of national communities have been employed in higher managerial positions such as in the public service sector, the judicial system and in the state controlled sector of the economy.

(4) The audio-visual council controls the electronic media, represents the will of the political majority. Two of its members

are nominated by the head of state, three by the government and six by parliament. In this way, the television is completely dominated by the country's ruling political power. This situation and the rapid fall in the standard of living have resulted in a rejection of higher values and norms. This makes it virtually impossible to eliminate the communist legacy and change the mentality of the disoriented masses.

(5) An example of discrimination in the judicial system was the fact that in relation to the uprising of 1989 and the ensuing anti-Hungarian pogrom in Marosvásárhely (Tîrgu Mures) in March 1990, only members of the Hungarian gypsy community were condemned.

(6) The constitutional principle of decentralization does not work in practice. Because there are no laws which are specifically applicable to local governing bodies such bodies have to depend completely on the arbitrary decisions of the central authority in Bucharest.

(7) The guarantee to the right to own private property which is a fundamental constitutional principle (see article 41) is a subject for further legislation.

(8) The 1991 law on the redistribution of land is discriminatory, because it does not take into account property belonging to national communities that was confiscated from them under the communist regime after the Second World War.

(9) The sporadic legislation pertaining to economic activity serves only to increase the existing inequality. With the help of statistics it is possible to show that members of national communities who live outside the densely populated minority areas are the ones who are hardest hit by unemployment.

(10) A number of articles in the Rumanian constitution indicate in no uncertain terms that people belonging to national communities: the Hungarians, Germans and gypsies are not wanted in Rumania. Article 1 of the constitution declares that Rumania is a national unitary state. Article 4 states that the Rumanian nation is the only constitutional entity and article 13 declares that the Rumanian language is the only official language of the state. Amendments to these articles are prohibited by the constitution.

(11) The fundamental right of national minorities to retain and develop their identity is not guaranteed under the Rumanian constitution (see article 6). Even the rights accepted by the constitution are made ineffective under present law or non applicable as there is no effective legislation in that domain.
(12) The Rumanian language is the only language that may be used during court cases. Interpreters may only be called in if the accused does not possess a good enough knowledge of the official language. The authorities only offer compensation for translators who help out in criminal court cases. It is compulsory to speak Rumanian during meetings held by any administrative organizations even if all the representatives present speak the language of the national community, like for instance in Szeklerland. Civilians may submit verbal or written petitions to local authorities in their mother tongue, but written petitions must always be accompanied by a Rumanian translation validated by a notary public. All this amounts to considerable restrictions on the use of the mother tongue.
(13) Since communism ended, the infrastructure of Rumania's educational system has hardly changed. Trips abroad, even for professional courses are restricted by ministerial order. Refresher courses for non-Rumanian staff are not available in their mother tongue. The Hungarian national community does not have higher education institutions. The Hungarian Bolyai University was closed down de facto in 1959, but still exists de jure and has not been handed back to the Hungarians.
(14) Religious communities which do not fit in with the official denomination of the state, that of the Rumanian Orthodox Church, have been discriminated against insofar that the property confiscated from them under communism has not been returned.
(15) The authorities support institutionalized contacts between Rumanian minorities living in other countries and the Rumanian mother nation. Similar support is not, however, given to minorities of other nationalities living within Rumania.

The administrative measures taken to oppress the Hungarian community in Transylvania is not what constitutes the biggest danger. The atrocities and pogroms to which Hungarians, gypsies and other minorities have been exposed since communism fell in Rumania has been something much worse. In March 1990, shortly after the fall of Ceausescu in December 1989 Transylvania once again formed a backdrop to the organized attempted mass murder of Hungarians. On 19th and 20th March, there was an anti-Hungarian pogrom in the city of Marosvásárhely (Tîrgu Mures). It is important to note that the attacks upon the Hungarians were well-prepared and organized by the local authorities and fully supported by central government in Bucharest. The official version of the story which claimed that it had to do with clashes between 'extremists' from both camps, therefore, has to be rejected.

After the fall of Ceausescu, second rank communists in Rumania rose up and seized power. These communists set up the *National Salvation Front* and Ion Iliescu was to be their strong man. The new elite had a legitimacy problem, because they were clearly connected to and derived from the old communist elite. Would the Rumanian people who fervently believed in winning the revolution accept their new leaders? By organizing a pogrom in Marosvásárhely, the new Rumanian leaders could resolve two of their most acute problems. The Rumanian government used the anti-Hungarian rallies to mobilize the Rumanian population and win its support. These new politicians wanted to prove that they were strong enough to make the Hungarians buckle under. Beyond this the anti-Hungarian pogrom warned the Hungarians who had set up the RMDSZ in December 1989 to minimize their political objectives. The Rumanian government would not tolerate any Hungarian initiatives. It was Ion Iliescu himself who initiated the attack on the Hungarians. On 26th January 1990, the newspaper *Adevarul* published extracts from his speech that had been broadcast on television the previous day: "During the past few days we have received word from several provinces in Transylvania of events that give cause for concern surrounding the matter of separatist tendencies. This has given rise to tension and conflict between Rumanian state citizens and persons of the Hungarian nationality." In this quotation, the notion of **separatism** is crucial.

On 13th January 1990, the RMDSZ held its first meeting in Marosvásárhely. One of the party's resolutions related to restoring the Hungarian education system in Transylvania, which the Hungarians had been deprived of in the communist era. It was agreed that the Hungarian Bolyai University should be reopened in Kolozsvár and the Farkas Bolyai grammar school be taken over, that the publication of text books should be independently organized and that Hungarian history should be taught. The Hungarian teaching question, that is the demanding of cultural rights, fell under the 'separatist' tendencies referred to by Iliescu. The statement made by Iliescu was probably also partly a reaction to statements made by the French president Mitterand who was in Budapest on 18th and 19th January at the occasion of an official state visit to Hungary. While in the Hungarian capital, Mitterand recalled how during the course of two world wars the country had lost two-thirds of its territory. At any rate, by using the word 'separatism' Iliescu wanted to stir up anti-Hungarian sentiment amongst the Rumanian population. The insinuation was that the reintroduction of Hungarian into schools would prove to be a first step in the direction of wanting to separate from Rumania.

Hungarian claims for more cultural rights, for education in their own native language and for their own educational establishments to be reopened was strongly supported in the January period by students and school children in a number of cities throughout Transylvania. For instance, on 28th January 1990 members of the Hungarian students' union from the Medical and Pharmaceutical Faculty and the Drama Academy in Marosvásárhely compiled an open letter expressing their demand for Hungarian language teaching to be reintroduced. The students pointed out that "according to the foundation statutes of the Medical and Pharmaceutical Faculty of 1945 all lectures should be given in Hungarian. Nevertheless, in 1962 a department was added and all the teaching was done in Rumanian. Since then, we Hungarian students are required to follow more and more of our lectures in Rumanian. When it comes to laboratory studies, everything is in Rumanian." In this letter, the students urge that Hungarian language teaching be reintroduced, that they are given the right to sit examinations in Hungarian and that equal numbers of Hungarians and Rumanians are elected to serve on education boards. Finally, the Hungarian students requested that more Hungarians should be admitted to these higher education institutions. In 1989, a mere sixteen Hungarian students were admitted.

All these activities, the petitions, open letters etc. calling for the right to receive education in the Hungarian mother tongue came to a head when on the 10th of February peaceful protesting took place throughout Transylvania. Around 100,000 people armed with books and candles took part in the demonstration. The silent march in Marosvásárhely was led by the well-known Transylvanian-Hungarian writer András Sütő, who had long been an advocate of harmonious coexistence between Hungarians and Rumanians.

From the moment that Iliescu gave the 'go-ahead' for anti-Hungarian campaigning, negative feeling was rife in the Rumanian media and political circles. Dr. Octavian Stanasila, underminister of Education, actually announced in the Rumanian language newspaper *Cuvîntul Liber* of 15th February 1990, which is circulated in Tîgru Mures and serves as a platform for the ultra-right organization Vatra Romaneasca, that an anti-Hungarian pogrom was about to take place. In the interview, Stanasila expressed his concern about the donations of books from Hungary: "In Rumania many text books have arrived from Hungary. Truck loads full of entire collections. This makes us very uneasy. Take for instance *The History of Transylvania*, thousands, no, tens of thousands of copies are being distributed.[144] The Rumanian people should not accept this! If something occurs that is anti-Rumanian and a threat to the state we must take action! There are laws! We have prisons! We are not joking!" Stanasila further explained his thoughts on the matter and announced the start of the anti-Hungarian pogrom: "It has nothing to do with me, but rather with Vatra Romaneasca that will never forgive something like this as I can tell from their reactions. We do not want to see those ethnic Rumanians living in the mountains near Tîrgu Mures coming down from the mountains and storming Cluj or Tîrgu Mures." In this quotation, the allusion to the ethnic Rumanians living near Tîrgu Mures is clearly very deliberate. In quashing the Hungarian revolutionary movement in 1849 these people, led by Avram Iancu, had slaughtered many Transylvanian Hungarians. Stanasila was, therefore, implying that the Rumanians might once again descend upon the Hungarians from the mountains and that Vatra Romaneasca would be the driving force behind the attack. An analysis of the events of 19th and 20th March proves that the underminister was certainly familiar with the scenario of the anti-Hungarian pogrom.

The organization *Vatra Romaneasca*, established on 1st February 1990 in Tîrgu Mures, functioned as a kind of battering-ram. Vatra soon proved itself to be an unequivocally ultra-nationalist organization subscribed to by local public servants from the Rumanian army, police force, the judiciary and the health service. On 6th February, the *Cuvîntul Liber* published the Vatra Romaneasca's programme. The organization declared that its objective was to defend the rights of Rumanian people living in Transylvania. Vatra also wanted to combat nationalism, chauvinism and separatism. In its programme, the organization announced that Hungarian autonomy would be rejected, since that would restrict the rights of the country's Rumanian majority and that Rumanian was to remain the only official language in Rumania.

Vatra Romaneasca's first big rally took place on 25th February 1990 in the southern Transylvanian city of Gyulafehérvár (Alba Julia). It was no coincidence that they chose this city. For a long time, Gyulafehérvár had been the Hungarian administrative centre in Transylvania. National Transylvanian Hungarian princes, like Gábor Bethlen, lie buried in the city's cathedral. This was one of the reasons why, on 1st December 1918, the Rumanians chose this city to proclaim Transylvania's union with Rumania. The man who became the target of the aggression when the hysterical masses gathered together on 4th March 1990 was the Hungarian László Tőkés, he was the 'spark that lit powder keg' of the Rumanian uprising. On video images one can clearly see how the crowd, goaded on from a balcony in Gyulafehérvár's central square, chanted abuse directed at the minister: "traitor!", "kill Tőkés!" Tőkés had stirred up the wrath of the Rumanians when, during a visit to America he had spoken out for the rights of Hungarians in Rumania. For Tőkés achieving true democracy in Rumanian society and equal rights for the Hungarians are inextricably intertwined.

The secret agenda of Vatra Romaneasca surfaced during the month of February.[145] In a 21 point manifesto dated 20th February 1990 in Tîrgu Mures Vatra revealed its ideology and the strategy to realize all its aims. It is a typical sample of a Rumanian version of fascism. Vatra wants to establish a homogeneous Greater Rumanian state by means of ethnic cleansing amongst non-Rumanians in which members of Vatra and Ceausescu's security service, the Securitate, would play a leading role (point 10). The organization's ultimate aim was to establish an ethnically pure Great Rumanian State (point 15): "Our organization can be promoted all over the world and made popular by means of propaganda campaigns. The hostile feelings towards Hungarians, gypsies and Germans, which are deeply rooted in Rumanian people's hearts must be carefully cultivated so that each and every Rumanian understands our objective: Greater Rumania where there is no room for foreign elements and where these will not be tolerated. The moment has come when we will solve, by any means, for ever, irreversibly and with certainty the problems of the minorities. "In the view of Vatra Romaneasca, Transylvania belongs solely to the Rumanians (point 16): "Transylvania has always belonged to us, it is still ours and it will always be ours! Unfortunately, the holy Rumanian territory is still trampled under foot by Asiatic Huns [i.e. the Hungarians, LM], gypsies and other riffraff. We must unite and drive them out of our country. Out with the Huns, those wanderers who have never really belonged here and with the gypsies who are only a disgrace to our country! We want our country to be pure and great! We want to get back all the areas that have been stolen from us! It's now or never! Do not be afraid to fight nor to spill the unclean blood of foreigners! Those hairy apes have no place in our precious homeland. Now is the time to rid ourselves of them and of all in whose veins no Rumanian blood flows. We have already driven out many of the Germans, but there are enough other people we could well do without. Let us do our utmost to get rid of them too. Ceausescu does not have enough time left to get rid of them, but our nation must not give up the fight! We do not want our country to be like Switzerland! We do not need Europe! We are Rumanians. Do not let yourselves be misled by pro Europe slogans for these slogans will lead to the destruction of our country. We are a sensible people! The common European house means nothing other than the destruction of our national unity and Rumania's territorial integrity. Unity! Unity! Unity! We all need Vatra Romaneasca and nothing else. The Rumanian language must be the only dominant language! We no longer want to hear gibberish we only want to hear Rumanian words! We hereby call up all Rumanians who are interested in the good of their country to join in our actions which at present are exclusively concentrated on Tîrgu Mures, but we trust that with the help of the Rumanian people these actions will spread to cover the whole area of Greater Rumania in 1918."

The Vatra manifesto also explains why the pogrom in Tîrgu Mures is going to take place. Point 17 states: "In view of the population composition of Tîrgu Mures where 50% of the population is Rumanian and 50% Hungarian our organization will continue its activities in this city until Rumanian public opinion is sufficiently permeated with patriotism and until everyone is of the opinion that the demands of the Hungarians must be rejected. In connection with the composition of the population we believe that Tîrgu Mures is the most suitable place to put our ideas into practice." Marosvásárhely is an important city, because it is the gateway to and an important centre of Szeklerland, the area in which, since olden times the Hungarians in Transylvania have been in the majority. If Marosvásárhely is conquered by the Rumanians this would mean that Szekler-Hungarians would be isolated from all the other Hungarians in North Transylvania and, thus, also that the Hungarian corridor leading to the Hungarian border would be severed. Therefore, the

Rumanians invest so much energy in altering the city's ethnic balance.

In August 1993, the RMDSZ published a secret document of the provincial council of the former Rumanian Communist Party in the Mures province. The document which dated from 1st November 1985 and was entitled *Memo relating to the nationality structure of the population of Tîrgu Mures* contained the following details on the ethnic balance in the city. According to the 1977 census, the 130,000 persons living in the city could be divided as follows:

46,558 Rumanians	35.8%
81,151 Hungarians	62.4%
2,342 other nationalities	1.8%

According to the same document, Tîrgu Mures had 154,904 inhabitants on 1st January 1985 made up of the following groups:

66,420 Rumanians	42.9%
85,176 Hungarians	55.9%
2,342 other nationalities	1.2%

The memo states that if, indeed, the number of Rumanians living in Tîrgu Mures is to rise above the 50% mark within the next two years it will be necessary to offer 7,600 people of Rumanian nationality employment in socialist enterprises. Presuming that there are on average roughly three people to a family this amounts to some 22,800 people. This quotum had to be reached within five years so that the Rumanians would make up 58-60% of the total population in the city.

What may be deduced from these statistics is that within a short period of time ten thousand Rumanians were pumped into the city. These masses of people who were pushed into grey, socialist-style concrete jungles became easy prey for those wishing to indoctrinate and manipulate. A mural in a Rumanian Orthodox Church situated on the central square in Tîrgu Mures provides us with evidence that the Orthodox Church, Rumania's established church, was party to the arousing of an anti-Hungarian psychosis long before Hungarians in Marosvásárhely demanded to be given back their Farkas Bolyai high school (see photo).

The mural that was painted in the second half of the eighties shows a Rumanian saint being tortured. The men to the right who look angry and are making aggressive gestures are clothed as Hungarian aristocrats and so symbolize the Hungarians. The people weeping for the saint are dressed in Rumanian national costume and so represent the Rumanians. The message is obvious. For centuries the Hungarians have oppressed the Rumanians and their religion. Rumanians beware of the Hungarians! It is, indeed, curious to find such a mural in a church that was painted at a time when the country's official ideology, communism, was one of equality. It is, therefore, not surprising that the representative for the Orthodox Bishopric of Alba Julia, Stefan Urdea, was a spokesman at Vatra's mass gathering of 4th March in Alba Julia and that he openly professed his solidarity with Vatra and its objectives.[146] Strategically and ideologically Marosvásárhely was, from the Rumanian perspective, the most ideal setting for an anti-Hungarian pogrom.

The objective of the pogrom is revealed in point 18 of the Vatra manifesto. "The main aim of our organization is to find different ways and means to terrorize our adversaries. We shall begin by removing the most capable political and intellectual leaders from office or neutralizing their influence. This is the most important and most urgent task ahead of us. We must then make it perfectly clear to all non-Rumanians that there is no place for them in Rumania and that in the future neither their physical nor their psychological integrity may be safe. If these methods work, then our holy Rumanian country will surely be purified of these blots on its reputation, because these alien elements will leave the country. As far as those who remain behind are concerned, we shall find drastic ways of dealing with them at a later date."

The pogrom began on 16th March 1990 in the Tudor quarter of Tîrgu Mures. A drunken mob of some 200 Rumanians descended on pharmacy number 28 protesting at the fact that the chemist had a board in his window with a Hungarian text on it, namely the word *gyógyszertár,* which is Hungarian for pharmacy. The drunken mob removed the board and then proceeded to ransack the whole pharmacy. A trabant that was driven into the crowd injured a number of people. The chemist László Győrffi declared that there was nothing illegal about his notice board, because he had gone through the correct channels to obtain permission for placing the Hungarian language board. The next day, on the basis of a news report issued by the Rumanian press office Rompress, Rumanian papers reported that the notice in the pharmacist's window had read "Rumanians will not be served" and that the trabant in question had been driven by an ethnic Hungarian.

Tension continued to mount in the city and on 19th March the anti-Hungarian pogrom began. Below is an extract from the eye-witness account of J.H. Geerts of the Eastern European Contact foundation, a Dutchman who happened to be in the city on Monday 19th March:

"In the company of Tibor Kusztos, a Hungarian minister from Covasna, we drove from Covasna to Cluj-Napoca. We passed through the towns Toplita, Reghin, Tîrgu Mures and Turda. Our first stop was in the village of Brincovesti where we had an appointment with the local minister József Székely. About ten kilometres before reaching Brincovesti we caught up with an open-backed truck with 100 to 150 men in it who were all armed with sticks, steel bars and the Rumanian flag. They were shouting various slogans in chorus! In Brincovesti I had the chance to take a couple of photographs. They continued towards Reghin.

Later in the afternoon we had another appointment, in the village of Miercurea not far from Tîrgu Mures. We reached the outskirts of the city at about 4.30, approaching from Brasov/Sighisoara (E15). We headed for the city centre driving along the B-dul 1 decembrie 1918 and turned right at the first set of traffic lights. One of the buildings in this street was a Reformed Church. Already we could sense the tension. The street was dotted with small groups of people engaged in animated conversation. Windows were closed and entrances had been barricaded. While I was parking my car, several people dashed towards me gesticulating wildly. Clearly they wanted to warn me of impending danger. They advised me to park my car elsewhere, out of sight, which was what I did.

We went to find Kálman Csiligyi, the minister we had come to visit. Because of the tension, he was hardly able to talk with us. Even on the vicarage grounds and in the vicarage, the necessary precautions had been taken. Windows had been closed, curtains drawn and here, too, the main gate had been barricaded. There were several persons in the fore court. A woman and her child sought cover in the forecourt. From where I was behind the wall

I could see several people on the other side huddled together at the back of the garden. We and several others just waited to see what would happen. After less than half an hour a gang of men came past by armed with sticks, bars, stones and flags. I estimate that around 1,000 demonstrators passed down the street yelling in Rumanian: "Kill the Hungarians", "Tőkés must be hanged", "We want blood, Hungarian blood", "Out with the Hungarians".

It took 10 to 15 minutes for all the demonstrators to pass by. They were on their way to a Hungarian radio station that was on the air. I could see fear in the faces of Hungarians who had been hiding behind their houses and sheds. Here and there, I noticed people peering out from behind drawn curtains. They were not simply upset they were also angry!

Even though the atmosphere was tense and there were threats of violence, we were able to talk with someone and share our feelings, not with the minister, though, he was speechless. After a brief exchange we left. I consciously wanted to go to the city centre that was closed to vehicular traffic. After making a detour, we managed to reach Hotel Continental. On the way, we were stopped by two Rumanians who threatened us and made obscene gestures. They made it clear that we should go away from the place otherwise we would be killed. They were quite unscrupulous and emphasized what they said with throat cutting gestures.

As I mentioned, we managed to reach the Hotel Continental in the city centre. I parked my car on the grounds of the hotel and we continued on foot towards the centre of the city. We saw only Rumanians on the streets and heard only Rumanian being spoken. As we walked diagonally across the square behind the hotel and got nearer to the centre, we noticed that several windows had been broken and that several statues had been daubed with red paint. At the end of the street, roughly opposite the Hotel Grand, several lorries were forming a roadblock. A few thousand demonstrators were assembled here. I was threatened by people several times more and just as I was about to take a photograph the situation seemed to become very dangerous. That was when I decided to return to the hotel.

The coffee bar in the hotel was closed and it seemed as if the restaurant was also closed. Several Hungarians had sought cover in the coffee/drinks bar and were in a state of great anxiety. It was calm in front of the hotel. A few tourists from Norway were busy unloading their baggage from a car, obviously they had just arrived in the city. At the instigation of my fellow traveller we decided to quickly make our way out of the city. We did not take the direct route, through Turda, but went back the way we had come. Once again, we passed a police station. Several policeman were standing on guard in front of the building with firearms at the ready. About two hundred metres further up a policeman was directing the traffic, there we turned left. At the end of the street to the left, a military truck was parked. A few armed soldiers were in the truck. When we arrived there, some six cars were in front of us and ostensibly intended to turn right. We drew up behind them, but suddenly panic broke out. All the cars seemed to want to reverse quickly at the same time which was of course impossible. We soon realized what was going on. A huge group of demonstrators was running towards us waving wildly with their sticks and iron bars. Some people were running in front of them in an attempt to flee. As we were at the back of the queue of cars it was at first relatively easy for us to make our get away. We reversed and turned at a T-junction then drove down a side road which at first sight seemed to be free. At the end of the road, however, about 250 metres further, the road took a left turn and was blockaded.

At this point, I witnessed the following events. A group of extremely fanatical demonstrators was in hot pursuit of a small group of people. A corpulent man (short and fat, dressed in an orange T-shirt and dark trousers) was literally running for his life. He was kicked and beaten. While running he was hit with a wooden stick and a metal bar. There was blood pouring from his head. Apart from this one man, there were also others who were being chased, kicked and beaten as well. As I watched and slowly drove away, I hit a stationary vehicle parked on the left-hand side of the road. A few people who were walking in front of me asked for a lift, they were young Hungarians. There were also some other people who asked for a lift, but they could not get into the car. I then opened the back doors of the car to let in several other pedestrians. Two women, a man and several children jumped into the car. One of the women turned out to be pregnant. They were all in a state of panic and had fear written across their faces. I then tried to get away from this awful place as fast as I could but with little success at first, because the road was totally blocked. Finally, we managed to escape and I dropped the Hungarians in my car at the above-mentioned police station. One unpleasant detail was that throughout the rallying all the policemen and soldiers on duty just stood by and watched things happen. The military vehicle we had seen did move at one point when the demonstrators ran into the particular street, obviously there had been some change in the route. During the lynchings, a number of people must have been badly wounded. At first sight, it seemed as if many had been seriously wounded. I also saw several men (at least two) jump over high walls/fences in their blind panic. One man got caught as he tried to negotiate a high fence, as far as I could make out he was already badly wounded. As this happened at a street corner, I could not tell whether or not the demonstrators actually caught up with this man.

As we again passed through the city centre, at least past the Hotel Continental again, we were set upon several times by enraged Rumanians. Many a time fists were raised at us in a very threatening way and many a Rumanian assured us that we were in imminent danger of losing our lives. We kept driving and managed to get out of the city without further incidents."

Geerts reported, as indeed did a number of other eye-witnesses in their accounts of the anti-Hungarian pogrom in Marosvásárhely, that huge numbers of Rumanian aggressors had been brought in from surrounding villages such as Hodac, Deda Bistra and Ibanesti to launch this massive attack on the Hungarians.[147] Indeed, these villages lie in the Görgény (Gurghiu) valley between the mountains to the north of Tîrgu Mures (Marosvásárhely), exactly as Stanasila the underminister had foretold. The fact that the Rumanian demonstrators were ferried into the city in municipal buses and state factory lorries and that the police and army stood by showing the attackers the way in the city seem to indicate that it was a planned and co-ordinated campaign.

On the afternoon of 19th March, the Rumanian assailants assembled at the RMDSZ's headquarters in the city centre. At that moment the provincial council of the RMDSZ just happened to be holding a meeting on the matter of Hungarian education in the province of Maros. Sixty to seventy RMDSZ members were present at that particular meeting, one of whom was András Sütő. The Rumanian crowd, that had swelled to several thousand during the course of the afternoon, stormed the building. The Hungarians barricaded themselves in at the top of the premises. After repeated pleas neither the police nor the army proved willing to release the Hungarians. From 4.00 in the afternoon until 8.00 in the evening, the Hungarians were left to fend for themselves. The Rumanians rampaged through the building destroying everything in their path including the Hungarian library.

By eight in the evening, the Rumanians obviously had decided that the Hungarians had waited in fear long enough. At that point, colonel Ion Judea, retired army officer and chairman of the National Salvation Front and the provincial council in the province of Mures, appeared on the scene accompanied by twenty soldiers.[148] The colonel made it clear to the Hungarians who were still hiding in the attic that they must leave the building, because he could not guarantee that the Rumanian demonstrators would not set it on fire. The members of the RMDSZ fell into Judea's trap. Colonel Judea promised András Sütő, the man with whom he negotiated about the Hungarian's escape from the besieged building, that he would personally guarantee their safe passage. He promised that they would be driven out in closed lorries as

March 1990: Colonel Ion Judea inciting people to acts of anti-Hungarian violence.

March 1990: Rumanian soldiers occupy the centre of Tîrgu Mures after the anti-Hungarian pogrom.

they had demanded. However, once the Hungarians were outside the building Judea and his men withdrew leaving them in the hands of the seething crowd. The Hungarians were viciously attacked by the Rumanians and the truck provided by Judea was open and, therefore, offered little protection. Many of the Hungarians were badly wounded, Sütő included. He was blinded in one eye and had bruises and fractures all over his body. On the next day, Tuesday 20th March, there was to be even more bloodshed.[149]

Bloody Tuesday
The day after the attack on the members of the RMDSZ and their headquarters Hungarians started assembling at ten in the morning on the square in front of the city hall. The crowd which had swelled to about 15,000 people by the afternoon demanded that the ethnic Hungarian, Előd Kincses, be reinstalled as vice

chairman of the National Salvation Front and of the provincial council in the province of Mures. Judea had removed Kincses from office at the beginning of March.[150] The crowd also pressed for president Iliescu to come to Matosvásárhely to help restore law and order and to condemn and prohibit the activities of Vatra. Iliescu did not, however, turn up. During the course of the day, bus and truck loads of Vatra Romaneasca supporters trickled into the city from the surrounding villages armed with farm implements, bars, sticks and stones. The Vatra group, which was about 3,000 man strong, was gathered on the left-hand side of the square. The Hungarians and Rumanians were separated from each other by a row of some fifty policemen. While the Hungarians chanted "Bring Kincses back!", Bring Timisoara back!" and shouted for Hungarian education the Rumanians yelled "We'll fight and die for it, but you'll never get Transylvania." To which the Hungarians retorted "Who asked for it?" The Vatra supporters and the police signalled to each other by making a *V* sign, the *V* for Vatra being the Rumanians' sign of recognition.

As the afternoon progressed, it became increasingly obvious, in view of the overheated mood in front of the city hall, that the whole confrontation would degenerate into a bloodbath. Towards the end of the afternoon, the Vatra supporters broke through the police cordon and began attacking the Hungarians. Csaba Bátonyi an employee of *Fekete Doboz,* an independent film company in Budapest, was an eye-witness who recorded the events of *Bloody Tuesday* on video. When the Rumanians started their attack Bátonyi ran up onto the balcony of the city hall, but returned to the square when the Hungarians started to fight back. "As I went down the steps I heard people saying that many people had been badly injured and that one person had even been killed. I saw one old man who was still alive. He groaned as blood poured from his stomach that was cut open. A little further on a woman was trying to resuscitate her dead husband who had obviously been bashed to death with something."[151] Bátonyi also noticed that as soon as the Rumanians launched their attack the Rumanian police disappeared. He also filmed how a number of Rumanians, whilst pulling back from the surging Hungarians, were given cover by a couple of armoured vehicles that had their machine guns trained on the Hungarians. When the Rumanians gathered to mount a fresh attack the armoured vehicles took the lead and the Rumanians followed behind, just as the Russians used to do, commented Bátonyi. At seven o'clock in the evening, seven or so tanks arrived, ostensibly trying to split up the two warring factions. According to Bátonyi, the Rumanians filled their Molotov cocktails with fuel tapped from the tanks. Obviously, the tanks had, therefore, not come to restore order, but rather to support and supply the Rumanians. The fighting continued through the night and gradually the Hungarians gained the upper hand after receiving reinforcements at two in the morning when 150 armed gypsies turned up on the scene. At first, it was quiet because no one was quite sure what the gypsies were going to do. Then to the relief of all the Hungarians present they heard: "Hungarians don't be afraid, the gypsies have arrived!" The gypsies had come to help the Hungarians and they provided them with arms. By the end of the night, the Hungarians had taken over the city hall and imprisoned a number of Rumanians. The Rumanians had occcupied the hotel on the opposite side of the square. The damage was very extensive. Reinforcements from the Rumanian army did not appear until daybreak.

In the anti-Hungarian pogroms in Marovásárhely that took place between 16th and 20th March about 10 people were killed and around 1,000 were wounded, many of them seriously. Regrettably, there were casualties on both sides. The poor Rumanian peasants were misguided by their own authorities. When one reflects on the sequence of events leading up to this, one can only conclude that the Rumanian authorities were fully responsible for everything that happened. The Rumanian government made no effort whatsoever to prohibit the anti-Hungarian activities and hate campaigns mounted by the neo-fascist organization Vatra Romaneasca that had been going on in the months of February and March. The country's official leaders, the Rumanian president Ion Iliescu and the prime minister Petre Roman, encouraged Vatra Romaneasca's activities and even publicly defended the organization after the Marosvásárhely pogroms. In not sending troop reinforcements to Marosvásárhely the central government failed in its duty. The local police force and the army failed to offer the Hungarian population of the city protection when they were under attack. Thus they also failed to fulfil their legal duty. On top of all this, the Rumanian army and police took sides with the Rumanian attackers even fighting alongside of them. The offical Rumanian press agency, Rompress, heightened the tension by circulating disinformation. The Rumanian media also tried to lay the blame for the escalation firmly on the Hungarians and the Hungarian government in Budapest. Bucharest tried to make the Hungarians at least jointly responsible by making a neutralization move. After the events of 16th to 20th March, 'negotiations' chaired by government representatives were begun between Vatra Romaneasca and the RMDSZ. Those with political power in Bucharest, the second rank communists, had achieved their goal. They had succeeded in mobilizing Rumania against the Hungarian 'danger' in order to strengthen their position of power. Vatra had opted to function as a battering-ram and in return for its efforts would be allowed to retain its powerful position in Transylvanian politics. Another important achievement on the part of the Rumanians was that they had managed, temporarily at least, to break the Hungarian movement for education in their own native language. The Hungarians had by now realized that the education issue was a highly contentious one that could very easily lead to pogroms. If they wanted to prevent escalation of large-scale violence, it would clearly be best to drop the struggle for Hungarian language education from the agenda for a while at least. Until now the Hungarians have been given back very few of their schools and the reopening of the Bolyai University seems to be further away than ever.

The cynical anti-Hungarian and anti-gypsy attitude alive in Rumania today remains evident in present court procedures relating to the anti-Hungarian pogrom organized in Marosvásárhely.[152] The judicial aftermath of the pogrom is being felt in the provincial court of justice in the province of Maros

(Mures). What one has to take into account here is the ethnic composition of the whole judicial system in a province inhabited by almost as many Hungarians as Rumanians. Of the 24 public prosecutors only two are ethnic Hungarians. Out of the 27 judges only five are ethnic Hungarians and the police force is 97% Rumanian. No ethnic Hungarians are employed at the public prosecution's municipal and provincial offices. Partiality in matters relating to the anti-Hungarian pogrom is apparent not only from the nature of the cases brought to court - and from the heavy sentences that non-Rumanians have received, while acting in self-defence - but also through the fact that a great portion of the judicial power in the province of Mures lies in the hands of the neo-fascist Vatra Romaneasca. In 1992, five ethnic Hungarians were still detained in connection with events linked to the Marosvásárhely pogrom, their sentences added up to a total of 22 years of imprisonment. The judicial state of affairs two and a half years after the Marosvásárhely events was as follows:
(1) The Rumanian public prosecution has not yet succeeded in tracing and prosecuting the people responsible for organizing and carrying out the anti-Hungarian pogrom. Nobody has been charged for the assault on András Sütő and the other members of the RMDSZ on 19th March 1990. Police officers and army officials responsible for public law and order and safety have noticed no ill effects in any way for having failed to carry out their jobs. In fact, most of them have been promoted since then.
(2) In eleven court cases in which more than 28 people came up before the magistrates, ethnic Hungarians and gypsies who had acted in self-defence were charged in every case for criminal behaviour. On their way to Marosvásárhely, the Rumanian attackers had left a trail of destruction behind them in the Hungarian villages they had passed through. The villagers had tried to defend themselves against this agression. In such cases, the Rumanians became the claimants alleging that they needed to receive compensation for damage done to their vehicles. Those accused were charged with having 'infringed public decorum', of having 'vandalized public and private property' and in some cases of having 'created physical damage'. The sentences varied from six months to four years. In none of the cases did the public

prosecutor mention that the accused had a legitimate right to defend himself. Neither was any mention made of the damage incurred by the buses and trucks in the various villages.

(3) Until now, with two exceptions, only Hungarians and gypsies have been condemned for punishable acts during the Marosvásárhely events. While government representatives in Bucharest refer to the anti-Hungarian pogrom as one of 'inter-ethnic violence', the 'justice spoken' has been exclusively ethnically biased. In his official summing up of the legal proceedings, the chief prosecutor, Dan Petru, recorded that fourteen persons, twelve of whom were gypsies and two of whom were Hungarian are to be taken to court for having committed acts of violence with sticks, axes and other objects. All fourteen Hungarians and gypsies were found guilty. Even a nurse in the Marosvásárhely hospital, the Hungarian Ferenc Szabadi, was sentenced to five years in gaol for having allegedly beaten up victims of the violence who were admitted to the hospital "because they were Rumanian". The charge was having 'caused a public scandal and having disturbed the peace', 'abuse of power in the workplace' and having 'caused bodily harm'. The case brought against Pál Cseresznyés and Ernő Barabás was the most outrageous show trial of all the show trials connected with the Marosvásárhely events and one that clearly demonstrated that the Rumanian authorities were only out to make scapegoats of the ethnic Hungarians. On 7th July 1992, both men were sentenced to 10 years in prison for 'acts of extreme violence with intent to kill' and for 'obvious hooliganism' towards the Rumanian, Mihaila Cofariu, who came from the village of Ibanesti and who was beaten up in Marosvásárhely on 20th March. During the trial, Cofariu stated that he and a hundred other men had been transported by bus to Marosvásárhely at the instigation of the local Orthodox priest, because the situation in the city was apparently serious.

(4) The public prosecutor dropped the cases brought against three ethnic Rumanians who had been identified in connection with the murder of four people on 20th March. In all three cases the men were truck drivers who had driven their vehicles over ethnic

Hungarians. According to the prosecutor, these drivers were "not responsible" for the deaths of these people.

(5) Charges were brought against 47 ethnic Hungarians and gypsies. On 27th October 1992, it was certain that the following persons were still in prison serving sentences:

(a) Pál Cseresznyés (Marosvásárhely/Tîrgu Mures). Ten years. At present detained in Marosvásárhely prison.

(b) Ferenc Szabadi (Marosszentimre/Sintimbru). Five years. Location unknown.

(c) Arpád Füzesi, Albert Füzesi and Arpád Papp (Erdőcsinád/Padureni). Four years. Imprisoned in Marosvásárhely.

(d) Bálint Hanzi and József Galaczi (Maroszentgyrgy/Singeorgiu de Mures). Three years. Location unknown.

(e) Domokos Vajda (Sáromberke/Dumbravioara). Still one year to serve.

PART III

Towards a new Central Europe

"Historically Hungary was always known as a harmonious state, a safe place for people to live in and as a country that cushioned Europe against direct danger from the East. This mission, fulfilled by Hungary for some ten centuries was made possible by its organic unity. Those, at least, were the words of the great French geographer Elisée Reclus who believed that Hungary formed a perfect geographical entity which made it, as such, unique in Europe. The valleys and rivers running from the country's periphery to its heart create a powerful structure that can only be governed from a central point. The separate segments of the country are almost all inter-dependent with the central region forming a strong economic nucleus and the peripheral regions providing the various raw materials vital to the country's economic development."

This quotation comes from the speech made by count Albert Apponyi on 4th June 1920 during the time of the peace negotiations in Trianon.

The Trianon apologia

Even now, in this post 1989 era, the Trianon apologia still continues. The division of Central Europe into small states which expand at the expense of the Hungarian centre is something that is still happening today. Even now that the artificially constructed states, which may thank the power political constellations of both the world wars of this century for their very existence, have started to disintegrate, there is still no indication that the position of the Hungarian national communities is going to improve. Since communism fell in 1989, East Germany has disappeared and the Soviet Union, former Yugoslavia and Czechoslovakia have fallen apart. These developments have completely altered the geopolitical balance within Europe. The present situation is starting to resemble the situation of before the First World War when Germany was also powerful in Central Europe. Not only have states fallen apart and has Germany been reunited but, on the basis of the right to self-determination, a significant number of new states have come into being as well: the Baltic countries, the Ukraine, Slovenia, Croatia, Slovakia, Moldavia etc. In the process, the *pre-Trianon borders* have in certain instances been restored, such as, for example, in the case of the present Czech and Slovak border and in the case of the borders of Croatia and Serbia. The Hungarians, who were really discriminated against, in Trianon are again being threatened with a similar kind of discrimination. With this revival of the right to self-determination the Hungarians have, from a national point of view, become even more fragmented. Before the fall of communism, the Hungarians were dispersed over six states (Hungary, Czechoslovakia, the Soviet Union, Rumania, Yugoslavia and Austria). Now they live in eight states (Hungary, Slovakia, the Ukraine, Rumania, Rump Yugoslavia (Serbia), Croatia, Slovenia and Austria). Though the Trianon configuration might have been reduced by virtue of the fact that relatively powerful states, such as Yugoslavia and Czechoslovakia have disappeared and smaller, less stable states, such as Slovakia and Rump Yugoslavia have arisen in their place the Hungarian question has only become more complex than it was before.

The right to self-determination has not only manifested itself in the formation of new states, but it has also, in a number of cases, been implicated within existing borders. The first and most clear-cut instance is that of the German community in South Tirol which falls under Italian jurisdiction. After the First World War, this area was annexed from Austria by Italy. After forty years of negotiations, Italy and Austria have finally signed a treaty which assigns territorial autonomy to the German community (350,000) of South Tirol. This so-called *internal self-determination* has been applied in Central and Eastern Europe as well, for instance, amongst the Turkish Gagauziś in Moldavia, and amongst the Crimean Tatars of Russia. The Hungarian national communities of Hungary's neighbouring countries have not so far been able to profit in any way from the dynamic right to self-determination developments, even though all these particular Hungarian communities in Central Europe only claim a right to autonomy on the basis of the internal application of the right to self-determination.

In this part of the book, I shall demonstrate how the upholders and the apologists of Trianon, the *Trianonists,* still manage to dominate the scene in Central Europe and how they still approach the 'Hungarian question' in terms of stereotypes and prejudices. The Trianonist's agenda is no different from that of their predecessors from before the First World War. The objective is to keep Central Europe in a stranglehold position so that it is unable to regenerate politically, culturally and economically. This political objective has been put back on the Trianonist's agenda now that Germany has been reunited. German power in Central Europe must be kept strictly under control. It is an aim that can only be fulfilled if the region gets swept up in an endless downward spiral of internal strife that will ultimately lead to chaos and desolation. Consequently, the extreme nationalist forces in the region are allowed to go their own way as long as they basically support the Trianon coalition. This explains also why the Serb leaders Milosevic and Karadzic were given free rein to do as they pleased in the 'Serb' regions of former Yugoslavia.

By contrast, the Hungarians in Central Europe are given absolutely no room for manoeuvre whatsoever despite the dehumanizing activities discussed in the previous part of this book that continue to take place in Hungary's neighbouring states. Hungarian autonomy is seen as a threat to the Trianon configuration which is why the West closes its eyes to the many blatant violations of human rights against Hungarians. It is, of course, easy to simply say that the victims deserve their fate, because they are 'extreme nationalist', 'anti-Semitic', or even 'fascist' and to assert that such barbarians do not deserve the support of the West. In part one of this book, I have shown how deeply-rooted these negative stereotypes and images of the Hungarians are in Western culture. The mammoth task of demythologizing these stereotypes sometimes seems to be a totally impossible task. Suffice it to say, the Hungarains have not yet been successful on this front. In this chapter, I shall expound on a number of methods and strategies which are characteristic when it comes to 'controlling' the Hungarian question: *asymmetries, neutralization* and *the status quo.*

Asymmetries

Since the Treaty of Trianon, Hungarians living outside of Hungary have come to be classified as 'minorities'. This category was applied to all groups of people who were not a part of the constitutional nation state. During the Trianon congress, it was decided that all citizens who did not ethnically belong to a given nation state's majority group would be guaranteed cultural rights in an appendix to the Trianon Treaty. These so-called minority provisions, published in the *Journal Officiel de la République Française* were reluctantly signed by the new states of Yugoslavia, Rumania and Czechoslovakia after the First World War. What these special provisions implied was that there were big groups of citizens who, individually, were able to benefit formally from the civil rights to which everyone in the country was entitled while at the same time they were as a group an alien element within the unitary nation state. This was why the rights laid down in these minority clauses, such as the right to autonomy in the field of mother tongue education, were not honoured. Even the Entente Powers who had thought up these agreements in the first place and who, in signing the documents, had guaranteed to ensure that these regulations were abided by, did nothing to enforce them.

It is correct that in the successor states of Rumania, Czechoslovakia, Yugoslavia and Austria the Hungarians were, numerically speaking, in the minority. In the areas where they live, however, they are in the majority. In part two of this book, I furthermore demonstrated how the Hungarians living in compact concentrations in Hungary's neighbouring countries are, in most cases, in continuity with the Hungarian coreland. The term 'minority' so often used in Western literature to describe Hungarians living in Hungary's neighbouring countries is, therefore, misleading. Apart from anything else, the word 'minority' has all kinds of other connotations in the West.

In the West, the concept 'minority' has an extremely complex and vague meaning. The concept pertains to an endless list of different cases. For instance, there are national, ethnic, cultural, religious, immigrant and language minorities. There are the Basques of France and Spain, who form a national minority, in Alsace-Lorraine there are the Germans, who form a language minority, the Frisians in the Netherlands are recognized in the Dutch constitution as a linguistic minority but not as a national or ethnic minority. The Catholics of Northern Ireland constitute a religious minority. In most Western European countries, gypsies are seen as belonging to a social minority. Finally, there are the immigrants and foreign workers who have been settling in states in the West since the Second World War, who are considered a minority. In the Western context the concept 'minority' is ambiguous and, therefore, it cannot be unequivocally defined.

Since the list of possibilities is endless, it is thus virtually impossible to define exactly what one means by 'minority'. Hence the conclusion that all terms derived from 'minority' such as: minority rights, minority statutes, minority protection have an empty meaning. The term 'minority' furthermore has a rather derogatory undertone in Western society which has to do with the fact that in the West our notion of what constitutes a state is linked to the concept of a homogeneous nation state. Minorities are seen as elements that disrupt internal harmony which in turn leads to tension within a state. Therefore, 'minorities' that fight for cultural freedom and autonomy are, a priori, given a negative image. They are often branded as being 'intolerant' or 'extremist'. Furthermore it is so that existing states refuse to give minorities separate language rights, because conducting administrative systems in two or more languages would be too expensive. 'Minorities' are, therefore, not only seen as a threat to the cohesion of a nation state, but also as creating extra expenses.

Because of its heterogeneity, it is, therefore, difficult to unambiguously define the term 'minority'. Solutions to the problem are, therefore, also difficult. Often factors other than the compliance of the relevant state are responsible for resolving the problems surrounding the rights of minorities in an amenable way. Below are a few examples to illustrate my point. The different national groups of people in Switzerland who together compose the Swiss state: the Germans, French, Italians and Rhaeto-Romans constitute equal status portions of the Swiss nation each with their own territorial and cultural autonomy. This symbiosis is partly made possible by Switzerland's geographical circumstances. The country lies isolated between mountain ranges. It is a symbiosis with a long history, Switzerland provides us with a prime example of tolerance in a country. Last but not least, Switzerland, one of the wealthiest countries in the world, can financially afford to operate with four official languages. The Swedish minority in Finland that constitutes approximately 10% of the population is also in a relatively favourable position as far as rights are concerned. This has to do with the fact that Finland is a large, but thinly populated country. From an economical point of view, the Swedish minority is important to Finland. As the Swedish minority is concentrated in the south of Finland and is separated from the mother country by a stretch of water, there is no danger of separatism occuring. For the German minority living in Denmark (20,000) and the Danes domiciled in Germany (40,000) things have been more or less satisfactorily resolved for two reasons, firstly because relatively low numbers of people are involved - only several tens of thousands - and secondly, because the proportions are roughly comparable. This is, therefore, a well-balanced situation. These minority groups have the function of a bridge between the German and Danish nations and of thereby contributing to good relationships between these two neighbouring states. In most cases, though, the legal positions of 'minorities' are far from well organized.

When applied to the Hungarians living in the Carpathian Basin, the term 'minority' infers an asymmetry which does not correspond to reality. It is incorrect to apply the term 'minority' to the Hungarians of the Carpathian Basin for the following reasons:
- national communities of people living next to their coreland who only find themselves in their present unnatural 'minority position', because of *falsely* taken political decisions can easily return to being in a majority position, if country borders are simply changed. This constitutes a qualitative difference between, for instance, the Slovakian Hungarians and the gypsies and Germans of Hungary. Such groups may, therefore, not be casually lumped together.
- the concept of what constitutes a minority is relative to the territorial area to which it is related. If one takes the Carpathian Basin as a territorial criterium then all the Hungarians living in that area can be seen as belonging to the majority nation. Viewed from this angle the only Hungarians forming an ethnic minority in Eastern Europe are those living in Moldavia in Rumania, the Csango-Hungarians (200,000).
- because of their numbers, the Hungarians living outside of Hungary's present territorial boundaries cannot be rightly termed 'minorities', if one considers that there are European states, for example Luxembourg (250,000) with fewer inhabitants than the number of Hungarians in North Vojvodina (400,000 Hungarians) or newly created states, for instance, Slovenia (two million people), with equal or less people than for instance the number of Hungarians living in Transylvania (over 2.5 million). Therefore, it

is necessary to establish a 'critical number' so that above this number there can no longer be talk of a 'minority'.

If a stop is going to be put to the unmotivated asymmetrical situation, it will be necessary to stop regarding the Hungarians of the Carpathian Basin who live outside of Hungary as a 'minority'. It would be more correct to refer to them as 'Hungarians living outside the country' or 'Hungarian national communities'.

Slovakia became independent on 1st January 1993. In part two, I explained how it was that the disintegration of the Second Czecho-Slovak Republic was not the result of a democratic decision. The Slovak leader Meciar did not think it necessary to call for a referendum. The international community simply accepted the division of the Second Czecho-Slovak Republic as an accomplished fact. When the country was split in two, the Slovaks claimed their right to self-determination. What was interesting about this claim was that it remained exclusive. It should, furthermore, be noted that the area of southern Slovakia which is inhabited by Hungarians has never previously come under Slovak authority. Before the First Slovak Republic was established, this area had in the meantime been returned to Hungary on the grounds of the First Vienna Award of 1938. It is, therefore, not absolutely certain upon what grounds, historical (?), self-determinatory (?) or otherwise the Slovaks claimed that the south of the country was rightfully theirs.

The Slovaks had been free to choose to separate from the rest of the country, but they could not accept that similarly the Hungarians domiciled in the south of Slovakia might conceivably be allowed to decide to which state they wanted to belong. On the basis of the democratic principle: 'what goes for one must go for another' the Hungarians had envisaged the following two options. Either they could establish a new Slovakia together with the Slovaks, obviously on a basis of equality within a democratic federation of Slovakia, or they could choose to break away in much the same way as the Slovaks had separated from the Czechs, namely by exercising their right to self-determination.

The Hungarian community living in Slovakia received nothing whatsoever from the Slovaks. No referendum was held which would have given the Hungarians a possibility to air their views, nor was their constitutional position improved in any way. The preamble to the Slovak constitution made matters quite clear. The Hungarians need not expect to receive equal treatment in the new Slovakia which had sunk to the level of an apartheid state in which huge portions of the population were to be systematically discriminated against. Slovak nationalism had barred its teeth and claimed for itself rights that it withheld from others. The Slovaks had only intensified their asymmetrical relationship with the Hungarians.

The preamble to the Slovak constitution states that independent Slovakia is the historic successor state of the Great Moravian Empire.[153] According to aberrant Slovak irredentist theory, the borders of this ancient empire bisect present day Hungary. Historians affiliated to the Slovak Academy of Sciences maintain that the southern boundary of the Great Moravian Empire follows lake Balaton in Hungary.[154] From a purely scientific point of view, it is absolutely uncertain whether or not this Great Moravian Empire ever even existed, but the people of Bratislava firmly believe in this myth. Hence the Slovaks were not afraid to lay indirect claims on Hungarian territory in the preamble to their constitution. Furthermore, the Slovak emblem and flag contain the double cross, a symbol which originates from the coat of arms of the Hungarian royal Árpád dynasty and which is as such a centuries-old component of Hungary's national emblem. The question is, on what grounds does the new and independent state of Slovakia claim the right to use the heraldic symbolism of another existing state? Finally in October of 1992, Slovakia blatantly ignored all international agreements in going ahead with unilaterally changing the course of the Danube. The river was redirected to flow into the Danube canal, needed to drive the newly built hydro-electric power station at Gabčikovo/Nagymaros.[155] Béla Lipták, an American-Hungarian expert and environmental activist stated in a lecture given in the Netherlands in March 1995 that, when the course of the Danube was changed the Slovak army had stood by, presumably to stave off possible Hungarian intervention, but this precaution had been quite unnecessary as the Hungarians had not intervened. Slovakia, therefore, made a unilateral decision to alter the Hungarian-Slovak border, a border which, according to a peace agreement of 1947, is created by the river Danube. As a consequence, there are places where Hungary no longer has free access to the river Danube. Different independent studies have demonstrated that the long-term effects of the hydro-electric power station will be catastrophic for the wider regional environment. Rare kinds of flora and fauna will eventually disappear. The power station, which is very uneconomical also consumes huge quantities of water with the result that vast tracts of southern Slovakia, notably the Csallóköz (Žitny Ostrov) region, inhabited by many Hungarians whose livelihood depends on agriculture, will dry out. It is highly probable that the Hungarians living there will be forced to give up agriculture and look elsewhere for an income. In the western part of Hungary, the ground water level is dropping which means that domestic water supplies are under threat as is the whole agricultural industry. Another problem is that the actual hydro-electric power station construction is showing major structural faults which means that the nearby cities of Komárom (Komarno), Győr and Budapest might one day be in very great danger. If any major technical problems occur at the power station all these cities would be flooded or, worse still, because of the fall of the water of twenty metres, these cities would be in danger of extinction.

The Danube dam project is just one in a chain of ploys to ecologically surround Hungary and to destroy the area of southern Slovakia which is predominantly inhabited by Hungarians. In February 1995, the Slovak government announced that its nuclear power plant in Mohi (Mochovce) on the Danube, just over the border with Hungary, was nearing completion. Meciar alleged that if European financiers had not been forthcoming then the Russians would be prepared to lend money for the completion of the nuclear power plant.[156] When the Slovak government announced that they were planning to finish building this nuclear power station, a storm of protest broke out amongst Austrian,

Slovak and Hungarian environmental activists. The power plant, which is situated about 140 kilometres to the north of the Hungarian capital of Budapest, is similar to the one that was built in Chernobyl and is fitted with French safety valves. Apart from the perpetual risk of a meltdown occuring the atomic reactor at Mochovce will be dumping its radioactive waste in the Danube which means that Budapest's drinking water supplies will automatically become contaminated. If this happens, the genetic make-up of the inhabitants of that city could be altered within a generation.

Until now Hungary has not reacted to any of these violations of international agreements and threats of danger generated by the Slovaks which is incomprehensible if one bears in mind that Hungary's legitimate rights are clearly being seriously violated. One would expect some kind of reaction from the Hungarian side if only to prevent a freshwater shortage occurring in the country. According to experts in the field, there will be a worldwide shortage of freshwater before very long.[157] It is, therefore, in every state's best interests to protect its clean drinking water and freshwater supplies. All states react differently in similar cases. If, for instance, the course of the river Jordan, which forms the border between Jordan and Israel, were to be unilaterally changed the Israelis would regard this as an open declaration of war.

The nature of the conflict continuing between Slovakia and Hungary is not dissimilar to the one going on between independent Macedonia, a federal republic of former Yugoslavia and Greece. In three different ways Greece felt threatened by the new Macedonian Republic and so refused to give the state international recognition. In the first place, the Macedonian constitution contains a clause which declares that Macedonia will do everything in its power to free fellow Macedonians living in neighbouring countries. In the second place, the Macedonian emblem and flag represent a star like the one found in the grave of the father of Alexander the Great in Verghina which is situated in what is now Greece. In the third place, the fact that Macedonians refer to Thessaloniki as a Macedonian city indicates, so the

András Ágoston

Greeks believe, that they would like to annex it. Such a move would give the Macedonians free access to the Aegean Sea. Though Greece admits that the Macedonian state is militarily very weak at present, it still feels threatened by this young state and reserves for itself the right to give priority to its own national interests and pursue a preventative policy. What it amounts to is that Greece is not prepared to recognize Macedonia's independence only, perhaps, if it changes its name. Greece has finally endorsed its politics by introducing an economic boycott against the young state that contravenes all international agreements.

During one of the Yugoslavia conference meetings supervised by the European Union held on 4th November 1991 in The Hague, the so-called Carrington paper, which aimed at building up new relations in former Yugoslavia, was accepted. Article 2/paragraph 3 stated that people who belong to a national or ethnic minority have cultural rights and may not be discriminated against because of their national or ethnic affiliations. The Carrington paper went a step further. In paragraph 5 of the same article, special status in the form of autonomy is given to people of national or ethnic groups who form the majority in the area in which they live. This autonomy makes allowances for the following matters: (a) the right to have national symbols, (b) a separate education system that respects the values and needs of the group in question, (c) legislative, judicial and administrative bodies including regional police forces and (d) facilities in the field of international monitoring.

On the basis of this proposition, the EU offered the Serbs in Croatian Krajina cultural and territorial autonomy. The Serbian leader Milosevic agreed to this proposal on 9th January 1992 in Brussels.[158] The EU's Council of Foreign Affairs Ministers made the recognition of Croatia dependent on the granting of autonomy for the Serbian Croats living in Krajina. In this way, Croatia was compelled to recognize the cultural and territorial autonomy of some 400,000 Serbs living on Croatian territory in its constitution. The Serbian community was treated quite differently from the Albanians living in Kosovo or the Hungarian community in North Vojvodina. The chairman of the Democratic Community of Vojvodina Hungarians (VMDK), András Agoston, made clear in letters addressed to the conference chairman, Lord Carrington, exactly what kind of pressure and threats the Hungarians and Croats of Vojvodina were having to live under. In a letter addressed to the Serbian leader, Slobodan Milosevic, Agoston pointed out that Serbia was not prepared to keep to its side of the bargain where the Carrington proposals were concerned: "The draft text of the constitution does not correspond with reality which is that both Serbia and the federal Republic of Yugoslavia are multinational communities. In fact, the proposal represents an anti-democratic procedure in the legislation process. Furthermore, the constitution drafted out does not account for the collective rights of ethnic groups. They are not recognized as legal or political subjects. These omissions constitute a direct contravention of the agreements laid down in The Hague on which the peace negotiations are to be based. No mention is made of autonomy as a possible solution to the nationality problem in the whole new European system."[159]

The Serbian leader Milosevic was obviously successful in persuading the international community to accept that the Krajina Serbs living in Croatia should be given autonomy, while simultaneously not being required to make any concessions for the national communities within his 'Greater' Serbia. The asymmetry of the Trianon configuration towards Hungarians (400,000 of them) and towards the Albanians of Kosovo (2 million) is thus perpetuated. Obviously, this completely goes against any kind of democratic and just approach to this kind of problem. It also gave an indication of what the power balance situation was like within the EU. At the time of the peace talks the Serb Milosevic was given a free hand. The Dutch prime minister, Ruud Lubbers, confirmed this in an interview with *Vrij Nederland* on 23rd January 1993 when he said: "From the beginning the Germans have felt very involved in matters concerning Slovenia and Croatia. They had a limited idea of Yugoslavia. Because of its past Germany was unable to take part in any kind of military intervention. France has found itself in rather a dilemma; the French knew the Serbs well. For a long time, France found it best not to offend Milosevic. From that point of view it was pure good fortune that our ambassador in Paris, Henry Wijnaendts, was able to play such a prominent role as mediator, because the Netherlands just happened to be chairing the EU at the time. He agreed with the French and was keen to keep on negotiating with Milosevic."

In their struggle for more rights and greater autonomy, the Hungarians living in Transylvania have so far received no support from international public opinion and politics. Whenever the Hungarians raise the Transylvania question, the propaganda mongers immediately get going. The Hungarians are then branded as 'nationalists', 'anti-Semitics', 'revisionists', etc. It is a different matter, though, when the Rumanians start to raise the question of reuniting Rumania with the former, but now independent Soviet Republic of Moldavia (Moldova) and bring forward territorial claims for a particular section of the Ukraine. During the secret Ribbentrop-Molotov Pact of 1939 a section of Rumania covering approximately 50,500 square kilometres with 3.7 million inhabitants was handed over to the Soviet Union. In 1940, Stalin turned the greater part of this area of the Soviet Union into the Soviet Republic of Moldavia and the remainder was added to the Ukraine (South Bessarabia and North Bukovina). Together the former Soviet Republic of Moldavia and these parts of the Ukraine formed what was historically known as Bessarabia and what had, until the First World War, belonged to Tsarist Russia. Only after the war, did it become a part of Greater Rumania.

The former Soviet Republic of Moldavia (Moldova) is inhabited by ethnic Rumanians, Russians, Ukrainians and Turkish speaking Gagauzis. On 6th May 1990 when the independent state of Moldavia was still a part of the Soviet Union, the border between Rumanian Moldavia and Soviet Moldavia, formed by the river Prut, was opened for six hours at eight different points. So it was that ethnic Rumanians living on both sides of the border were able to cross over without having to show any identification papers. The day was organized by Moldavian cultural societies in both countries and was named the 'bridge of flowers' day. In the international press much was written about this 'bridge of flowers' day: "On Sunday the millions of flowers that were thrown over the bridge converted the river into a beautiful field of blooms. There were just as many tears as flowers, though, as the deep emotions of a divided people were poured out."[160] The articles written about this occasion when 'the Moldavian people were reunited for one day' were accompanied by a photo of a Rumanian border soldier shown throwing flowers into the river Prut from the bridge, into 'Moldavia's wound' as the caption read. When the border opened "many people took the school books with them that had been banned in the Soviet Republic for a long time. It is only since last year that Soviet Moldavians have been allowed to publish books and newspapers in Latin script."[161] In all these instances nothing other than understanding is shown for the Rumanians who have been separated from each other by an artificial border. That also applied to the declaration made by the 'liberal' opposition in Rumania, the so-called Democratic Convention, that concerned itself with the question of "the Rumanian regions on the other side of the river Prut that were forcibly occupied by the Soviet Union, but which remained an inextricable part of Rumania."[162] It was logical that the Rumanians were delighted to be reunited with their Moldavian brothers for one day and that they took with them school books to give to the Rumanians in Moldavia who had been deprived of such books for so many decades. Why then should Hungarians be called 'extreme nationalists', when they do similar things for their brothers in Transylvania? Why also is there no '-flower bridge' at Komárom (Komarno) where the Danube forms the Hungarian-Slovak border as this is also one of the many 'Berlin walls' of the Carpathian Basin where a city extending over both banks of the river Danube is chiefly inhabited by Hungarians?

The Rumanians have even managed to go a step further without being reproached by the international community. On 29th November 1991, the Rumanian government claimed that "it could not accept that these areas [South Bessarabia and North Bukovina, LM] might be integrated into the Ukraine, an independent state."[163] The Rumanian government tried to mobilize the international political machine in order to give their demands international publicity. The underminister of Foreign Affairs, Adrian Dohotaru, was for instance sent to the Netherlands to further explain the territorial claims: "Bucharest demands South Bessarabia and North Bukovina", regions that until now have belonged to the Ukraine. According to Dohotaru his country would only use "peaceful" means to achieve their goals. "We shall do our utmost to win back those regions through the channels of international justice open to us. Our history-based arguments are very strong. The Stalin-Hitler pact of 1939 that had allocated these areas to Russia was invalid and the world knows that. The pact has never been fully recognized by Rumania which regarded the taking over of these tracts of land within 24 hours as outright theft" and "The new government in the Ukraine has not yet voiced its official view on the matter. Everybody is still too preoccupied with the new-found independence. We respect the Ukraine's independence, but we also want to see that an end is put to historical injustice."[164] The reverberations felt in the West that emanate from such 'revisionistic' utterances on the part of

257

Rumanians are quite different from those of Hungarian politicians who simply seek spiritual 'reunity', like József Antall in 1990 the first democratically elected prime minister who said that "in spirit he felt like a prime minister for all the fifteen million Hungarians everywhere in the world." It was not only the Rumanian politicians that were lobbying for the recovery of South Bessarabia and North Bukovina, but also Rumanian religious leaders. The head of the Rumanian Orthodox Church, the patriarch Teocrist, declared on 19th November 1991 that "the plea of the Rumanian people" in these areas, their "basic human rights" and the "right to be part of their native country" had been ignored.[165] In these cases, no further qualifications. This contrasted sharply with, for example, the label 'extreme nationalist' that was instantly given to the spiritual leader of Transylvania's Hungarians, bishop Tőkés, as soon as he called for autonomy for his people.

Neutralization

Another strategy of the Trianon apologia, alongside of the strategy to perpetuate Hungarian/non-Hungarian asymmetries, is the neutralization of the Hungarian question of which there are many instances. I shall discuss here two particular examples of neutralization. The first relates to the fact that Hungary's neighbouring countries behave as though Hungary has or has had the same minority numbers as they have within their borders. The second example has to do with the fact that in an official respect the legitimate representatives of the Hungarian national communities are equated with extreme right organizations in neighbouring countries.

The issue of the number of Slovaks living in Hungary provides a good example of the first neutralization strategy. The former Slovak minister of Foreign Affairs, Milan Knažko, said the following when once interviewed: "I would be glad if this myth about the repression of our Hungarian minority could be banished. Slovakia is the only country where the Hungarian minority is increasing. After the First World War there were 400,000

Hungarians left behind in Slovakia and in Hungary a similar number of Slovaks. At the moment, there are 560,000 Hungarians living in Slovakia, but Hungary has no more than 9,000 Slovaks. These statistics surely demonstrate what the policy towards minorities is like in the relevant countries."[166] As Slovaks in academic circles share this opinion it would seem that what Knazko said was not just something of the spur of the moment. Ladislav Deák who is affiliated to the Slovak Academy of Sciences wrote the following in his article entitled *Die slowakische Minderheit in Ungarn von 1918 bis zur Gegenwart:* "According to estimates around half a million Slovaks were left in Hungary making them, together with the Germans, the country's biggest national minority."[167] The anti-Hungarian ploy underlying such assertions is obvious. First, the number of Slovaks left behind in Hungary after Trianon is inflated in relation to the number of Hungarians who, after the Great War, suddenly found themselves living in the First Czechoslovakian Republic against their will. The next conclusion to be drawn is that the number of Hungarians has remained more or less stable whereas the number of Slovaks has fallen 'spectacularly'. This can only imply that the policies employed by the Slovaks towards the Hungarians have been extremely humane while Hungarians have forced Slovaks to assimilate. The whole argument does not hold water, because the first assertion is not sound. The Slovaks are unable to produce a single document proving that hundreds of thousands of Slovaks were left behind in Hungary after Trianon. The most likely conclusion surely is that the Hungarians living in Slovakia constitute a resilient and closely-knit community which, after 75 years of state nationalistic oppression, is still intact.

The tactic of neutralization in order to control the Hungarian problem is not only used by Slovak Trianon apologists, but also by international political 'mediators' who readily fall back on this same method. In a letter sent by the High Commissioner for National Minorities of the OSCE, Max van der Stoel, to the Hungarian Minister of Foreign Affairs, Géza Jeszenszky, the High Commissioner made a problem of the Slovak minority living in Hungary.[168] The High Commissioner's experts found out that

Slovak language education had suffered at the hand of the assimilation policies enforced by former Hungarian administrations and that the Slovak cultural and linguistic identity had been significantly watered down in the assimilation process that had taken place after Slovak national consciousness had started to manifest itself more clearly during the course of the 19th century. This would in fact explain why Hungary's Slovak minority has such a poorly developed national identity. The High Commissioner's experts had also managed to unearth a number of representatives of Slovak organizations who had made it quite clear that they wanted to receive guarantees that Slovak culture and, in education, the Slovak language would be preserved.

By appealing to the Hungarian's 'sense of guilt' the High Commissioner argued for implementing a generous Hungarian law for national and ethnic minorities related to Hungary's Slovak minority. Van der Stoel put the following propositions to the Hungarian government: (1) the above-mentioned law would have to be explained better to minority groups, (2) the Hungarian government would have to see to it that the additional clauses needed to make the law on minorities acceptable be quickly passed through parliament, (3) the Hungarian government would have to adopt a generous financial policy, so that the laws for minorities could be successfully brought in and (4) the Hungarian government would have to give special attention to the status of the Slovak language in the Hungarian education system. If necessary, positive action should be taken to promote Slovak as a teaching language for Slovak pupils. It is especially this last point that is rather amazing, the suggestion that the Hungarian government should stimulate the use of Slovak. Surely it is rather so that a minority must apply to its own government for mother tongue education. Van der Stoel's 'recommendations' strongly create the impression that in Slovakia the Hungarian question must be neutralized by increasing the status of the Slovak minority in Hungary, if need be with the support of the Hungarian state. This was painfully illustrated in the reply of the Hungarian Minister of Foreign Affairs, Géza Jeszenszky.[169] In his letter Jeszenszky mentioned that he had studied the history of Hungary's Slovak population in detail during his university career. He, furthermore, added that he knew of no possible legal or financial obstacles standing in the way of using Slovak as a language in which to teach. Professor Jeszenszky explained that Slovak organizations had voluntarily chosen to have a bi-lingual Hungarian/Slovak school. According to Jeszenszky the biggest opposition had come from Slovak parents who preferred to see that their children were taught German, English or French rather than Slovak. For years teachers had been doing their utmost to persuade Slovak parents to let their children be taught in Slovak. Apart from anything else such a move was financially attractive to the school. The government gives more than a 40% subsidy per child for pupils who receive education in minority languages.

Another example of neutralization was the 'Neptun scandal' that was directed by the American *Project on Ethnic Relations* (PER). Three top members of the RMDSZ: György Tokay, László Borbély and György Frunda met a number of times in 1993 with the Rumanian government for secret negotiations. Their meetings took place in the Swiss town of Gerzenzee and in the country residence of the former dictator Ceausescu at the resort of Neptun on the Black Sea. These secret negotiations had been convened by the PER without the RMDSZ presidium knowing about them. Once knowledge of the secret meetings had leaked out the chairman of the RMDSZ, Béla Markó declared that "negotiating on behalf of the RMDSZ might only take place, if permission was received from the chairman. These politicians had not been given such a mandate in Neptun."[170] PER was supported in these activities by the American ambassador in Bucharest, John R. Davis, the man 'known' from the book written by David F. Funderburk, also a former US ambassador in Bucharest (1981-1985).[171] Funderburk whose reports of the shameful acts of the Ceausescu regime were ignored by his own State Department noted that at that time Davis had been director of the Bureau for Eastern European Affairs and that he had been a supporter of the Conducator's regime (p.23). It would now seem that he had supported the secret negotiations for which the Hungarian participants had received no mandate from their own party.

Bishop Tőkés who was the first person to write about the PER scandal argued that these talks did not have the character of private discussions. From the press reports that came out towards the end of July 1993, it was obvious that those who participated in these talks regarded them as official. Traian Chebeleu, the official spokesman for president Iliescu, commented during one press conference that "during the talks solutions had begun to emerge".[172] On 23rd July 1993, one Rumanian newspaper reported that a "Rumanian-Hungarian settlement" had been reached in Neptun. Tőkés wondered what exactly had taken place during those meetings.[173] What Tőkés is certain about is that the three representatives had worked together for a long time with high representatives of the Rumanian government without the RMDSZ having knowledge of this. We, furthermore, know that this illustrious group was allowed to use the country house of the Swiss Ministry of Foreign Affairs in Gerzenzee and what was formerly Ceausescu's country residence in Neptun. The *New York Times* also gave its full support to the Neptun negotiations. The journalist David Binder wrote a positive article about the negotiations in that paper on 21st September 1993. The RMDSZ leadership tried to rectify the article, but the *New York Times* refused to publish any such amendments. Once knowledge of the secret negotiations in Neptun had leaked out John R. Davis, US ambassador in Bucharest, tried to convince representatives of the RMDSZ that it would be better to support PER's moderate line than to go for 'autonomy' and 'unrealistic demands'.

In his above-mentioned article László Tőkés summarized the negative effects of the PER deliberations as follows:

Tőkés first of all blamed the 'Neptun trio' and the PER delegates for being prepared to come to an agreement with the Rumanian authorities. The problem is that the Rumanian leaders do not seriously entertain the possibility of establishing a compromise. The Americans and the Neptun trio had absolutely no idea that in Byzantine culture the aim behind negotiating is often to trick the opposition into accepting agreement points only to later on flout them. Tőkés rejected the pragmatism and political realism of the PER representatives, because the politics of taking little steps will not lead to a compromise, but rather to a naive form of capitulation. According to the bishop, this political approach has been taken only too often during the past decades and it has never led to anything productive. The only way forwards is through adopting a political approach based on internal self-determination for the Hungarian community.

In the second place, Tőkés believes that the secret negotiations have deprived the RMDSZ of the opportunity to put pressure on the Rumanian government to take the Hungarian question seriously. The RMDSZ could have been recognized as a partner, because in the summer of 1993 Rumania was waiting to be admitted to the Council of Europe and was in line for being hailed 'the most favoured trading partner' of the US.

Finally, Tőkés claims that Rumanian foreign politics is based on a method of institutionally and expertly misleading the Western world. For a long time, the Ceausescu regime relied on this well-tested method. In this way, the Rumanians were able to conceal their domestic problems and the way in which they were keeping down the Hungarians until the fall of Ccauscscu. PER supported this politics of disinformation as well. In April 1993, the go-ahead was given to start up a propaganda campaign targeted at the West with the intention of creating a positive image of Rumania so that it would be accepted in the Western organizations. What also fitted into this campaign was the notion of creating an image of Rumania as a state that was prepared to reach compromises with the Hungarian community. From July 1993 onwards, the world was, therefore, bombarded with enthusiastic articles on the 'Neptun agreement' which the Rumanian government claimed to have settled with 'moderate' Hungarian minority representatives. For instance, *AP* and *New York Times* correspondents reported on 20th July 1993 that "Rumanians and the Hungarian minority have agreed on the steps that need to be taken to improve minority rights" and "Official representatives have agreed to the improving of rights for minorities". In Munich, George Stein reported on PER on 21st July 1993 stating: "Ethnic agreement places a small, hardly known group in the spotlights." Not only the American papers and the press agencies were involved in this whole propaganda campaign on the Neptun 'agreement' but also government representatives and the Neptun trio. It was Tokay who beat the lot when he proclaimed: "I shall tell my people that we are making constructive progress and that we have been able to prove that Rumania is no Yugoslavia." As far as Tőkés is concerned, all three Neptun participants also contributed as private persons to losing respect and to destroying the RMDSZ's chances because of legitimizing the success of Rumanian fake politics that is diametrically opposed to Rumanian reality. One could easily fill many pages with such examples.

This fake agreement also boosted courage in international political circles. John R. Davis, US ambassador in Bucharest was very enthusiastic about Rumania when he said: "It is a fantastic country with a great future ahead of it."[174] Asjborn Eide, member of the UN Human Rights Commission noted in his report to this commission by referring to 'positive developments in Rumania'. Most of what he knew was based on the Binder article.[175] Max van der Stoel, High Commissioner for National Minorities declared that he was "satisfied with the progressive nature of the democratic efforts of the Rumanian government". The High Commissioner even said that he expected that "the Rumanian nationality question would be resolved within a year" and that he, therefore, found it "motivated" for Rumania to be accepted as a member of the Council of Europe. The PER collaborators were also satisfied. Livia B. Plaks claimed: "Rumania is one of the countries that is in a position to resolve the problems surrounding minorities."[176]

Finally, bishop Tőkés noticed that while this positive Western image of Rumania was carefully being created by important Western press agencies, newspapers, the PER and by certain politicians of the Hungarian community and the RMDSZ at the same time a negative Hungarian image was built up. Tőkés wonders why the Rumanian government did not negotiate with the legitimate RMDSZ representatives. Why had they never organized a Rumanian-Hungarian round table conference to resolve all the problems? According to him, the answers are simple. Rumanian nationalism is still not prepared to recognize the Hungarian question and, in connection with its 'national unitary state' doctrine it, therefore, pursues, where the Hungarian community is concerned, a politics of homogenization, assimilation and discrimination. With a degree of bitterness Tőkés concludes that the whole PER shake-up has at least achieved that for the first time ever the Rumanian government has acknowledged the Hungarian problem.

This 'success formula' of PER's that was set out by George Stein was based on the doctrine that "ethnic tension is stirred up by militants who invariably do not represent the opinions of the majority", PER, furthermore, "sought out the moderate opposing party representatives and brought them into contact with each other". The implication here is that the Rumanian government representatives and the Neptun trio were viewed as 'moderates' while the legitimate Hungarian delegates who were looked upon as 'radicals' were rejected from the negotiating process. In this way, Hungarian discussion partners were 'selected' by the Rumanian government and by outsiders while all the rest were regarded as 'extremist' and cast on one side. Thus, the RMDSZ was discarded as well as illustrated in many press articles of the time, here below are just a few such quotations from David Binder and John R. Davis. For instance, Binder wrote: "There is also an extremist element on the Hungarian side in the form of the RMDSZ that makes no secret of the fact that it wishes to see Transylvania reunited in the way that it was before the First World War."[177] The ambassador to the US, John R. Davis, told the RMDSZ that they were to support the PER approach and he called up the RMDSZ leaders who "hold on to unrealistic demands" and who make "extreme comments" to "give up their radical points of view". He had "difficulty understanding the demands for autonomy" and warned that "no tension should be created that might lead to a Yugoslavia-like situation." The threats of the Hungarian 'radicals' were also taken seriously by *Le Monde Diplomatique*: "If they do not respect our rights then the radical wing of the Rumanian Hungarians might well resort to taking up arms."[178] According to Tőkés it is not difficult to see where this image of the "bloodthirsty" Hungarians comes from, namely from the Securitate and its successor organization, the SRI. The aim underlying this whole smear campaign was, to keep the West from offering help to the Hungarian community in Rumania, which was portrayed as being "rebellious", "destabilizing" and "poised to shed blood" so that the Hungarians would be seen in an unfavourable light in the eyes of the "civilized", "freedom-loving" world.

The PER affair perfectly illustrates how the tactics of neutralization work. The legitimate Hungarian representatives were labelled 'radicals' and compared to extreme nationalists and fascists. In the case of Transylvania, those were the Hungarian representatives who sought autonomy and on the Rumanian side the extremist parties like PUNR and Romania Mare. In Hungarian circles the political discussion partners selected were people who were prepared to go along and 'play the game'. Such politicians were depicted as 'moderates' and allowed to engage in official talks. In the PER affair they were the Neptun trio and delegates from the Iliescu administration. The overall effect was that the legitimate Hungarian representatives in Rumania were put on one side and official Rumanian politics were upgraded. The bogus negotiations are used to legitimate the anti-democratic and nationalistic regime as 'salonfähig' for the outside world and to sow the seeds of internal discontent among Hungarians. This kind of neutralization is also established by means of deliberate and co-ordinated press campaigns which, consciously or unconsciously, affects international politics. It is clear that the PER actions had the approval of a certain line within the State Department, probably the same faction that had embraced Ceausescu's politics in the eighties. Such neutralization scenarios are easy for other countries with big Hungarian minority communities to reconstruct. The aim of neutralizations is to paralyze the Hungarian struggle for emancipation and to maintain the status quo in Central Europe.

The status quo

On 6th December 1991, Hungary and the Ukraine signed a treaty in the Ukrainian capital of Kiev on good neighbourliness and co-operation. The agreement also contained a 'territorial clause'. In article 2, it was stated that "the parties involved will respect each other's territorial integrity and that they, furthermore, declare not to have any mutual territorial claims now or in the future." In article 17 of the agreement, the text of a previous declaration is incorporated on the rights of national minorities that was signed on 31st May 1991 by both parties entitled: *Declaration on the principles of co-operation between the Hungarian Republic and the Ukrainian Socialist Soviet Republic on the matter of guaranteeing the rights of national minorities*. It is a declaration that recognizes the cultural rights of national minorities.

One can well understand that Hungary strives to good neighbourliness with the Ukraine, because it is a massive country with many inhabitants (55 million) that is equipped with nuclear weapons. Apart from this, when the Soviet Union fell apart the Ukraine became a part of the Trianon configuration. From the point of view of security and defense needs, the Antall administration was right to block the possibility of an anti-Hungarian Serb-Rumanian-Ukrainian-Slovak alliance developing by easing the Ukraine away from this camp. Once the Hungarian-Ukrainian pact had been signed Slovakia, Rumania/Serbia were no longer able to make a geographical 'link up'. The fact of the Hungarian-Ukrainian pact was sound, but the way in which it was executed was not quite right.

For a long time, the text of the pact remained secret. There was no discussion on the procedure that was to be followed either in the Hungarian parliament or within the main governing party of the Hungarian Democratic Forum (*Hun. Magyar Demokrata Fórum*, MDF). Public opinion was kept out of it altogether. In fact, no discussion or agreement really took place in Antall administration circles either. The KMKSZ, the organization representing Hungarian interests in Subcarpathia was also kept out of the picture.[179]

The Hungarian parliament ratified the treaty in the spring of 1993. The clause referred to above only leaked out then. The ratification was pushed through parliament with the help of votes from the opposition parties, the ex-communist MSZP party and the leftist liberal SZDSZ, the liberal left. The Antall government was already governing with a minority at this time and so was unable to push such an issue through parliament on its own strength. The agreement had by now doubtful democratic support and so it amounted in effect to a matter between Antall, the prime minister and Jeszenszky, his minister of Foreign Affairs. These politicians, therefore, made far-reaching decisions behind the backs of the Subcarpathian Hungarians and created precedents which, in the future, would be referred to by the other Trianon configuration countries.

Apart from the curious and, in the international political arena, unusual formulation of the 'territorial clause' establishing that there would be no further territorial claims made in the future, the Hungarian minister of Foreign Affairs neglected something else. The agreement was signed on 6th December 1991 in Kiev after a referendum had been held on 1st December in which the Ukrainians had voted for independence. In the same referendum the Hungarians living in the Subcarpathian district of Beregszász (Beregovo) had overwhelmingly voted in favour of establishing an autonomous Hungarian district (81.4%). The referendum results were published in the local newspaper *Beregi Hírlap* on 5th December which meant that the Hungarian Foreign Affairs minister knew the results before leaving for Kiev. One cannot help wondering, therefore, why Jeszenszky did not defend Hungarian interests and why, with the referendum results in his inside pocket, he did not make a fair deal in Kiev. Hungary recognizes the present borders and the Ukraine in its turn guarantees that it will safeguard Hungarian territorial autonomy in Subcarpathia. Instead of negotiating on this option Jeszenszky left the Subcarpathian Hungarians standing in the cold. The KMKSZ signed a declaration protesting at the fact that the autonomous Hungarian district of Beregszász is not mentioned in the common declaration relating to the guaranteeing of rights for national minorities that was ratified by the Ukrainian parliament on 25th June 1992.[180]

The Hungarian government, led by a prime minister who had once claimed that he felt like the spiritual prime minister of all 15 million Hungarians, not only let down the Hungarians of Subcarpathia, but also all the other Hungarian national communities in the region and gave off a wrong signal to Slovakia, Serbia and Rumania. Antall implied that in exchange for the very minimum, with respect to rights for Hungarian national communities, Hungary would be prepared to recognize the present borders. Instead of establishing a precedent that would break down the Trianon encirclement, while preserving the existing borders the Antall administration created a dangerous anti-Hungarian precedent. The fact that this 'missed' chance was no mere coincidence was clearly evident from the fact that this same man, Jeszenszky, had supported the secret PER negotiations in the summer of 1993 without other government members knowing it and had, together with the Rumanian government, tried to marginalize the legitimate RMDSZ representatives.[181] It was the Antall administration, which gained no international credit for the Hungarian-Ukrainian treaty, that paved the way for what was to be known as the Balladur Pact.

In 1993, the former French prime minister, Balladur, launched the so-called "Pact for security and stability in Europe'. The objective of the Balladur Pact was to set up clear European boundaries to achieve greater stability in exchange for the respect of the collective rights of national minorities. In the first version of the pact of 9th June 1993, the Quai d'Orsay entertained the idea of introducing small border changes, probably just to see how this notion would be accepted. However, *rectification mineures de frontiéres* quickly disappeared from the text. In March 1995, the Balladur Pact was signed by the member states of the OSCE. As a follow-up to this Hungary and Slovakia drew up an agreement on good neighbourliness, the borders and the rights of the Hungarian 'minority' in Slovakia. As no fixed guarantees on the rights of Slovak Hungarians were given, the Balladur Pact could not be seen as anything other than a verification of the Treaty of Trianon. The Balladur Pact does, of course, fit in with the long tradition of French national interest politics.

What has stood in the way of the process of reinforcing Central Europe or what has even sometimes sought to destroy its system with the help of allies in the East has been the particular basic doctrine of French foreign policy that has persisted for centuries. The French kings were always on a good footing with the Turkish sultans and the Russian tsars. The French Republic that preached liberty and which was prepared to secure such liberty abroad, with weapons, if necessary, leaned on Tsarist Russia's 'prison of peoples' and later the imperialist Soviet Union that sought to expand in an imperialist way. The encouragement offered by the present French president, Jacques Chirac, to Russia to quash the Chechenian's current struggle for independence should be viewed as part of this same tradition. The 'peace treaties' that brought down Austria-Hungary fitted in with the policy to encircle Germany. The socialist president Mitterand who was responsible for France's foreign policy spent the fourteen years that he was in power either being overtaken by events or simply making blunders. The French could not bring themselves to admit that the Yalta system had collapsed. After the fall of the wall in Berlin, Mitterand sped to Kiev for talks with Gorbachev. While in Berlin, Mitterand refused to walk under the Brandenburger Gate and he even made an official visit to the German Democratic Republic that was only to exist for a few more days at that stage. Mitterand had supported Gorbachev up until the very last moment. Monsieur le président did not want to witness the fall of the Soviet Union.

During the crisis in former Yugoslavia, it once again became evident that the state model of French politics is based on the Jacobin view of a nation state. From the very start, the French were not prepared to recognize that Yugoslavia was an artificial construct that had from the very beginning served the needs of Greater Serbian imperialism and had been held together with the help of terrorist organizations. For a long time, the French refused to acknowledge the independence of Slovenia and Croatia, they also denied that the 'ethnic cleansing' actions were really going on and French officials continued to make grand speeches about how close and firm Franco-Serbian relations were. French UN soldiers tolerated the fact that while under their protection a Bosnian politician who had been travelling through Serbia in an armoured vehicle was dragged out of the vehicle and murdered before their very eyes. Subsequently, the commandant responsible for the armoured transportation was not in any way held responsible for the incident. The French even proved to be prepared to conceal the identity of Serbs who attacked French and other UN soldiers reporting that it is simply difficult to 'identify' snipers. They could be Serbian or Bosnian. The official policy now pursued by France in former Yugoslavia is to guarantee humanitarian goals, but in doing so France does not lose sight of its main objective, namely to recognize Serbian territorial conquest as an accomplished fact. French endeavours to stall American proposals in favour of lifting the weapon embargo against Bosnia should be seen in this light, as should efforts to immobilize international power political organizations, such as the UN Security Council and the international contact group set up for former Yugoslavia. While impeding the finding of a possible solution to the problems in former Yugoslavia, the French are also preventing the US from rapidly extending NATO towards the East arguing that the Russians will never tolerate this.

Gabriel Robin's book *Un monde sans maître. Ordre ou désordre entre les nations* well illustrates the degree of continuity that exists in French foreign politics.[182] Robin, advisor to the former French presidents Georges Pompidou and Valéry Giscard d'Estaing, was removed from office as head of the French NATO mission in 1986 after having criticized the politics of president François Mitterand in his book *Le diplomate de Mitterand ou le Triomphe des apparences (1985)*. In the first part of his new book Robin analyzes the Yalta system that was based on 'anti-German leverage'. Anti-German leverage dominated all else: strategies, ideologies, institutions etc. In the second part of his book, he discusses the new world order after the Yalta system. Robin finds this order, despite the Gulf War, the disintegration of Yugoslavia and the events in Somalia, Rwanda and Burundi safer than the previous world order. Robin acts as an apologist for the Iraqian leader Sadam Hussein and for the Serbian leader Slobodan Milosevic. The Gaullist, Gabriel Robin, calls out for the same things as the socialists.

One can never pin down the French or the British to admitting to bearing major responsibility for any main developments in the world today. Yet almost invariably the hotbeds of world conflicts are seated in areas where the imperialist great powers were responsible for erecting new frontiers after the First World War. The irreconcilable discrepancies stem from the fact that France and Great Britain refuse to accept responsibility for their criminal politics. The present Balladur Pact works as a kind of panacea for peace, while at the same time masking where the original responsibilities lie. However, in point five of the Pact's declarations the reasoning already becomes shaky: "A stable Europe is a Europe where people are able to democratically exercise their will and where human rights, also for those who belong to national minorities, are respected, where sovereign states co-operate in harmony regardless of where the frontiers lie and where all neighbouring states strive to establish good relations."

The new and sovereign states of Central and Eastern Europe want to become a part of European organizations, because after decades of Soviet Russian dominion and with the present aggressive actions emanating from Russian imperialism, they will only be able to feel relatively safe when sheltering under the wings of Western Europe. When it comes to matters of membership, the EU and NATO both have as a prerequisite that countries wishing to join their organizations must first sort out the mutual problems they might have pertaining to borders and minorities. Among these countries are the countries that have profited from the 'peace' treaties of the First and Second World Wars and countries which have suffered damages. In the framework of the Balladur Pact, which makes provision for greater security, the countries that have suffered damages are to sign agreements with countries that have benefited. Though perhaps a strong term, the only correct word for this is *blackmail politics*. The victims of these unfair peace pacts are required to resign themselves to their unjust fate and once again - this time voluntarily - forgo their right to moral redress. This point may be well illustrated by what Balladur himself once said when he declared in an interview with a correspondent from the French newspaper *Derniéres Nouvelles d'Alsace of* the 31st January 1995 with regard to the negotiations being carried on with the members elect for the EU after the EU restructuring of 1996: "Things will go more smoothly if the border and minority problems relating to the stability pact are settled beforehand." Diplomats, too, have voiced similar opinions on this matter. In reply to a question put by a reporter from the Hungarian newspaper *Magyar Nemzet* as to whether the European security conference in Paris could be successful if agreements on good neighbourliness were not signed before the conference Bertrand Dufourcq, secretary at the Quai d'Orsay said, during a visit to Budapest in February 1995: "We would not like to see such a situation arise because the solution to this matter is in the interests of all of Europa, not just Hungary and its neighbouring states."[183] The US ambassador in Bucharest, Alfred H. Moses, declared during a visit to Budapest at the end of February 1995 that during the meeting organized by the American undersecretary for Foreign Affairs, Richard Holbrooke, in which US ambassadors stationed in Central and Eastern Europe participated, the point of view generally expressed was "that countries contending with heavy ethnic conflicts inside or outside of their frontiers may not join NATO. Hungary must collaborate with Slovakia and Rumania to resolve the position of the Hungarian minorities."[184]

The Balladur Pact was signed on 20th March 1995 in Paris. The text of the pact makes absolutely no mention of obligations. The EU presumes that the recommendations made by the Council of Europe will be abided by and further entrusts its execution to the OSCE which is participated in by both the Americans and the Russians. The OSCE was incapable of resolving the Yugoslavian crisis and the Russians have shown a disregard of human rights in Chechenia. Hungary's Horn administration, composed of ex-communists and leftist liberals, was in a great hurry to have the pact with Slovakia and Rumania signed. When the appointed day arrived, only the Slovak-Hungarian agreement was ready for signing. The copy of the text which was distributed by the Slovak Ministry of Foreign Affairs had an 'accompanying text' that differed from the content of the agreement. The Rumanians did not succeed in drawing up and signing the agreement. The Rumanians found the Council of Europe's 1201 Resolution which guaranteed collective rights for minorities unacceptable because, in the words of Ion Iliescu, the Rumanian president himself: "The Resolution has, on the one hand, no internationally recognized legal status and on the other hand it includes the concept of an ethnic territorial separatist vision."

At the time of the signing of the Balladur Pact, it occurred to nobody to demand that the Czech Republic and Slovakia declare the Benes decrees null and void, decrees in which the Czechoslovakian Germans and Hungarians are accused, en masse, of being war criminals. The decrees that should particularly have been withdrawn were, the cleaning up edict of 19th June 1945 and the resolution of 21st June 1945 on "speeded up distribution of and expropriation of agricultural land belonging to Germans, Hungarians and any other enemies of and traitors to the Czech and Slovak people." The other decrees were equally discriminatory: the Germans were forced to wear white armbands, they received the same food portions as the Nazis had measured out for the Jews, the Germans were not allowed to seek any contact with persons in other countries or to make use of public transport.[185] If the Munich Agreement of 1938, officially signed by British and French heads of state, is to be rescinded then it would be reasonable to expect that the Benes decrees, which smack of the Nuremberg laws, also be declared invalid, because these decrees particularly contradict the human rights' agreements. The Czech and Slovak authorities do not want to withdraw the Benes decrees, because they do not want to have to meet the claims for damages lodged by the victims of these regulations. It would be more correct to detach the nullification order, which is a judicial-moral act, from the damage claims problem.

In conclusion, one can say of the Balladur Pact that it amounts to a fake victory. After all, a degree of moral-political pressure was placed on several states to sign the pact in their *own* interests. On the other hand, however, the moral-political factors that clashed with human rights were not taken into consideration.

Hungarian revival

In this chapter, we shall discuss what the Hungarians and the international community have done to oppose the Trianon configuration and what the consequences of Trianon have been. With Yalta, which was effectively a reaffirmation of Trianon, there was little prospect of being given the chance to raise the Hungarian problem. After the Hungarian uprising of 1956 had been quelled, in which the communist János Kádár had played a prominent part, his regime made clear that the affairs of the Hungarian minorities were matters of internal concern to be resolved within the socialist 'brother'states and that Hungary should no longer make any territorial claims. Until the latter half of the eighties, communist Hungary left the Hungarian minorities to fend for themselves. During the era of communist rule in Central Europe, the Hungarian national communities were hardly given a chance to air any of their grievances. Because of the fact that the communist rulers had a strong totalitarian hold on the people of the various states, which meant that there was virtually no room for manoeuvre whatsoever. In connection with the need to promote communist interests, alibi organizations such as *CSEMADOK*, the society of Hungarian workers in Czechoslovakia, were set up. This organization consisted of the communist cadre that adhered completely to official communist ideology and politics.

Hungarian heroes

Protests launched in the communist period were, therefore, often solitary affairs, sometimes organized within the framework of the official communist body. The first and only Hungarian politician to operate within the communist hierarchy was Károly Király who had climbed within the Rumanian Communist Party (RCP) to the level of Politburo member. Ion Pacepa, former head of the Rumanian intelligence service, the Securitate, who fled to the West explained in his memoirs *Red Horizons* how Király had managed to find his way into the Politburo of the RCP.[186] The cunning Szekler-Hungarian had managed to catch Ceausescu's attention by organizing big bear hunts in which the 'genius', who was mad about going on shooting expeditions in the Carpathians, was allowed to shoot the biggest bear. In 1972, Király wrote a letter to the Rumanian Foreign Affairs minister in which he protested about the way in which Hungarians domiciled in Rumania were discriminated against and afterwards he resigned as member of the Politburo. In the summer and early autumn of 1977, Király repeated his protests. He wrote letters to Politburo members and to the Central Committee in which he outlined his grievances on the oppression of Hungarians living in Rumania and listed a number of recommendations which could lead to improvements in the situation. His proposals were discarded and in October 1977 Király underwent a series of security police interrogations. Because of this, he subsequently decided to publish his letters in the West and in the last week of January 1978 reports of his protest were published in the international press. In reaction to this and also in order to repress the growing unrest among Hungarians in Transylvania, the Rumanian government took certain emergency steps. Rumanian army units were dropped in Marosvásárhely, the place where Király lived, with instructions to find possible copies of his letters. Even though Király's life was under threat and he was forced to distance himself from his letters he steadfastly held on to his convictions. In February 1978, Király was banned to the little city of Karánsebes. Even though he had been ordered to remain silent he still allowed himself to be interviewed by three Western correspondents and reiterated his objections. In October of that same year, Király was allowed to return to Marosvásárhely where he lived in complete isolation. Until the time of the Rumanian uprising in December 1989 Király remained under house arrest.[187]

The Hungarian from Slovakia, the geologist Miklós Duray, operated outside the communist bodies. He was one of the few people to sign Charta '77 in Slovakia. Duray set up the *Committee for the Legal Protection of the Hungarian Minority in*

Miklós Duray

Czechoslovakia and between 1978 and 1988 managed, together with a small group of supporters, to map out the situation for Hungarians living in Slovakia and to regularly organize protests against their oppression. The committee's study reports and various memoranda have been collected and published under the title *The double oppression: documents on the situation of and legal protection of the Czechoslovakian Hungarians.*[188] Apart from containing memorandums the collection also contains reports on and protests about anti-Hungarian acts of violence such as, for instance, the actions of 8th and 9th March 1987 (p.306) directed against four Hungarian cultural institutions in Pozsony (Bratislava). In the end, Duray was sentenced to a year in prison (1984/1985) because of his activities directed at democratizing Czechoslovakia and for standing up for the rights of Hungarians. Duray wrote of his struggles as an activist in his book *Kutyaszorító* 'In the Doghouse' (New York, 1983) and in *Kutyaszorító II* 'In the Doghouse II' (New York, 1989), he describes his trial and time in prison.

Though the overt protests of activists such as Király and Duray were rare, they were important when it came to the matter of keeping the Hungarian question alive on the international agenda. In the Cold War power constellation, the Hungarian diaspora in the free West played an important part. The Hungarian diaspora was instrumental in bringing the matter of the Hungarian 'minorities' to the attention of various parliaments and the international media. In Hungarian diaspora circles different organizations have been and still are active on behalf of the Hungarian national communities. These organizations made use of the room for interpretation offered in the UN treaties for the protection of human rights and, from 1975 onwards, the Helsinki Agreement that has clauses on human rights and on the rights of national minorities. These treaties were also signed by the various communist states.

The Hungarian diaspora

One leading organization that supported the cause of the Hungarians in Transylvania was the *Transylvanian World Federation* which has its seat in Brazil and is chaired by István Zolcsák. The many memoranda issued by the Transylvanian World Federation were designed to indicate that as far as human rights for the Hungarians were concerned things were not going all that well. The memoranda were aimed chiefly at the American Congress and Senate.[189] At the instigation of the Transylvanian World Federation resolution H. Res 415 was passed in the House of Representatives on 1st April 1992. This resolution relating to the human rights position of Hungarians in Transylvania was supported by 35 representatives and was aimed at the Foreign Affairs commission, went as follows:

Since the Rumanian government has signed international treaties and agreements - including the peace treaty of 1947 agreed to in Paris, the international covenant pertaining to civil and political rights, the international covenant on economic, social and cultural rights and the final act of the conference, the 1975 final act on security and co-operation within Europe which led to the 1990 Paris charter - which guarantees human rights for civilians without discriminating according to belief or national origins, due to the fact that the constitution of the Rumanian Republic of 1991 makes reference to the rights of the national minorities of Rumania, because the region Transylvania, inhabited by at least 2.5 million Hungarians who, for a whole millennium were part of the Hungarian kingdom before it was handed over to Rumania in the Treaty of Trianon (1920) due to the fact that the fate of the Hungarians in Transylvania has been exposed to denationalization by various subsequent Rumanian regimes - royalist, fascist or communist - and because of the fact that continued ethnic tension forms a threat to peace and security in Europe and so must be resolved before more blood is shed, as happened in Marosvásárhely in March 1990, the House of Representatives requests that the Rumanian government will abide by the present human rights treaties and decrees to guarantee the safety of minorities living in Rumania and it requests the president and the Secretary of State for Foreign Affairs to discuss the issue of the cultural rights and self-determination of the Transylvanian Hungarians with the Rumanian government, other governments concerned and the OSCE.

In the United States the group most actively occupied with Hungarian affairs was the *Hungarian Human Rights Foundation* (HHFR) situated in New York and led by László Hamos. This group, chiefly composed of second and third generation American Hungarians, managed to organize a big anti-Ceausescu demonstration near to the Waldorf Astoria Hotel in New York on 16th April 1978 which successfully ruined the Conducator's visit to America. It was largely thanks to the financial backing of the steel baron Thyssen-Bornemisza of aristrocratic Transylvanian Hungarian/German extraction that the HHFR was able to realize many of its activities. On a number of occasions, in follow up conferences that have taken place since the Helsinki Agreement, the HHFR has brought the Hungarian issue to people's attention.

In Europe, an important feat of arms was the condemnation of Rumania by the Council of Europe on 29th September 1984 in Resolution 5259. It was a resolution that heavily criticized Rumania's negative human and minority rights politics. In this resolution which had been conceived under the chairmanship of Blaauw, the Dutch delegate, the Rumanian government was called upon to "stop violating basic human rights in social, ethnic, cultural, economic and religious areas and to create an atmosphere in Rumania in which all nationalities can live without being discriminated against and are not being forced to leave their own country." Resolution 5259 which takes a critical stance on the position of all Rumania's minorities, its Hungarians, Germans, gypsies and Jews had the following to note about the Rumanian Jews: "The emigration of Jews which has been stimulated by the Rumanian government still continues. The Rumanian Jews have been forced into urban conglomerations. This community, composed now of many aged people, is doomed to die out. Rumania, the only country in Eastern Europe that recognizes the state of Israel will soon be without a Jewish community. In this way, Rumania will probably inadvertently revive the fascist *Iron Guard* slogan of the inter-war years: "Out with the Jews, down with the Hungarians!"

The plan announced by Ceausescu to 'systematize' the Rumanian countryside aroused a storm of protest throughout the world. The Conducator's grand plan had been to flatten 8,000 villages with bulldozers and transfer the villagers to agro-industrial complexes in concrete jungles. Apart from destroying an irreplaceable part of Europe's cultural heritage such a scheme would certainly have eradicated Transylvania's Hungarian community, notably the many traditional Hungarian villages of Szeklerland. The Conducator's plan, which involved obliterating country life, had been to create a new type of socialist human being. However, he had probably underestimated the opposition that such a bizarre plan would arouse. By 1988, it was clear that international public opinion turned firmly against such devastation of villages.[190]

Hungary awakes to reality

In Hungary, it was the first time since the Second World War that people were being forced to wake up to reality and to really think about Transylvania's problems. The change was partly instigated by the many thousands of Hungarians who had fled from Transylvania to Hungary during the latter half of the eighties. Gradually, the vicissitudes and the hardships of these Hungarians living in the Rumanian 'ideal state' came to light. It was only because of the political upheavals going on at international levels that it was possible to take an official stand against the anti-Hungarian Ceausescu regime. The moves made by Gorbachev had given the moderate communist contingent in Budapest the confidence to push through their reforms, while the hardliners in Bucharest lost their hinterland. As a result, the authorities for the first time ever decided to give their support to a big demonstration against a fellow socialist state. The huge 100,000 man strong rally staged in Budapest's Heroes' Square was not only supported by official communist civil organizations, but also by the organizations from which later, after 1989, Hungarian political parties would emerge. In the demonstration manifesto it was stated that the participants would "implore the Hungarian government to turn to the UN for help in this tragic matter."[191] The Rumanian threat to destroy Hungarian villages and the predicament of the Hungarian refugees recently arrived from Transylvania were what galvanized the Hungarians of the Western diaspora into swift action. By circulating memoranda the *SOS Transylvania Geneva Committee* tried to bring the plight of the Hungarians in Transylvania to the attention of representatives of the UN and the Council of Europe.

The effects resulting from the thousands of Hungarian refugees streaming out of Transylvania were not purely negative. Apart from arousing international public interest and mobilizing Hungary there were also, among the refugees, a number of intellectuals, who were able to provide insight into the situation and make rational analyses of the Rumanian danger. Because of communism and being cut off from their fellow Hungarians in Transylvania, Hungarian intellectuals living in Budapest had become oblivious to the dangers threatening the Hungarian nation and were not able to weigh up the interests involved. An important task, therefore, lay ahead for the Transylvanians. The Transylvanian Hungarian writer István Kocsis, who in 1984 was forced to leave Rumania with his family, played a prominent part. In a penetratingly brilliant analysis entitled *Our self-defence reflex do not let us down...* (February 1988, Budapest), Kocsis got to the bottom of the Transylvanian problem and revealed how the Rumanians really view the matter.

According to Kocsis the anti-Hungarian hatred generated by the Rumanians, notably by the political leaders regardless of political affiliations stems from the fact that the Rumanians have still not come to terms with the idea that such large parts of Hungary, Transylvania and eastern East Hungary and so many Hungarians suddenly became a part of Rumania in Trianon. Rumania's political leaders know quite well that the territorial decisions made were unjust and they have a guilty conscience about this. The way to escape from such a burden of conscience is by immersing themselves in anti-Hungary hate campaigns and convincing themselves, and the Hungarians, that the decisions taken at Trianon were fair. This guilt is manifested in the hate campaigns that extend across the borders, in the way in which the Rumanians falsify their own history by propagating the Daco-Roman theory which Rumanian historians know to be false, in the way in which they seek to destroy Transylvania's Hungarian community and in the way in which, clinging to the tactics that 'attack is the best form of defence', the Rumanians make ever new claims on Hungarian territory. During the Ceausescu period even the poet laureate Adrian Paunescu was allowed to appear on television and loudly proclaim that Rumania claimed from Hungary the area extending as far as the river Tisza. As long as Rumanians carry on living with such feelings of guilt and with such self-deception, they will not be able to break away from this nationalistic totalitarian system. The road to democracy will, therefore, remain closed to the Rumanians and they will continue their world-wide hate campaigns directed at the Hungarians.

Kocsis proposes that if the Rumanian's depression is openly discussed this will bring salvation for Transylvania's Hungarian population. For the Rumanians this will also be the only way to break away from nationalistic totalitarian dictatorship whatever its name or guise. The Rumanians can only put an end to anti-Hungarian politics and to having to resort to falsifying history and telling other lies to escape from their remorse if they adopt an attitude of openness. The advice Kocsis gave the Hungarians of Hungary (in 1988!) was almost prophetic: "The Hungarians of Hungary should delay no longer. Do they want to wait until anti-Hungarian pogroms commence in Rumania or large-scale riots. The least they can do, if no one else saves the Hungarians of Transylvania from ruin is to step in and help. This is the burning question that is to shape the future of the Hungarian nation."

Those who defended the interests of the Transylvanian Hungarians and Germans believed that with the dawn of the Rumanian politics of ethnocide by the Ceausescu regime the time was ripe for calling for Transylvania to become independent. Transylvania would have to become a communal state for the Rumanians, Hungarians, Germans and other nationalities living there. In a study entitled *Transylvania: Analyses and Proposals for Solutions,* published by the International Transylvanian Committee in Vienna that is presided over by the Austrian lawyer Eva Mária Barki, a constitution for an independent Transylvanian state is worked on. According to Dr. Barki the right to self-determination is a general international right that can become a secession right, if national communities live in states that discriminate against them so that in the end the government of the nation state no longer represents all its citizens. In the study many examples are given of cases where self-determination rights have been adopted in the form of secession or autonomy. Even in Switzerland, one of the wealthiest and most stable democracies in the world, this right has been exercised. The French-speaking community within the German-speaking canton of Berne broke away during the course of the seventies and set up its own French-speaking canton of Jura. Partly on the basis of historical arguments Dr. Barki urges that the right to self-determination should apply to Transylvania and its constitutional nations including the Hungarians, Rumanians and Germans. The oldest European right to autonomy was that granted to the German Saxons of Transylvania in 1224 in a document known as the *Andreanum.* In 1293, the Vlachs (the Rumanian's ancestors) were officially recognized as a separate nationality. The federalization of Rumania and the cantonization of Transylvania are not just empty slogans, this is reinforced by the way in which votes are distributed there. During Rumanian elections it has been evident, time and again, that Transylvanians vote differently from the rest of the country, from the parts on the other side of the Carpathians. In the parliamentary and presidential election of May 1990, Iliescu, the presidential candidate, and his crypto-communist National Salvation Front were able to win the election largely because of the support obtained from voters in Old Rumania. In the study carried out by the International Transylvanian Committee it was proposed that, taking into consideration the ethnic dispersal of the national communities, Transylvania should be divided into four autonomous areas as follows: (1) Szeklerland, (2) the border areas with Hungary densely populated by Hungarians, (3) remaining areas and (4) the Bánát region.

In August 1989, a summit was called between the Hungarian party leader Károly Grósz and the Rumanian dictator Ceausescu because of the tension being generated by the Hungarian refugees and the plans to flatten Hungarian villages in Transylvania. The Arad summit was a failure. The loss of face suffered by the Hungarian delegation turned out to be fatal for Grósz, the party leader. It marked the end of his political career. It was only then, during the summit in Arad, that the Hungarians started to realize how really threatened they were by Rumania. Mátyás Szűrös, the communist supporting reforms who had als been present in Arad admitted in an interview in 1990 that during the negotiations Ceausescu had tried to intimidate the Hungarian delegation. Szűrös alleged that Ceausescu had said at one point: "I can produce anything, even nuclear weapons" and that when nobody had reacted to the remark Ceausescu repeated his threat. So, the Conducator was even prepared to use nuclear weapons against the Hungarians ...[192]

The Hungarian struggle for self-determination

Since the fall of the wall in Berlin, the Hungarian national communities of Subcarpathia, Rumania, Lesser Yugoslavia (Greater Serbia) and Slovakia have organized themselves into parties and interest groups. These parties and organizations are made up of Hungarians of all persuasions and from all political sides who share the one objective of wanting to preserve Hungarian national identity. Day by day, they give myriad signs of wanting to fight the injustice that is being done to them. In recent years, the Hungarian national communities have produced hundreds of kilos of petitions, memoranda, protest letters etc. addressed to the governments of the countries in which they live, the Hungarian government, the great powers and to the international gremia in which they make mention of systematic discrimination and repression, of grave violations of human rights and even of the use of violence and terror towards them. In all these letters etc. pleas are made, often in vain, for the harshness of their cruel lot to be eased. The Hungarian national communities have not only put all their energy into fighting injustice and inhumanity, but they have also tried to give shape to their emancipation process in which autonomy is central. The parties of the Hungarian national communities have made a programme of the following points.

All these communities see themselves as an integral part of the Hungarian nation. In the respective countries in which they live, they wish to be treated as equal partners. This implies that Hungarians claim collective rights in accordance with the recommendations that have been made by international organizations, such as in the last document of the OSCE's follow-up conference on the human dimension in Copenhagen in June 1990, the European charter on regional and minority languages, the European charter on local self-government of the Council of Europe (1990), Resolution 1201 of the Council of Europe (1993) and statement no. 47 of the UN General Assembly, 1992 on the rights of people who belong to a national, ethnic, religious or language minority.

In repudiating the national unitary state the Hungarian communities, thus, automatically applied themselves to the democratization, federalization and regionalization of the countries in which they live. They aimed at achieving a federal state structure of the type that exists in Switzerland and Belgium. The Hungarian national communities, thus, wish to be seen as 'constitutional nation' partners. The partner-nation concept was conceived by Imre Borbély, RMDSZ member of parliament, who introduced the idea at his party's first national congress in Marosvásárhely. Since then, the claim for Hungarian autonomy for the Hungarian national communities has been developing at a rapid pace.

The Subcarpathian Hungarians first made public their claim for autonomy in the referendum of 1st December 1991. Where the district of Beregszász (Beregovo) is concerned the Ukrainian state still has not recognized territorial autonomy. The KMKSZ, the organization which represents the interests of the Hungarian community in Subcarpathia, keeps applying the necessary pressure. On 28th April 1992, the council in Beregszász passed a bill laying down the legal principles for the creation of an autonomous Hungarian district. The enactment was also supported by the Rumanian and Ukrainian delegates of the Beregszász council. The council has, furthermore, made an urgent appeal to parliamentary representatives in Kiev to adopt this bill. At the moment, things have come to a standstill, but this does not mean that the drive to regenerate Hungarian identity in Subcarpathia has in any way weakened.

On 2nd March 1995, the Hungarian Ukrainian parliamentary representative, Mihály Tóth from Beregszász, managed to get the Ukrainian parliament in Kiev to agree to restoring all the original Hungarian place names in the three Subcarpathian districts of Beregszász (Beregovo), Nagyszőllős (Vinogradov) and Ungvár (Uzsgorod). Hence-forth the Hungarian place names will be the officially recognized names instead of the Ukrainian equivalents or translations.

The Szekler-Hungarians planned to hold a people's meeting and a referendum on 19th October 1991 in Agyagfalva (Lutita) on autonomy for Szeklerland. This was the place where, in 1506, the Szekler-Hungarian's ancestors had decided during a people's meeting that Szeklerland was rightfully theirs and that, according to ancient royal privileges, the Szekler-Hungarians of *Terra Sicolorum* were entitled to aristocratic status. Until 1848, the Szekler-Hungarians had a separate constitutional status based on a system of self-government organized in territorial districts known as *székek* 'seats'. The initiator of this autonomy for Szeklerland and the organizer of the gathering in Agyagfalva was the art historian, Adám Katona originating from Székelyudvarhely (Odoreiu Secuiesc), the 'capital' of Szeklerland. In an interview with the Hungarian language newspaper *Erdélyi Napló* 'Transylvanian Diary' (8th, 15th, 23rd and 30th January, 1992) Katona explained why they were unable to go ahead with the planned referendum.

The first attack to their initiative came, strangely enough, not from Bucharest but from Budapest. On 7th October, Radio Kossuth began a smear campaign against the organizers of the referendum. The pattern followed was familiar. It was the Foreign Affairs minister, Jeszenszky, supported by the former Foreign Affairs minister and the prime minister of the day, Gyula Horn who led the attack. Katona and the other organizers of the initiative were stigmatized as 'radicals' and 'nationalists' and were excluded from both the Hungarian and the Rumanian media. At the same time, other Transylvanian Hungarians labelled as 'moderates' were pushed forward, the same representatives that were later to become the 'Neptun trio' and who would later negotiate in secret with Rumanian leaders without receiving a mandate from the RMDSZ. It was only after Hungary had opened up its attack on the Szekler-Hungarians that they fell prey to Rumanian politics, notably that of the extreme nationalist Romania Mare and Vatra Romanaesca. In the end, on 14th October 1991, Katona and his friends decided to cancel the meeting and the referendum. When asked to comment Katona said: "Since the crisis in Yugoslavia had led to a civil war, we decided that the tanks lined up in the Agyagfalva region, the machine-gun emplacements and the larger and smaller Rumanian army units that had been patrolling for days on end in our woods constituted a real danger. Therefore, we decided to put off the planned rally. Our minimal goal, however, namely that of making known our demands for autonomy for Szeklerland had been achieved, thanks to the 'help' of our opponents and enemies."

Since then, there has been much discussion on Hungarian autonomy in Transylvania. The RMDSZ declared on 25th October 1992 in Kolozsvár (Cluj) that the struggle for *internal* self-determination is a political doctrine. The text of this declaration reads as follows:

The Kolozsvár declaration of 25th October 1992
"One of the socio-political problems in Rumanian political life that most urgently needs to be resolved is the national issue. The bitter experiences and tragic events that have convinced us, the Rumanian Hungarians and our legitimate representational body, the RMDSZ, that until now neither political will nor political practice have been able to provide us with an acceptable solution. We accept our national identity, but will not retreat or shrink away. We regard this native homeland and soil as ours, but at the same time we do not want to be swallowed up by the Rumanian nation. Politically, the Rumanian Hungarians are a constitutional factor and so they are, as such, equal partners of the Rumanian nation. We are just as responsible for the future of that nation as any other citizens and when we see that in Hungarian circles the struggle is being given up and defeatism is starting to set in causing many to decide to leave the country it is our duty to intervene. We feel duty-bound to find a solution that will offer a way out of this crisis for us and for our country. The autonomy of the ethnic and religious communities is one cohesive whole in Transylvania's history. One might refer to the Saxon people's right to self-government that has existed for almost 800 years. Self-government was also pronounced in the Gyulafehérvár proclamation of 1918.

We believe that the solution lies in establishing internal self-determination. The principle of self-determination is one of forward-looking universal implications, in fact, many ethnic or other sorts of self-governing communities that have developed in the past or are developing now, already demonstrate the success of this principle in operating European democracies.

The Rumanian Hungarians will be integrated community by community into the society of our country within the wider context of our state's European integration process.

We are aware of the fact that the national issue will gain new dimensions that will go beyond the framework of human rights and which are already important in the matter of European security and stability.

We are convinced that the self-government of the various communities will contribute to strengthening the constitutional state and the civil social structures, while at the same time being an important aspect of the democratization process.

Finding a solution to the national question is of national importance. In carrying out this awesome task in which constitutional and legal frameworks have to be created we rely on the support from the democratic forces within this country."

The doctrine of internal self-determination, as formulated above by the RMDSZ, has been further elaborated by the Hungarian senator József Csapó. Csapó published a discussion paper on 31st December 1992 entitled *The internal self-determination of the Hungarian national community in Rumania*. In this paper, he gives a point by point description of what the Hungarians' internal self-determination scheme will have to look like. Since then, the whole internal self-determination debate has had its ups and downs. The Neptun affair, described in the last chapter, created two camps within the RMDSZ, namely that of the autonomists and that of the anti-autonomists.

So far the reaction of the Rumanian state to the Hungarian community's bid for autonomy has been one of fear and panic. In November 1994, the Rumanian intelligence service, SRI, declared in its annual report presented in parliament that it heavily condemned the "anti-Rumanian, irredentist and revisionist" activities of Hungarian individuals and organizations within and outside of the country. The three people specifically named in this connection were Dr. Barki, Dr. Csapó and Adám Katona. In December 1994, the Austrian security service made it known that the SRI was planning to murder Mrs Barki and it was also informed that there was a *blacklist naming* Tőkés and three other civilians from Hungary. All the people named on this list have managed to remain level-headed about the death threats, but remain perpetually on their guard.[193] The laconical remark made by Katona on the matter was: "To me it is like receiving an award from my country."

The key figure for the Hungarians of Transylvania has been bishop László Tőkés. The man who has withstood so many attacks, accusations, press campaigns, threats and attempts on his life has never given up the fight. When the tyrant Ceausescu fell, Tőkés became confident that with a firm belief in God and a clear conscience it would be possible to combat all evil forces. As far as Tőkés is concerned, making Rumania fully democratic and securing equality for the Hungarian community are simply two different sides to the same coin. It is as though the harder they push him the more the bishop starts to gain the same allure as black South African spiritual leaders or the Tibetan Dalai Lama who also became moral figure-heads in the battle for the emancipation of their people. This status was confirmed when recently Tőkés was invited by Jimmy Carter, the former US president, to travel to America to discuss the Hungarian-Rumanian question.

The Hungarian-Rumanian round table conference took place on 14th and 15th February 1995 in Atlanta. On this occasion, it was once again the PER that mediated. The PER had apparently learned from the failure of Neptun that no constructive negotiating could ever be established between the Rumanian authorities and the Hungarian community without the legitimate representation of the RMDSZ. The RMDSZ delegation was composed of 'radicals' and 'moderates', including bishop Tőkés, honorary chairman of the RMDSZ. In a written statement made before the proceedings in Atlanta began, Tőkés declared that he was prepared to negotiate with the Rumanian government even though he was aware that the conference would be full of 'pitfalls' that could be disadvantageous for the RMDSZ. Yet Tőkés found the risk worth taking since Jimmy Carter's reputation would serve as a guarantee for open negotiation. The bishop, furthermore, pointed out that the round table conference in Atlanta provided the first real opportunity for bringing the question of the Hungarians in Transylvania to the attention of the international public opinion.[194] In a personal letter written before he went to America, Tőkés called upon the former president "to do his utmost to ensure fair solutions." At the press conference held after the round table meetings, Jimmy Carter commented that "the conference may be regarded as a success, because both parties have agreed to continue the difficult discussions embarked on in Atlanta."[195] The Atlanta negotiations were rounded off with a joint declaration in which both sides promised to continue the dialogue, notably in the following areas: (a) to loosen up political tension and improve inter-ethnic relations, (b) on concepts of autonomy, (c) regarding the education law and teaching in the mother tongue, (d) on the issue of accepting the native language in local government, the law courts, public life and in economic and social areas, (e) in bi-lingual place and road naming, (f) regarding the law on minorities, (g) the law on religious denominations and the restitution of church property and possessions, (h) pertaining to the law on local spending, (i) the Pál Cseresznyés case and (j) the problem of economic discrimination.[196] Although the Rumanian parliament and senate had distanced themselves from the conference proceedings it was still, for bishop Tőkés and the other delegates, the first time that their problems were being recognized internationally.

The Vojvodina Hungarians' struggle for autonomy was recorded in a memorandum entitled On the Self-government of Hungarians in the Republic of Serbia that was adopted at the general meeting of the Democratic Community of Hungarians in Vojvodina (the VMDK) on 25th April 1992. The memorandum makes mention of Serbia, because the Hungarians feel threatened by Serb aggression and at this stage they do not want to provoke ethnic cleansing in Vojvodina. In the words of the community's president, András Agoston: "We are surrounded by sharks." Without armed protection, life for the Hungarians of Vojvodinia remains precarious. It was, therefore, very brave of the VMDK leaders to dare to accept the proposal relating to autonomy. The proposal contains detailed plans on establishing an autonomous Hungarian region.

The VMDK bases its concepts on the proposal of Lord Carrington who chaired the Yugoslavia conferences in The Hague and Brussels relating to the special status of 'minorities' that form a majority on their own territory. The VMDK refers to paragraph c of part II of the congress document adopted in The Hague to claim a special status for communities where Hungarians are in the majority. The preamble to the memorandum proposes that, in its capacity as the legitimate representational organization for the Hungarian community in Vojvodina, the VMDK should request that the Serbian parliament adjust its laws in such a way that the Hungarian majority is given special status with its own parliament, police force and schools and the freedom to use all its own national symbols. The autonomous Hungarian region is the ethnic conglomeration along the banks of the river Tisza, including the communities of Kanizsa, Zenta, Ada, Csóka and Óbecse, and in the Bácska district, including Kishegyes, Topolya and Szabadka and some other neighbouring communities. Here, the Hungarians constitute a compact bloc and they are in the absolute majority. The Vojvodina Hungarians are demanding nothing more than what the Serbian government is demanding for the Serb communities in Croatia and Bosnia. According to the VMDK, Serbia should not employ double standards. It may not back out of recognizing the constitutional rights of national communities and of guaranteeing different forms of self-government in accordance with the intentions of the peace proposal. Since 1992, there has been no progress in the matter of autonomy for Hungarians in Vojvodina. Now that the war in former Yugoslavia has come to an end, new possibilities are opening up for the Hungarian community. As international pressure mounts, the Serbs are making more and more mistakes even though they still enjoy the protection of powerful states. Now that war criminals are being brought before the international war tribunal in The Hague, even the most extreme of Serb tyrants, like Seselj, are proving willing to negociate with the VMDK about Hungarian autonomy.

The last of the autonomy declarations to be made was that of the Hungarian community in Slovakia. In Slovakia there are four Hungarian political parties: the liberal parties Coexistence (Hun. *Együttélés*) and the Hungarian Civic Party (*Hun. Magyar Polgári Párt,* MPP), the Hungarian Christian Democratic Movement (Hun. *Magyar Kereszténydemokrata Mozgalom,* MKDM) and the conservative rightist Hungarian People's Party (Hun. *Magyar Néppárt,* MNP) which all made an electoral alliance pact before the elections. With the return of nationalistic totalitarian politicians like Meciar not only common Hungarian interests need to be defended, but also the process of democratization. As a result, co-operation between Hungarian parties has been intensified. On 8th January 1994 3,000 elected Hungarian representatives, local council members, mayors and members of parliament assembled in Komárom (Komarno) to adopt a declaration relating to the future of the Hungarians in southern Slovakia. Policies were formulated in the field of politics, self-government, public administration and the constitution. The signatories of the 'Komárom declaration' emphasized that they want to regulate the legal position of the Hungarian Slovaks within the formal framework, while at the same time respecting Slovak territorial integrity.

The political section of the declaration states that the Hungarians and Slovaks have a long history of mutual tolerance and that they have developed common cultural values. The Hungarians of Slovakia want a stable and integrated Europe and they are oriented to the West. They want to avoid political conflict at all costs, but they do point out that on the Slovak side the political will to improve the position of the Hungarians in Slovakia is lacking. This is why it is required to look for new solutions and to, for instance, aim at establishing a partnership.

The declaration states that if local councils have extensive powers that is what forms the foundation of a democratic constitutional state. It, furthermore, states that the powers of the local councils in Slovakia are to be suspended by the constitution and central government. The signatories of the Komárom declaration want the local councils to be given more extensive powers and rights and more financial elbow-room. They call upon the Slovak government to sign the European charter on local self-government which introduces the principle of subsidiarity.

The declaration of Komárom also criticizes plans proposed by the Slovak government for the territorial restructuring of Slovakia. The Hungarians find this proposal unacceptable, because the districts would be restructured in a north-south direction which would mean that the Hungarians who are concentrated in a 'west-east' line would find themselves in the minority in all the new districts. In such a situation, the Hungarians would certainly no longer be able to organize their own affairs. In the memorandum, the alternatives put forward for the territorial restructuring of Slovakia do more justice to the number of Hungarians and their geographical distribution.

The constitutional position of the Hungarians can only be properly laid down when local self-government and territorial restructuring have been decided upon in a democratic way. The Slovak Hungarians want a collective status to be established in the constitution and they no longer want to be defined as a 'minority' but rather as a national community. They want to be represented proportionally in governmental bodies and they want the use of the Hungarian language to become legal. Where Hungarians are in the majority, their language must stand on an equal footing with Slovak and in regions where Hungarians are a numerical minority Hungarian should be recognized as an official second language. The declaration contains the four following political demands:
- the Hungarians are a political entity and as such demand to have local self-government.
- in areas where they are in the majority the Hungarians demand that article 11 of Resolution 1201 of the Council of Europe be strictly enforced which means that in all local government areas (in the civil service, police forces, the law courts) Hungarians will have to be represented proportionately.
- a principle of reciprocity should operate within the state. Slovaks who are numerically in the minority in a region where Hungarians are in the majority must have the same rights as Hungarians who are numerically in the minority, while Slovaks are in the majority.
- as a partner nation the Hungarians wish to live on an equal footing with the Slovaks.

In the declaration of Komárom the term *autonomy* has been deliberately avoided since that might lead the Slovaks to interpret this as a first step on the road to separatism. In that respect, in wanting to avoid provocation of the Slovaks at all costs the Hungarians have been very compromising. The signatories do, however, stipulate that if the Slovak government does not take the Komárom declaration seriously and if it shows no interest in realizing the proposals they must expect that tension will inevitably increase.

The Balladur Pact and the ensuing opposition

Until now the efforts made on the part of the Hungarian national community to achieve autonomy have not been taken very seriously and international politics have tried to hold back this process. One of the instruments used to realize this policy was the stability pact that was signed on 20th March 1995 in Paris under the chairmanship of the French ex-prime minister Balladur. The original idea had been to resolve the problems existing between Hungary and her neighbouring countries of Slovakia and Rumania by getting all the parties to sign bilateral treaties. A friendship treaty between Hungary and Slovakia was signed, even though both parties later went on to interpret the text differently. No treaty was signed with Rumania, because the Rumanians were not in agreement with the Council of Europe's 1201 Resolution upon which the rights of the Transylvanian Hungarians were to be based.

Resolution 1201 of the Council of Europe, which is an elaboration of the European convention on human rights for national minorities is, however, little more than a recognition of the cultural identity of national 'minorities' *individually* guaranteeing people the right to use their own native langauge, receive education in their own mother tongue etc. Resolution 1201 also recognizes people's right to local self-government in regions where the 'minority' in question is in the majority. If a state ignores such minimum requirements, one cannot really interpret this as anything other than its refusing to recognize a national community's right to existence on its own territory.

Before the agreement between Hungary and Slovakia was signed, much criticism was levelled at the Hungarian government for its way of dealing with the matter. The political parties of the Hungarian national communities and the Hungarian opposition parties had heard that the Horn administration wanted the treaties to be signed quickly. On 19th August 1994, the Independent Smallholders' Party (Hun. *Független Kisgazda Párt*, FKGP) organized a congress in which the Slovak Hungarians were represented as well. The congress was rounded off with a petition which suggested that a possible friendship treaty between Hungary and Slovakia should not be signed without the consent of the Slovak Hungarians. On 20th October 1994, prime minister Horn announced at the congress of the World Federation of Hungarians, in the presence of all the leading representatives of the Hungarian national communities, that no agreement would be signed behind the backs of the Hungarian minorities. This prompted Hungarian societies in the diaspora to bombard the prime minister with letters beseeching him to keep his promise.

The protest against a quick and unconditional signing of the friendship treaties between Hungary and Slovakia/Rumania was initiated by the World Federation of Hungarians who organized a meeting on 3rd March 1995. At this meeting, they once again stressed that Hungarian communities would have to give full permission for these treaties to be signed. Only a true consensus would guarantee peaceful co-existence for the people of the region. The declaration contained the following demands:[197]

(1) The Komárom (Komarno) and Kolozsvár (Cluj) declarations will have to be incorporated in the treaties of friendship.
(2) The parties involved will have to conform to the objectives and regulations that underlie European integration, also in their interrelations. The free interchange of persons, goods, services and capital must be guaranteed and unlimited streams of information, as well as active border crossing regional co-operation must be allowed.
(3) Slovakia and Rumania must return all the Hungarian property that was confiscated by the previous governments. This includes

private property as well as the property of churches, institutions, societies, educational establishments etc.

(4) The treaties must be signed in full accordance with the international agreements made in the context of the OSCE and the Council of Europe.

The protest letter formulated by the World Federation of Hungarians was followed by a series of protests on the part of the Hungarian political parties in Slovakia and the opposition parties in the Hungarian parliament. For the first time in a long while, the Hungarians were actually fighting back and opposing the Trianon encirclement. With the signing of the treaty looming ever nearer, the Hungarian political parties in Slovakia were drawn closer together. In a common declaration on 17th March 1995 Coexistence, the MKDM and the MPP announced that they were aware of the agreement between Horn, the Hungarian prime minister and his Slovak counterpart Meciar, but that they doubted whether in Slovak government coalition circles the political will existed to implicate the treaty. Before the ratification of the treaty in the Hungarian parliament, the Slovak Hungarians, furthermore, asked the Hungarian government to draw up a programme that would guarantee that the agreement would be realized. The Slovak Hungarians finally pointed out that it was not exactly clear to them how the financial resources for their own educational establishments were to be safeguarded.

The Hungarian opposition parties: KDNP, MDF and FIDESZ rejected the treaty in a joint declaration on 18th March 1995, just as the FKGP had done at an earlier stage. The Horn administration was sharply criticized for having acknowledged that the Slovakian Hungarians form an integral part of Slovak society and for not having mentioned that the Hungarian minority is a constitutional entity and that the Hungarians in Slovakia are a concrete part of the Hungarian cultural nation. According to the Hungarian opposition the treaty accepts the Slovak programme for a national unitary state. The Hungarian opposition parties also resented the fact that prime minister Horn's Hungarian government did not allow the Slovak Hungarians to have a proper

part in the shaping of the treaty and that they had to face accomplished facts. The opposition parties were finally disappointed that these parties were not consulted on issues of national interest. MDF, KDNP and FIDESZ proposed that the agreement be revised on the following points:
- the Hungarian national community in Slovakia must be liberated from the decrees made by Benes which hold the Hungarian people collectively responsible for the outbreak of the Second World War and for crimes committed during the war. Once these decrees have been rescinded the Hungarian community in Slovakia must be indemnified.
- the treaty's frontier clause must be brought into line with the border change options included in the Helsinki Agreement which accepts border changes as long as the parties involved agree to such changes and as long as they are resolved in a peaceful way.
- the problems surrounding the Danube dam at Gabcikovo have to be settled.
- the Hungarians living in Slovakia must be given autonomy in accordance with Resolution 1201 of the Council of Europe and Hungarian institutions must be sure of receiving financial support from the Slovak state.
- a system of international monitoring must be set up to see that the agreement is really observed in practice.

As a result of the treaty, coalitions were formed in Hungarian politics that had not been possible for a long time. FIDESZ, the young liberals party that had become more conservative in its inclinations just before the 1994 election and the World Federation of Hungarians organized their first official meeting. In a joint declaration issued on 20th March 1995, they turned down the treaty made with Slovakia.

The FIDESZ spokesman, the member of parliament Zsolt Németh, claimed in an interview that the Hungarian government had misled public opinion with their argument that signing the treaty with Slovakia was an absolute prerequisite for Euro-Atlantic integration. Németh said: "Prime minister Balladur announced somewhere in February that the signing of the treaties of friendship would be very important as far as the European integration process in Central Europe was concerned. The next day, Juppé, the minister of Foreign Affairs, announced that the treaties of friendship were not essential in the process of securing Euro-Atlantic integration. The French declarations were contradictory but this had to do with the imminent presidential elections. There was one other concrete point. The Secretary of State for Foreign Affairs, István Szent-Iványi explained at a press conference on returning from the US that the State Department did not regard the signing of the friendship treaties as essential, when it came to the matter of establishing Euro-Atlantic integration. It would, therefore, have been no disaster, if the treaty had not been signed. In giving the impression that Euro-Atlantic integration depended on the signing of the treaty the Hungarian Foreign Affairs Department wilfully misled public opinion.[198] In the same interview, the young FIDESZ member of parliament further mentioned that just before the treaty was signed the Slovak delegation handed over a memo to the Hungarian delegation, without discussing this at all beforehand. The Hungarian delegation, therefore, knew nothing of its contents and the Slovak delegation regarded it as being similar to the agreement: "...this move proved in no uncertain terms that the Slovaks were not motivated by an understanding of the minorities or by a desire to improve Hungarian-Slovak relations. The Slovak move gave the Hungarian government a last chance to decide against signing the treaty. In Paris, the first effects of this bad agreement were immediately felt. The day after it had been signed, Horn and Meciar started hurling abuse at each other in connection with the treaty in the presence of representatives from other countries. They, thus, made themselves ridiculous in the eyes of international public opinion. The treaty itself, therefore, started generating tension and instability. The Hungarians will refer to the treaty in order to defend the rights of their minorities, while the Slovaks, by contrast, reject every claim made by the minorities that is not specifically mentioned in the treaty."

The Hungarian government surmised that the signing of the treaty - in reality a one-sided confirmation of Trianon encirclement politics - and the promises made by prime minister Horn at the meeting of the World Federation of Hungarians, which he had not followed up, would go down badly in Hungarian diaspora circles. Therefore, the secretary of state in charge of affairs for Hungarians on the other side of the border, László Lábody, wrote a letter to the Hungarian diaspora societies on behalf of the government in which he endeavoured to rectify what had gone wrong in Paris. Through this letter, which was couched in old-fashioned communistic jargon, the Hungarian government recognized that the diaspora constitutes an important political pressure group.[199] The secretary of state enumerated the treaty's main assets: the agreement would increase stability in the region and raise the level of trust between Slovakia and Hungary which in turn would be beneficial for the Hungarian minority living in Slovakia. The treaty would make Euro-Atlantic integration more supple and finally, Hungary showed that it was capable of and prepared to arrive at compromises in a civilized way in line with internationally laid down norms and legal customs and according to mutual and rational interests without in any way transgressing national interests, etc., etc., etc.

The last point gave clear insight into the opinions and attitudes of this particular government. What should Hungary, the country that since the Ausgleich with Austria of 1867 had established an impressive number of agreements with its neighbouring countries, that in 1956 had bravely stood up against the Soviet Union and which had fulfilled a leading role in the upheavals of 1989 that had ultimately led to the fall of communism still have to 'prove' that it is interested in seeing a Central Europe that is civilized, stable and democratic. What nonsense! It is high time that the neighbouring countries that have been expanding at Hungary's expense ever since Trianon treat their Hungarians better. The best proof of the defective reasoning of Horn's administration emerged from the fact that within a month of the signing of the agreement Slovakia had already cast it on one side.

Only if Hungary adopts a hard political line towards the neighbouring countries that oppress their Hungarian national communities, will the respect of nationalistic leaders be won. Slavishly signing treaties that offer no compromise, but which rather provide one-sided recognition, on Hungary's part, of the positions of Hungary's neighbouring countries is not the solution. Taking the lenient and soft approach will only encourage the Slovaks to pursue anti-Hungarian policies and place increased pressure on their Hungarian community. After the treaty with Slovakia had been signed, the Slovak Ministry of Education started increasing pressure. In contravention of what had been agreed in the Balladur Pact and in the Council of Europe's 1201 resolution, the Slovak Ministry of Education resolved to stop financing Hungarian language education. The subsidy of 80 million crowns that had been paid out to the Hungarian community each year in recent years was withdrawn. Government subsidizing of Hungarian cultural societies and magazines also ceased.

On 22nd April 1995, the Hungarian national community in Komárom (Komarno) organized a massive demonstration against the anti-Hungarian measures being taken by the Slovak government. Some 7,000 people took part in the protest. In a petition drawn up during the protest, the Hungarian community claimed that such measures taken by the Slovak government constituted a danger to Slovakia's Hungarian community and to the future of the country. The Hungarians came up with the following suggestions for ways of improving the situation:

- The government must drop the introduction of 'alternative education in Slovak' in the case of bilingual Hungarian/Slovak schools.
- The president of the Slovak Republic must reject law number 542/1992 already accepted by the Slovak parliament as it directly contradicts the self-determination principle.
- The Ministry of Education ought to recognize the validity of higher education given at the municipal universities of Komárom (Komarno) and Királyhelmec (Královsky Chlmec).
- A separate Hungarian faculty should be set up for teachers in training at the Nyitra (Nitra) college.

- Subsidies should once again be provided for general basic education and mass communication in the Hungarian language.
- The Ministries of Education and Culture should take back all employees dismissed for political reasons before December 1994.

It is right that the Hungarians in Slovakia protest at the cuts being made in education and culture as far as the Hungarian language is concerned, but it is, of course, frustrating for them to have to demonstrate every time they want to make some amendment. It would be much better if the Hungarians of Slovakia were to stick to the idea of a federal structure in which the country would consist of Slovak and Hungarian republics. In this way, Hungarian education and culture would come to be regulated in a proportional way.

In international politial circles reactions to the Balladur Pact were optimistic. The attitude being that every problem that seems to be solved is a problem less. This explains why, against their better judgement, the representatives of international politics welcomed the Balladur Pact with open arms. International politics had been putting pressure on the countries concerned. Lábody, the secretary of state, remarked in his memo to the Hungarian diaspora that "before the commencement of the stability conference of 21st March the leading NAVO and EU powers had placed pressure on Slovakia and Hungary to sign an agreement to establish good neighbourly relations. The German, French and Spanish prime ministers wrote a joint letter to the relevant governments. Even Clinton, the American President sent letters to Pozsony, Bucharest and Budapest. Both French and American diplomacy was very active."[200] International politics did not offer solutions to the *internal* Hungarian questions. Because of the above-mentioned objections to the agreement, it was to be expected that the treaty drawn up between Hungary and Slovakia would not work, at least not in its present form. As a result, certain Western politicians who were not convinced of the durability of this agreement, also because of the opposition it had received from Hungarians, put searching questions to their own ministers of Foreign Affairs.

The Dutch MP, J.D. Blaauw (of the VVD party, the liberal right) put his questions on the Hungarian-Slovak treaty to Van Mierlo, the Dutch Foreign Affairs minister, in parliament on 24th March 1995. The six questions raised in the House related, amongst other things, to the matter of whether with so much opposition to the treaty, political stability could be influenced in a positive way. Another important point was the question as to whether Hungarian-Slovak representatives should be involved in the monitoring process in view of the fact that it was a treaty between states. On 13th April, the Dutch Foreign Affairs minister reported that he was aware of the opposition but that "in view of the political situation in the country [Hungary] one should not attach too much importance to this." The minister, furthermore, said that "while it was true that this agreement did not solve all the problems it was important that both governments nurtured a wish to improve relations. In this way, the agreement could contribute to further concilliation and political stability in the region." Blaauw absolutely disagreed with the nonchalant replies of the minister. Together with Gabor (MP of the Christian Democratic Party) Blaauw posed a new series of questions in the House on 12th May which were again directed at the Foreign Affairs minister. This time the minister was forced to go into the issue in more depth, because there was the possibility of a parliamentary majority arising. Clearly, it was not worth having a cabinet crisis about this matter. Blaauw and Gabor wondered whether, in view of the 'social and historical processes' at stake here, it might not be best if these questions were given the greatest possible consensus and whether criticism should not be examined from the point of view of content, regardless of who had produced it. The minister and his civil servants were again given a lot of homework to do.

What had been called a 'stabilizing pact' had led to big differences of opinion in the very first parliamentary debate on the matter in a Western parliament. It underlined the fact that what had happened in Paris on 21st March had been nothing more than a charade. It was important that the political discussions had taken place in the Dutch parliament, because they had put the

Hungarian question on the international political agenda. For instance, in its spring congress the Liber International was unable to decide whether or not to support the treaty between Hungary and Slovakia. This was partly due to the activities of the Dutch VVD faction and one of its assistants, Geert Wilders. It seemed that where the Hungarian question is concerned, changes are taking place in the international political arena. Since the dictation of this treaty, change has been discernible within the Hungarian parliament. People have started to talk about the injustices of Trianon and the untenability of that treaty.

In May 1995, the MP of the FKGP, Sándor Kávássy, wrote the following to the Hungarian Foreign Affairs minister, the ex-communist Lászlo Kovács. "I should like to draw your attention to a major injustice and to a situation that definitely needs to be rectified. In the Treaty of Trianon, seven Slovenian villages remained under Hungarian jurisdiction while 25 villages inhabited entirely or almost entirely by Hungarians were annexed by Slovenia. They were the following villages: Kámaháza, Lendvahidvég, Bánuta, Csckcfa, Kisszerdahely, Alsólakos, Felsőlakos, Petesháza, Göntérháza, Radamos, Kebeleszentmárton, Zsitkóc, Lendvavásárhely, Szécsiszentlászló, Völgyifalu, Kapornak, Őrihódos, Kisfalu, Alsólendva, Csentevölgy, Kapca, Kót, Pártosfalva, Lendvahosszúfalu and Zalagyertyános. Why the Hungarians of these villages should be living in Slovenia remains a complete mystery. Furthermore, all the problems of the Hungarian minority in Slovenia could be instantly resolved, if the border was just moved one 1-2 kilometres. Why not simply exchange these villages for those to the south of Szentgotthárd? Hungary could offer the following villages populated by Slovenian majorities in exchange: Alsószömölnök, Felsőszömölnök, Apátistvánfalva, Kétvölgy, Orfalu, Rábatótfalu and Szakonyfalva. Obviously, this would have to be done in consultation with the inhabitants of these villages. Any villages wishing to remain where they are, either in Hungary or Slovenia, should not be forced to change allegiances against their will..." In his letter, Kávássy asks the minister to start negotiations on this issue with Slovenia.

The Hungarian MP put pressure on the minister by inquiring about the situation in conjunction with Hungarian autonomy in Beregszász (Beregovo) in Subcarpathia. On 8th May, he wrote the following to minister Kovács: "No one who thinks and feels in a humane and democratic way can possibly remain indifferent to the endeavours of Hungarians in the district of Beregszász. No one has the right to ignore the referendum results, if human dignity, popular sovereignty and the rights of peoples and nations to self-determination means anything to them. If there is one power organization in the world that should not take the easy way by being a quiet observer and burying its head in the sand, then that is the Hungarian government. I would, therefore, ask the Hungarian government to support the Hungarians of Beregszász in their quest for autonomy..."

With the debate on the ratification of the Hungarian-Slovak treaty the cycle of spiritual revival was complete. During the interpellation on 23rd May, the vice president of the Hungarian parliament, Agnes Maczó-Nagy (FKGP), presented a number of strong arguments for why the treaty between Hungary and Slovakia should not be signed. For the first time ever, the situation of the Hungarians in the Carpathian Basin was being lucidly and sharply defined. For the first time, the psychological shackles that had held the Hungarians mentally prisoner since the Treaty of Trianon were being cast off. At last, Maczó had revealed the sad truth that the Carpathian Basin is full of *Berlin walls* that keep the Hungarians divided. "How many of you here in this House know that Berlin was not the only city that was split in two? Not very long ago, the whole world witnessed the collapse of the Berlin wall and saw how people's souls were set free. How many of you really know that the city of Sátoraljaújhely [a city on the Hungarian-Slovak border in north-east Hungary, LM] is also divided in two by a river that flows through the city, a river that should be navigable. [See the Treaty of Trianon, LM] Now even a rowing boat is too big for that 'river'! The 'big wall' at Sátoraljaújhely was opened, but not like at that time in Berlin... But at the time nobody shouted out the words irredentist and chauvinist not even here, none of you did!... Even today, the great iron gate that separates Sátoraljaújhely has remained closed. Patiently and apathetically, people stood and waited on both sides of the border. A small door was opened, but everything else remained the same as before. Sátoraljaújhely has become Europe's new Berlin, a city you can only move about in with a passport. In the words of president Kennedy who once said: "Ich bin ein Berliner", we might all say: *We are inhabitants of Sátoraljaújhely.*"

Europe's hinge: Hungary

In the twentieth century, the destiny of the Hungarian people has been determined by two major historical-political events: the Trianon peace dictate (1920) that came after the First World War and the Soviet-Russian occupation of the country of after the Second World War.

The Treaty of Trianon destroyed the 1000 year-long period of Hungary's functioning as Europe's *hinge*. Because of Trianon, the Hungarians of the Carpathian Basin were separated and came to be dispersed throughout Lesser Hungary and the successor states of Czechoslovakia, Yugoslavia and Rumania. The various parts of the Hungarian nation went their own way. It was a situation that only ended for a brief period when, during the Second World War, these parts were successfully reunited. After the Second World War, the Hungarians were forced to 'integrate' and become part of the communist East Bloc. In Hungary, a reign of terror began that was driven by communist internationalistic ideology and every effort was made to fragment Hungarian society.

Lesser Hungarian particularism

By the end of the era of communist oppression, Hungarians everywhere in the Carpathian Basin had been effectively marginalized. Internationalistic, communist ideology was traded in for an ideology of globalized internationalism. The switches in orientation and ideology left the power political structures untouched, some of the characteristics being:

- that citizens have no real influence on the exercise power. Political decisions are taken behind the scenes. A good example of this was the pact made between prime minister Antall several days after his MDF had won its first free elections in April 1990 and the liberal left opposition party, the SZDSZ. Neither the electorate, his party nor the presidium had given

him the authority to do this. Together with the secret pact made earlier on with the communists pertaining to 'transfer of power', this pact has shaped the Hungarian politics of recent years.[201]
- the marginalization of the Hungarians has enormously affected the mental-moral atmosphere in the country. Hungary is an inward looking and socially unstable country. The pessimistic mood has penetrated deep into Hungarian culture. Artists expressing feelings of loneliness and losers have been given a prominent place in Hungarian culture. The Hungarian culture is full of metaphors for 'desolation', 'sorrow' and 'loneliness' and the country has numerous statues and other depictions of fallen revolutionaries. The post-communist system cultivated this 'Hungarian sorrow' sentiment and the image of 'Hungarians as losers'. The trend reached its height with the recent erection of a massive effigy in honour of the Turkish sultan Sulijman who beat the Hungarian army in the battle of Mohács and then went on to ravage huge regions of Hungary. The argument was that the statue symbolizes the peaceful relations now existing between these two peoples who had for centuries been at war with each other. If a statue of Hitler were to be erected in the West to symbolize the renewed friendship with Germany, this would surely also be seen as taking matters too far...

In Hungary's neighbouring countries where anti-Hungarian policy was practised clandestinely in communist times, these kinds of political strategies have now been given a free hand. The nationalistic regimes of these states are not afraid to mobilize their followers by propagating anti-Hungarian policies. The anti-Hungarian politics adopted in the neighbouring countries are still a success and Hungarians are still unable to defend themselves against the *indirect* strategy tactics commonly employed by these countries. This tactical approach towards Hungary is admirably illustrated in the following quotation which comes from the diary of the American general Harry Hill Bandholtz who headed the Entente mission in Budapest after the First World War:

13th November 1919. "Yesterday morning there appeared in the papers a notice from Roumanian Headquarters that they proposed to distribute large quantities of food to the inhabitants of Budapest. In characteristic Roumanian style, they broke into the food depôts belonging to the Hungarian government and distributed these supplies right and left, thereby completely upsetting the ration system of Budapest, but during the process being photographed as international philanthropists...they turned out some company kitchens, then robbed a near-by restaurant of food supplies and called together a lot of children in order to be photographed while feeding the poor. As no wood was handy, they got some newspapers, crammed them into the stove and, while they were burning, had a rapid photograph taken in order to complete the picture."[202]

Even Slovakia was not afraid of using ecological means to indirectly prolong the war. For the Slovaks, this opened up new ways of putting pressure on Hungary. It is incorrect to believe that the Hungarians were not aware of ways in which they could deploy indirect strategy to defend their national interests. During the era of dualism, the Hungarian elite had been the biggest supporters of the Austro-Hungarian Dual Monarchy. This was not because the Hungarians were so-called 'Danube-patriots' or irrepresible admirers of the Habsburg dynasty, but rather because Austria paid 70% of all the communal expenses incurred within the Dual Monarchy. As a result, money flowed into Hungary from Austria. Dualism was, therefore, in Hungary's interests.

During the inter-war years, there was head-on confrontation with the Trianon constellation. The Hungarians trusted that, on the basis of moral criteria, the 'civilized' world would see that the Hungarians of the Carpathian Basin were in an intolerable position. Emphasizing Hungarian cultural superiority, however, was ineffective. In international relations, it is power that counts and moral-cultural considerations are immaterial. Taking direct military action, like in the Second World War, was useless as well in the long-term. Today, taking direct military action to compensate for not having a strong army is impossible. Hungary will need to maintain strong defensive forces though, capable of combating possible aggression from neighbouring countries in a suitable way. The Hungarians do, however, have a number of other trump cards in their hands.

Post-communist Hungarian administrations have sought to flee from the Trianon constellation and to resolve Hungary's economic problems by attaching themselves to the EU and to NATO. It has sometimes been suggested that one need not bother with 'national' problems, because soon we shall have an American-like Europe with no distinct nations. This is, however, not supported by the facts. German unity, for example, was in the first place about reuniting East and West Germany and not about linking East Germany to the EU. Great Britain is the country generating most anti-European sentiment with its 'Euro scepticism' that is clearly gaining support and France has again started nuclear testing, just to assert its independence. The borders of a 'united' Europe can be felt and are visible. Sooner or later Hungary and Europe will, therefore, be confronted with the Trianon legacy and will be forced to think up solutions. If that does not happen, Hungary and Europe will have to find a way to take care of the millions of Hungarians who, in continually fleeing from the endless repeated ethnic cleansings reigned upon them, will ultimately be forced away from their native soil. With preventive policies, however, the situation should not come to this.

It has also been suggested that present day Hungary follows a policy that is designed to overcome the Trianon problem based on indirect strategy. Until now this strategy has proved to be completely counter-productive. For instance, the Hungarian constitution does not state that Hungarian is the country's official language which is unusual when one compares this to other European constitutions. The writers of the Hungarian constitution wanted to 'set a good example' for the Rumanians, Slovaks and Serbs by encouraging them to drop their nationalistic policy. The problem with such 'solutions' is that they tend to weaken Hungarian national consciousness. At the same time, it has become clear that Hungary's neighbours will make no concessions unless pressurized. The same applies to the generous law on minorities accepted by the Hungarian parliament. It was basically right of Hungary to introduce this bill, but if the underlying reason for introducing it was to 'set a good example' for neighbouring countries with Hungarian minorities then the effects will only prove to be counter-productive. The small minorities in Hungary will become unnecessarily upgraded and 'put on a par'. with Hungarian national communities. It is clear that the agressive expansionist politics adopted by Hungary's neighbours will only be ended and concessions will only be made to Hungarian national communities, if these countries are forced to do this.

Today, Hungary still holds on to notions of Lesser Hungarian particularism. Under communism, Hungary was unable to defend her national interests, because the ruling elite served the interests of a foreign power. With the Hungarian desire to become a member of the EU "as quickly as possible and without preconditions" Lesser Hungarian particularism has been given a new projection. If Hungary were to turn its back on Central Europe, this would not only be detrimental to the Carpathian Basin and to the nations living there because of, for instance, the huge numbers of refugees and the great stream of migrants this would precipitate, but it would also be detrimental to European integration as a whole. A 'fleeing' Hungary is no longer able to function as a stabilizing force and be an economic asset to the Carpathian Basin. Hungary would no longer be an integrative regional power able, together with Hungarian national communities, to strenghten cohesion in Central Europe and Hungary would no longer be able to fulfil its traditional role as a bridge between East and West. If Hungary once again wants to become a reliable hinge of Europe, then its potential will have to be exploited to the full and given a conscious geo-political slant that the West may possibly be able to support.

Global Hungarian potential

In the immediate future, Hungarian strategy will have to be based on the following spearheads: economic, political, social, cultural, demographic and defensive reinforcements and supporting the right that Hungarian national communities have to self-determination. To realize all these aims - while not in the possession of defence forces, natural assets and raw materials - Hungarians will have to start seeing themselves as a spiritual-cultural global community, or, as constituting a 'global village'. Hungary's economic prosperity and modernization will be decisive in the matter of creating chances for a stable and well-developed Carpathian Basin. But how should Hungary orient itself? The EU has become a gigantic economic power, because the individual member states have further developed the strong points which allowed them to dominate in the first place. Before Hungary is ready to integrate into the EU, its strong points will, therefore, also first have to be identified. The future does not lie in industrial and agricultural production, but rather in communication, information and computer technology, financial and other service industries and in the infrastructure that binds East to West. In innovating these new technologies the Hungarians may draw on their high standard of education in the sciences. The Hungarians have after all received twelve Nobel prizes, eleven of which went to researchers in the field of the sciences and they have been responsible for typical Hungarian inventions, such as, for instance, the ingenious Rubik's cube.[203] The Hungarians are, furthermore, an ambitious, hard-working and disciplined people. Hungarian brainpower has huge unknown potential that still needs to be tapped. Hungary will, therefore, need to invest in human resources and education.

Now that the communist regime has collapsed in Central Europe, the Hungarians have at last gained access to their own culture and history once again. In the first part of this book, I demonstrated how, through their culture, Hungarians are able to utilize their old collective fund of knowledge and such mental-moral imperatives as: integration, tolerance, the drive for freedom, a willingness to compromise and constitutionalism. I do not naively assume that in the international politics of the next century such mental-moral and cultural values will be more important than pure power politics even though the fall of communism has shown that mankind is moving towards a more political culture that also respects these values. In gaining renewed access to their own culture, traditions and history the Hungarians have discovered that they certainly do not stand alone. The Hungarians possess fruitful networks which may well, in the near future, be a positive political-economic asset.

Because of the changing power constellation in Central and Eastern Europe Hungary's relations with its neighbouring countries have not only become tense, but also have intensified and improved. The friendly relationship that exists with the Ukraine has already been outlined. The Ukrainians are interested in maintaining good contacts with Hungary, because for them Hungary is a window to the West. Friendship treaties were signed with the former Yugoslavian federal republics of Slovenia and Croatia bordering on Hungary, soon after these states had become independent. In their struggle against Greater Serbian aspirations both these new states obviously want to feel certain of peace on their northern borders with Hungary. As far as establishing the rights of the Hungarian minority living in the Mura region of northern Slovenian and the Slovenian minority in the Rába region of southern Hungary goes, Slovenia and Hungary signed an agreement on 6th November 1992 in the Slovenian capital of Ljubljana. This treaty guarantees to preserve the rights and identity of these minorities. The Croatian constitution of December 1990 evaluated the common Hungarian-Croatian past from 1091 until the time of the collapse of the Austro-Hungarian Dual Monarchy.

On the whole, the 825 year history of the Hungarian-Croatian confederation is viewed positively by the Croatian constitution, even when it comes to describing the events of 1848, the most sensitive issue in the common Hungarian-Croatian past, when the Croats sided with Austria against Hungary at the time when Hungary was fighting for independence. In sharp contrast to the positive way in which Hungarian-Croatian relations are viewed, criticism is now being levelled against the way in which former Yugoslavia came into being. Not all the details on this have yet come to light. In the Croatian constitution one can read about how in 1929 the Sabor, Croatia's parliament, never actually sanctioned the uniting of Croatia with Serbia and Montenegro within a Yugoslavian kingdom composed of Serbs, Croats and Slovenes.[204] Hungarian-Croatian relations are now so good that the old Hungarian royal free port of Fiume on the Adriatic coast, now known as Rijeka, constitutes a free trading zone with Hungary, just like in the past when Hungary was a kingdom. Goods may now be shipped to and from Hungary via Rijeka free of customs charges. Central European infrastructural connections and customs free zones are, thus, reverting to the way they once were.

Through the Roman Catholic Church, Hungarians maintain contacts with the Vatican and the Latin Catholic world and through their Hungarian Protestant connections they keep up their contacts with Protestants, notably of the Calvinistic denominations in the Anglo-Saxon world, Switzerland, the Netherlands and Scandinavia. These church ties are also very important to the large communities of Protestant and Catholic Hungarians living in Transylvania. The Vatican has agreed to the proposal that the Hungarian Catholic bishopric of Gyulafehérvár (Alba Julia) should revert to being an archbishopric once again. This archbishopric now falls directly under the Vatican, it no longer comes under the diocese of Bucharest. Though all the other Hungarian bishoprics in Transylvania still remain under Bucharest's authority the Hungarian Catholic community sees this step, on the part of the Vatican, as a recognition of Hungarian Catholic interests in Transylvania. The Catholic world now needs to turn its attention to the Hungarian Catholics of Moldavia in Rumania, the 200,000 Csango-Hungarians who are still being oppressed.

Perpetuating contacts with Calvinist church communities throughout the world is important, especially in the matter of strengthening the position of the Hungarian Calvinist Church in Transylvania. The Hungarian Reformed Church belongs to the World Association of Reformed Churches (the WARC) which, unlike the World Council of Churches, did protest heavily against the plans to destroy Hungarian villages and churches in Transylvania. In April 1995, the Hungarian Calvinist Church organized itself into a Hungarian Reformed World Synod under the auspices of the WARC. These Hungarian Calvinist connections provide some support for the Reformed Church's bishop, László Tőkés and his struggle to emancipate Hungarians in Transylvania.

Because of their early history, the Hungarians have contacts with a large number of cultures and peoples throughout Eurasia. Their 'links' are not only with the so-called Finno Ugric 'peoples' but also with the Turks, Tibetans, Japanese and Persians. This is being symbolized by the stupa that was recently consecrated in Hungary by the Dalai Lama. Most peoples of the Asian continent, such as, for instance, the Japanese, see the Hungarians as brothers. The Hungarians are therefore one step ahead where Japanese contacts are concerned and Japan is now a factor of enormous political and economic significance. The Tibetans are grateful to the Hungarians because it was the linguist Sándor (Alexander) Kőrösi Csoma (1784-Darjeeling 1842), who originated from a small village in Szeklerland, who was responsible for opening up their culture to Westerners. After having completed his studies at the University of Göttingen Kőrösi Csoma travelled to China in 1819 to study the Uigurs. Kőrösi Csoma was driven by the hypothesis that the Uigurs might be able to teach him something about the origins of the Hungarians. In fact the linguist never got as far as where the Uigurs lived, but he got stuck in Tibet where, in Tibetan monasteries and completely isolated from the outside world, he worked on a study of the old Tibetan language and culture. The result of all his efforts was the first ever description of Tibetan in the English language and the first ever Tibetan-English dictionary.

The Hungarian's early history gives them 'access' to China as well, a country which is certain to undergo enormous economic expansion in the next century. The Hungarian links with China have also been acknowledged in the West. On 8th February 1995, the *International Herald Tribune* reported that in 1986, in the Urumchi region of north-west China, Hungarian researchers carried out excavations in an old graveyard that contained the remains of people from a Turkish-speaking tribe, dating from 900 AD, the Ugars. The objects found there resembled objects found in Hungarian graves in the Carpathian Basin dating from the 9th and 10th centuries. Furthermore, the Hungarian expedition, led by the anthropologist István Kiszely, discovered that the Ugars, who live in the Urumchi region, knew more than seventy folks songs that were also familiar to the Hungarians.[205] Kiszely told me that, after the article had appeared in the above-mentioned American paper, the Hungarian Academy of Sciences decided that the research findings of his expedition to north-west China should be published in China as soon as possible. It was no coincidence that in 1995 the *International Herald Tribune* was the paper to carry reports of 'recent' discoveries creating links between China and a European nation. This American newspaper has a reputation for identifying and exactly registering political-economic changes in the world. It would appear that through their culture the Hungarians are at the centre of these changes. The 'Chinese' link is just one of the secrets to be disclosed in the future related the early history of the Hungarians.

Now that the Soviet Union has disintegrated the geo-ethnic distribution of the Russians is rather similar to that of the Hungarians. Today, there are huge communities of Russians living outside of the Russian coreland. This means that when it comes to the Hungarian question the Russians may be regarded as potential allies. In April 1994, Alekzij II, the patriarch of Moscow and of all Russians, paid a visit to Hungary and met with top ranking political and religious functionaries. In an appeal made to the Hungarian people, he confessed that his fellow countrymen were wrong to have treated the Hungarians as they did in 1956. He also met Sándor Csoóri, chairman of the World Federation of Hungarians. Alekzij II told Csoóri that many of his spiritual children now live outside Russia's borders and that he, therefore, well understood the predicament of the Hungarian national communities.

In this century, Hungarian history has been changeable to say the least with the result that the Hungarians have become dispersed throughout more than forty different countries. Many Hungarians left their fatherland because of the First and Second World Wars, because of the Hungarian uprising in 1956 when around 200,000 young Hungarians fled the country and because of nationalistic oppression in the Hungarian populated areas of the successor states. The Hungarians have found themselves in a situation not unlike that of certain other national and religious groups, such as the Jews and Armenians who also live in big diasporas. The Hungarian fate has not had purely negative consequences. Everywhere in the world the Hungarian global community has set up support points aimed at representing the Hungarians and their culture. In practice, this global network has functioned well like for example when an international protest was organized against violating the human rights of Hungarian national communities. It is striking how many Hungarians of the diaspora have become prominent scientists and politicians. In the autumn of 1994, the Republican politician George Pataki was elected governor of New York State, the biggest American state. Governor Pataki, a third generation Hungarian American, wrote in a letter addressed to the World Federation of Hungarians that one of the reasons for his electoral success was the support received from Hungarians in the state where the Hungarian ratio is high.

For the Hungarians this world-wide distribution is a relatively new situation in their history, but in this age of information technology the possibilities open to them are endless. There are two organizations holding the Hungarians together in their 'global village': the World Federation of Hungarians, which has one million members and the Hungarian Reformed Church World Synod already mentioned above. At present, the World

Federation of Hungarians is busy developing a computer network system that should provide the basis for a *global Hungarian on-line-electronic-village*. The possibilities for distributing and collecting information through Hungarian contacts are indeed great. Because they are also so well represented everywhere else throughout Central Europe the Hungarians are in a good position for setting up data file bases on Central Europe. Below are some good examples to illustrate this. In Central and Eastern Europe, Hungarians are represented in the six national parliaments of Budapest, Zagreb, Belgrade, Bucharest, Kiev and Bratislava. With a mere press of a button legal information may be called up in Hungarian in any one of these countries. Hungarian language newspapers are available in many Central and Eastern European countries. With Hungarian one can, therefore, cover the whole Central European region. Outside of this region there are new challenging possibilities as well. The Hungarian satellite channel *Danube T.V.* can be received all round the world. By contacting Hungarian societies throughout the diaspora, information may be instantly gained on political, economic and cultural events elsewhere in the world. This might well give the Hungarian community a certain prominence in the world in the next century. The radiating of the positive values of Hungarian culture might then become globally significant. Before the potential of the geographical distribution, the 'human resources' and brainpower, the moral-cultural values and the contacts being developed all over the world between all kinds of regions and cultures, can be fully exploited a struggle for emancipation has to be fought in the Carpathian Basin that will, of course, have to be based on 'Realpolitik' and power.

Greater Hungarian strategy

Hungary's present elite, which evolved during the communist era, is not suited to realizing a programme that has as its objective the restoration of Hungary to its former glory as Europe's 'hinge' and which aims at enabling the global

Hungarian community to become a positive force on a world scale. The only kind of elite suited to such a role is one that can think and deal freely. On the basis of what political doctrines can Hungarian politics be shaped in the future?

(1) *Hungary must follow the guiding principles laid down by count István Széchenyi*

Hungary must become a modern nation that is democratically, economically and culturally strong and which has the character of a social constitutional state. It must be a nation based on its own thousand-year old pluriform Hungarian culture and on its long constitutional tradition. One of the most important facets of the new Hungary will have to be economic power. In developing a powerful economy, the important components are human resources, infrastructure, distribution centres and financial services. Because Hungary is situated centrally in Europe, the Carpathian Basin can once again be turned into an economic link between East and West.

(2) *Hungarian foreign politics must gain priority over domestic political questions*

In view of the fact that Hungary is in a rather vulnerable position, because it is partly surrounded by hostile countries that are not prepared to reach settlements by compromising in any way, Hungary cannot take the risk of functioning as a Central European experimental station in domestic politics, social affairs or in any other areas. Foreign policy must be given absolute priority over and above other government matters. This also means that the circumstances for supporting and executing foreign politics should not be neglected. For instance, Hungarian defence must not be reduced on the grounds that it is too expensive and the Hungarian military tradition must once again be given its rightful place in society. Obviously, it must not be reinstated for the purposes of agression, but rather on the grounds of needing a legitimate self-defence response mechanism and to support international peace operations.

(3) Hungary should exercise an independent and self-conscious foreign policy

For centuries, it has not been possible for Hungary to exercise an independent foreign policy. Since the battle of Mohács (1526), Hungary has always been under the wing of greater powers and used to unilaterally orient itself to a greater centre of power. One of the reasons why the Treaty of Trianon (1920) hit the Hungarians so hard was, because up until the time of the First World War Hungary, as part of the Dual Monarchy, had been almost exclusively oriented towards Vienna and had built up hardly any political connections with the West. It is a mistake that must not be repeated. Hungary must adopt a multi-tracked foreign policy. In the geo-political situation of the present, it would be incorrect to aim at being only one-sidedly oriented to the West. It would be better if, alongside of its affiliations to the West, Hungary also sought to establish good relations with Russia, the Middle East and the Far East. If they want to build up meaningful contacts with these regions, the Hungarians do already have quite a few advantages.

The Hungarians can easily integrate into the West, because of their cultural-historical ties, their shared Christian norms and values, their geographical position and the economic cross connections that have been developing rapidly since 1989. As far as Russia is concerned, Hungary can easily build up ties, because of its geographical situation, because of economic interests - the KGB, the Russian intelligence service is one of the biggest investors in Hungary - and because of the fact that, like Hungarians, many Russians now live outside their own heartland. Another important point is that, on the whole, Russians look up to Hugarians. Since the Hungarian uprising of 1956 and because of the leading role taken by Hungarians in the changes of 1989 the Russians have come to respect the Hungarians. This was also reflected in the map of Europe drawn up by the Russian aggressive extreme nationalist Vladimir Zjirinovski. According to Zjirinovski, Hungary might be justified in taking Transylvania away from Rumania.[206] Hungary has access to the Far East because of cultural-historical links that are now being rapidly exposed. Hungarians will, therefore, easily be able to form ties with countries in the Far East such as Korea, China and Japan, all of which will expand rapidly during the course of the next century. Conversely, such countries as these will be interested in investing in Hungary in the future because of its 'neutral' status as a region surrounded by Slavic, Germanic and Latin peoples.

(4) Hungary should take the lead when it comes to the matter of reconstructing the Carpathian Basin

Hungary must work on restoring the Carpathian Basin, which is a perfectly balanced geographical, economic and climatological entity. If the Carpathian Basin becomes a strong and independent region offering no threat to other countries it will be important to both the West and East. Such a stable entity will also be militarily-strategically easier to defend and is, thus, preferable for reasons of security. Regenerating old cultural, economic and human ties and networks is in the best interests of all the peoples living in the Carpathian Basin. A number of nations there, such as the Croats and Slovenes, have started re-evaluating the history of Central Europe and their own history, since the wall fell and have started ridding themselves of manipulative, falsifying and distorting influences. It is a step in the right direction. The Slovaks and Rumanians of Transylvania have not yet reached that stage.

The Slovaks are currently still on an anti-Hungarian political course and oriented predominantly to the Byzantine East. The preamble to the Slovak constitution of 3rd September 1992 states that the Slovak people accept the spiritual legacy of the Orthodox apostles Cyril and Method. What exactly this Orthodox Byzantine myth of the Slovaks means in the light of the thousand year long Hungarian-Slovak co-existence is completely unclear. The alleged legacy of the Orthodox apostles Cyril and Method and the Great Moravian Empire abberation cannot replace this. If Slovakia wants to find its rightful place in Central Europe and become a fully accepted nation then it will have to stop misusing history for nationalistic ends. The same applies to the Rumanians who cling to their Daco-Roman myth. It is the moral duty and obligation of Hungarians to refute such myths, not only in the interest of human and historical dignity, but also for these nations themselves. The Slovaks and Rumanians will have to accept their own history and roots, if they are to become fully fledged nations. On 4th May 1995 Hungarian intellectuals from the Carpathian Basin made a collective appeal to the neighbouring peoples of the region during the *IV. Workshop on Bilingualism and Cultural Ecology* held at the Agricultural University of Gödöllő. In this appeal, it was argued that a 'new' Carpathian Basin should be created free of the present cultural-ecological war that is ruining the culture and environment of the Carpathian Basin and is detrimental to all the peoples in the region.

(5) Hungarian foreign policy must be 'Realpolitik', just like that adopted by every other state

National interest should be the issue underlying Hungarian foreign policy. Hungary should only support the interests of the West and the EU insofar as they correspond to Hungary's interests.

With respect to the neighbouring countries that oppress Hungarian national communities and employ expansionistic politics towards Hungary the only suitable kind of political approach is to adopt an offensive strategy instead of signing empty treaties aimed only at confirming the status quo by Hungary for the umpteenth time. As is the custom in international relations, there will have to be means of pressure to push back this expansionism directed at the Hungarian heart of the Carpathian Basin. Such pressure politics will not of course involve direct military confrontation, but the setting up of political and economic 'levers'.

The only kind of politics that will work with *aggressive* Slovakia is the politics of containment and encirclement. Hungary must start co-operating more closely with Slovakia's neighbouring countries of Poland, the Czech Republic, Austria and the Ukraine in order to isolate Slovakia. What is, furthermore, important is that Slovakia is included in Central Europe's economic network. It was, therefore, a good move on the part of the Antall administration to purchase Interbanka, the Prague bank which has a branch in Bratislava. If necessary the economic lever can always be brought down.

An *aggressive* Rumania must be dealt with in the same way as an aggressive Slovakia, namely by being contained and encircled. Hungary can bring pressure to bear on Rumania by co-operating with the powerful neighbouring countries with which it lives in discord. Rumania has territorial claims directed at the Ukraine and long-term plans to establish unity with independent Moldavia (Moldova). This will certainly meet with resistance from Russia, which will not tolerate the fact that within its sphere of influence a Greater Rumania might emerge that could operate as a bridgehead for other major European powers such as France. In the eastern region of Moldova, Russians and Ukrainians have already proclaimed the existence of the Dniester Republic. The independence of this republic is safeguarded by the presence of the Russian army. In this way, Russia has effectively defined the borders of Rumania for the future. Both Russia and the Ukraine are Hungary's allies, when it comes to matters concerning Rumania. The same goes for Bulgaria, which flanks the southern side of Rumania where Rumania is also in territorial conflict because of Dobrudja that has been annexed by the Rumanians.

Sometimes there has been doubt as to whether Rumania that extends over the regions of Wallachia, Moldavia and Transylvania can be regarded as one and the same nation. Culturally and historically there are rather many differences between the Rumanians of Transylvania and the Rumanians of Old Rumania. Those living in Transylvania have been influenced by Western Christian culture through Hungary and their own Rumanian Uniate Church, while the Rumanians of Old Rumania have been much more influenced by the Eastern Byzantine tradition. As was particularly clearly illustrated by the distribution of the results of the presidential election of 20th May 1990, this divided historical development

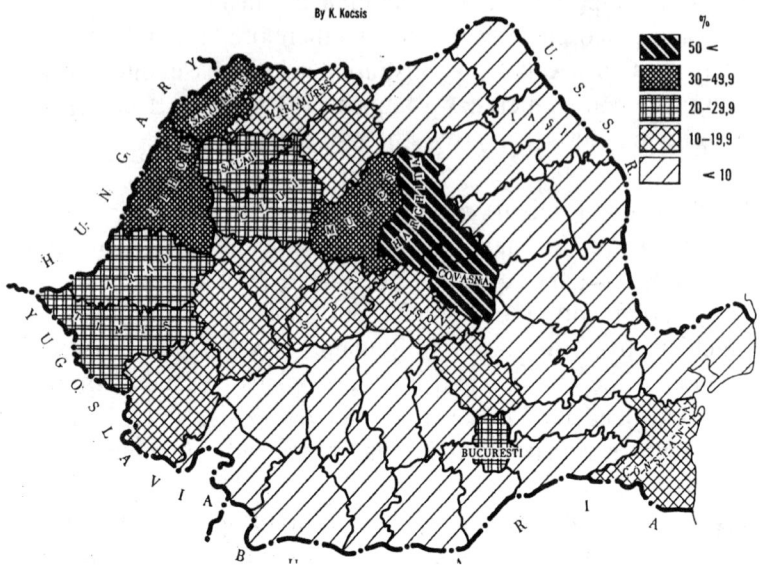

RATIO OF THE VALIDATED VOTES GIVEN FOR THE CANDIDATES OF THE OPPOSITION (R. CÂMPEANU AND I. RAȚIU) ON THE PRESIDENT ELECTIONS IN RUMANIA ON 20.05.1990

corresponds exactly with the natural geographical division existing within Central Europe in the form of the range of mountains known as the Carpathians.

The map shows that the eastern part of Rumania, historic Rumania, reflects more or less equal distribution, that is to say, a high score for the ex-communist Iliescu. There was a sharp contrast with the results in western Transylvania, where the opposition candidates did considerably better. The distribution of the election result would, therefore, indicate that regional-historic factors had much more influence than national-ethnic factors. The way in which Transylvanian Rumanians voted was much closer to the way that Transylvanian Hungarians - who did not have a candidate of their own - voted than to the way in which the ethnically connected Rumanians of Old Rumania voted. The economic interweaving of Hungary and Transylvania will reinforce the Transylvanian 'separatist' tendencies that will highlight internal Rumanian ethnic differences. It is not inconceivable that in Rumania a similar process will take place as has taken place in Italy where, through federalization the wealthier north has tried to shake itself free of the poorer south. It would seem fair to assume that the inherent cultural-historic realities are deep-rooted. Because of the increasing regionalization taking place in Rumania, Hungary will be able to develop a buffer against the expansionism radiating from Bucharest. The only way in which Rumania could protect itself from Hungary's influence in the matter of internal regionalization would be by hermetically sealing itself off from the outside world. This would be like placing a time bomb under the country's social-economic structure which might turn out to be catastrophic.

As far as the containment of Serbia goes, encirclement politics would not be the best option. Because of the war with Croatia and Bosnia-Herzegovina, western access to the West will remain blocked for a long time to come. Hungary has, thus, become Serbia's window to the West, which puts it in a powerful position where Serbia is concerned. In order to prevent Serbia's expansion politics from continuing at the expense of the Hungarians, Hungary will have to make use of Russia's influence on Serbia. This political line was first laid down in a treaty signed between Hungary and Russia on 11th November 1992 in Budapest on the rights of national or ethnic, religious and linguistic minorities. With this treaty Hungary succeeded in breaking down the Trianon-coalition between Russia, France and Great Britain existing within the international contact group for ex-Yugoslavia. It is partly thanks to this treaty with Russia and partly thanks to the perseverance and tact of the Vojvodina-Hungarians themselves that the Hungarian community in Lesser Yugoslavia did not fall victim to the massive ethnic cleansing conducted by the Serbs. Had Western politicians, such as Lord Carrington been the only decisive factor, the Hungarians of the Southern Lands would have been wiped out long ago. It is true that such politicians have done little to free the Hungarians and also the Albanians of Lesser Yugoslavia from the deplorable situation in which they have found themselves.

In the light of the conflict between Russia and Rumania the joint Russian-Hungarian treaty on minority rights came to be regarded as a threat. President Iliescu criticized the treaty saying that he found it dangerous and not in line with internationally recognized norms on minorities. To counteract this Russian-Hungarian axis the Rumanian media declared itself in favour of establishing a new Little Entente with Slovakia and Serbia along the lines of the anti-Hungarian alliance set up in the inter-war years between Yugoslavia, Czechoslovakia and Rumania.[207] It will be difficult to introduce such a Little Entente, because it will be in Russia's interests to put moderate pressure on Serbia on Hungary's behalf.

As far as the Ukraine is concerned, it will be best for Hungary to continue the policy of partnership and co-operation. Using peaceful and economic means Hungarian foreign policy will have to be aimed at achieving autonomy for the Hungarians of Subcarpathia and special status for Subcarpathia by, for instance, insisting upon creating a free trade zone. The arguments, notably the economic ones, that Hungary can produce for the Ukrainians are impressive. The Ukraine can never expect to become a member of the EU, but Hungary's membership is inevitable. In exchange for securing autonomy for the Hungarian national community, Hungary could offer to champion Ukrainian interests in its future capacity as a member of the EU.

(6) Hungary will have to support the Hungarian national communities in their struggle for the right to self-determination

Hungary must not revert to pursuing revisionistic politics, neither must it give up the fight until the Hungarian national communities are able to enjoy autonomy safeguarded by the great powers of the US, Russia, France and Great Britain. Hungary will have to push back the expansionistic policy that has been pursued since Trianon at the expense of the Hungarians where the primary aim was to destroy Hungarian national communities and blackmail Hungary. Supporting self-determination and autonomy for Hungarian national communities, therefore, increases Hungarian security. Together with her natural 'allies', the Hungarian communities, Hungary will have to work on reconstructing the Carpathian Basin. If, instead of relying on the Hungarian national communities Hungary depends on the nationalistic-expansionistic forces existing within its neighbouring countries, the Carpathian Basin will turn into a European disaster area.

The Hungarian national communities will have to follow their own course. They will have to find peaceful and democratic ways and means of effecting their emancipation struggle for self-determination and equality. In this struggle the Hungarian national communities will have to be chiefly self-reliant. All they can do is to keep on reminding the European and mondial forums of their grievances until these are universally recognized. Because of the fact that in recent years different post-communist Hungarian administrations have given higher priority to integrating into the EU and NATO - hence displaying a lack of realism - than to the situation of the Hungarian national communities, these communities will have to adopt an independent foreign policy. This has already been demonstrated well by the Hungarian Christian Democratic Movement in Slovakia which, by becoming a member of the European organization of Christian Democratic parties successfully opened up its own political and information channels. Hungarian national communities can only possibly hope for the support and sympathy of international public opinion, if they are prepared to carry out active politics in their own interests and make sacrifices. Where necessary the Hungarian diaspora will be prepared to help the Hungarian national communities in their endeavours.

A consequence of Hungary's *Einzelgang, it* might well be that new Hungarian nations emerge in Central Europe. It is the contention of the Transylvanian Hungarians that all the ingredients needed to create a nation are present. The Hungarian community in Transylvania is almost 2.5 million strong and has enormous intellectual potential at its disposal, structures and institutions of its own and even its own traditions, when it comes to political independence. The Szekler-Hungarians are politically independently aware and Transylvania has been an independent state. At present, the appeals for the formation of an independent Transylvanian nation are weak, but as the struggle for autonomy gets under way these pleas will strengthen. It might even be in Bucharest's best interests to carefully start supporting such separatist Hungarian tendencies. In his 1995 report (Nagyvárad, 1995) on the position of the Transylvanian Hungarians, Zsolt Mester wrote the following: "If the Transylvanian Hungarians keep on being rejected by their mother country then a process will be started that will ultimately result in the emergence of a new 'Transylvanian-Hungarian nation'. Culturally, such a nation will be Hungarian, but it will also have its own unique characteristics and it will become ever more different from Hungary. Thus, the resultant Transylvanian-Hungarian community will not only be a partner-nation for the Rumanians, but also for the Hungarians of the Danube-Tisza region. The German-Austrian relationship might be cited as analogous."

If internal regionalization continues within Rumania, possibly boosted by the economic attraction that Hungary has for Transylvania, and if the Transylvanian Hungarians start to form a nation of their own partly because of the dismissive attitude adopted by Hungary towards them and their problems, then it is conceivable that a new Transylvanian nation might emerge that would be composed of Rumanians, Hungarians and other nationalities that have lived in the region for a long time. This would explain why the Bucharest regime encourages the activities of extreme nationalists who create discord between Transylvania's native Rumanians and Hungarians. Until now these activities have stood in the way of effective dialogue between Transylvania's Rumanians and Hungarians which might have led to the establishment of common interests against centralized power in Bucharest.

The international perspective

Now that the Second World War is behind us for good the consequences of the system drawn up in Versailles that deeply influenced all the political and ideological structures of this century, are becoming visible. As far as international public opinion is concerned ever more people are coming to the conclusion that the injustices of Trianon should be questioned and that Central Europe should be given a new place within Europe. The well-known French commentator, Thomas Schreiber, recently wrote in an article that Georges Clemenceau and his friends "had believed that in creating the successor states and in annexing three and a half million Hungarians the nationality questions in the region might be resolved. But what happened was exactly the opposite. The folly of the Trianon 'recipe', of blindly creating boundaries is now coming to the surface. During his lifetime one particular inhabitant of Kassa (Košice) found that he had been a citizen of five different states and the Hungarian writer Sándor Gál and his grandmother, aged respectively 9 and 82 years of age, were both proclaimed to be war criminals."

The Dutch researcher, J.W. van der Meulen of the Netherlands Institute of International Relations 'Clingendael', concluded that Eastern European peoples' right to self-determination might not be *a priori* refused.[208] Van der Meulen observed that in the West there is resistance to introducing and supporting concepts such as 'collective rights for ethnic minorities', because such concepts cannot be reconciled with the constitution of Western democracies. Hence his conclusion that "proposals to allow ethnic groups to operate as legal entities conflict so sharply with the democratic norms that they might just as well be immediately dropped." (p.41). Van der Meulen is also sceptical about the general feasibility of achieving territorial or other kinds of autonomy for national communities. When it becomes apparent that territorial or personal autonomy provides no workable solution, then it seems to Van der Meulen that border corrections and border changes are the only solution.

According to Van der Meulen, applying the right to self-determination must be restricted by a few conditions, such as, for instance, liberating a national community from an oppressor state. It was a point of view that was also shared by the Dutch Christian Democratic Party (CDA) which stated, in 1992, that: "When a national community forms part of a bigger state body in which another national group dominates, when there is no guaranteeing that an identity may be preserved when the state can only remain intact by oppression and the violation of human rights and when those involved have been able to express their wishes democratically then the right to self-determination must be able to lead to constitutional independence, to liberation or to joining up with another state" (p.40). The circumstances surrounding the Hungarian national communities of Central Europe, as sketched in part two, match this criterium perfectly. In view of the systematic oppression to which these communities have been subjected applying and honouring the right to self-determination is the only way of securing freedom. Van der Meulen contends that it is also important to look at the way in which the borders that are to be changed came into being in the first place. "If the borders were established before the right to self-determination applied, like in the nineteenth century, then the decision made could turn out to be different from the one made about borders decided upon by external powers that have contravened the then already applicable rights to self-determination. The latter situation was the case with the borders of Hungary after the First World War" (p.40).

Europe now takes into consideration the possibility of border changes. When former Yugoslavia crumbled, the Swiss newspaper *Neue Zürcher Zeitung* headed one of its articles "On the road to new borders in Eastern Europe."[209] In this influential Swiss paper, it was argued that "maintaining borders may never be a goal in itself, but only a way of seeking to keep the peace. The original claim about the inviolability of borders put forward by the Soviets was aimed at the OSCE in order to retain their territory fought for in 1945. The conference did not, however, exclude *peaceful* border revisions." Raising the issue of peaceful border revision is, of course, not a matter of specific Hungarian interest, but rather one that opens the possibility to the reconstruction of Central Europe.

Central Europe is currently faced by the following problems: (1) small nations wrestling with nationality issues, (2) the small nations of Central Europe are themselves too weak to successfully counteract German and Russian expansion drives in the region and (3) because of lack of co-operation in economic areas, limitations where free trade and traffic are concerned and, in some states, because of investing in nationalistic programmes aimed at homogenizing and anti-Hungarian ethnocide the prospects of economic revival are bleak. Sooner or later, the EU and NATO will be forced to deal with these unresolved problems. Problems (1) and (2) relate to security and stability in Central Europe and are, therefore, important to Western Europe. Neither the EU nor NATO will be able to resolve the national and ethnic conflicts existing within Central Europe. If any of the Central European nations joins NATO this will weaken the organization, because all the mutual conflicts will be brought in and because Russia will grow suspicious if the West expands towards the East. Problem (3) relating to the lack of economic growth in the region, will also be disadvantageous to Europe. Western Europe cannot have an explosive social-economic situation in young developing democracies on its periphery. But bear in mind that this periphery is in the middle of the European continent.

For a number of publicists the solution to this collection of almost irresolvable problems lies in restoring Central Europe to its former state, to the dimensions and composition of the former Habsburg Empire.[210] Such a conglomeration of states, which to my mind would also be preferable, would be strong enough to counterbalance Russia and Germany politically. Because of the fact that a politically and economically powerful Central Europe does not need to belong to NATO, it would, thus, not form a threat to Russia. Having open borders in the region could be of help in solving the nationality problems and in improving economic and trade relations in the region. What might a renewed Central Europe look like?

The Hungarian political scientist, Gusztáv Molnár, sees possibilities for realizing Central European integration on a regional scale.[20] The sovereign states situated on the territory of the former Habsburg Empire could form a Central European confederation consisting of Croatia, Slovenia, Hungary, Austria, the Czech Republic and Slovakia. As a consequence, these states would have to give up part of their national sovereignity. When it comes to the matter of resolving the Hungarian question, a small Central European confederation would also offer possibilities because Molnár claims, it is unlikely that the Hungarian national communities, which have lived separated from Hungary since Trianon and have been through different historical and emotional developments, could possibly be simply reintegrated into the Hungarian nation state.

The falling apart of Yugoslavia has made it crystal clear that the fractures in political civilization and the continuity of the existing judicial system are stronger than the supposed homogeneity of linguistic nations where the various parts have been through totally different historical and cultural developments. It is simply impossible to merge together into one single state regions with a Western Christian culture and regions that belong to the Eastern Christian culture. Should such a small Central European confederation adhering to Western Christian culture come about then regions that were once also a part of the Western Christian sphere of influence, but which fell under Eastern Christian rule after the First World War, including Subcarpathia, Transylvania and Vojvodina would once again be able to join Central Europe. For the Hungarians, this would be extremely important. Hungary should, thus, support the political aims of the Subcarpathian Ruthenians, the Transylvanian Rumanians and the Serbs of Vojvodina all of whom would certainly be interested in developing economic and cultural ties with the Central European confederation in their struggle against Ukrainian, Rumanian and Serbian nationalists. These nationalists are already conducting a preventive campaign against the Subcarpathian Ruthenians, the Rumanians of Transylvania and the Serbs of Vojvodina in which they are accused of treason against the state. Ultimately, much will depend on the outcome of these struggles between Ukrainians and Ruthenians and amongst Rumanians and Serbs whether the Ukraine, Rumania and Serbia, in their entirity, will seek alliance with Europe.

The autonomy of Subcarpathia, Transylvania and Vojvodina will also depend on Russia which, it would seem, has special vested interests in the Ukraine, Rumania and Serbia. It is probable that Russia will support the autonomy of these regions as long as it receives a guarantee that Subcarpathia, Transylvania and Vojvodina will not be used as bridgeheads for anti-Russian expansion. In such a case, it might be possible to create a buffer zone between the Western Christian and the Eastern Christian spheres of influence in south-east Central Europe that would surround Hungary like a protective skin. Redefining Europe in terms of Western and Eastern Christian spheres of influence and marking a buffer zone is, therefore, my answer to the problem posed by Hugh Seton Watson *'What is Europe, Where is Europe?'* discussed at the beginning of this book. With a buffer zone there would be the guarantee that the Western and Eastern Christian cultural areas would no longer be able to expand at one another's expense as has been the case in previous centuries. Thanks to Trianon, Orthodox Christianity has seen westward expansion during the past 75 years at the expense of Western Christian cultural areas. The Hungarians were, and still are, the victims of this expansion. If a buffer zone is introduced between the Western and Eastern Christian spheres of influence, then this might help Europe to regain its old shine that has been dulled during the course of this century. Only when such a buffer zone is introduced can Western and Eastern Christianity begin working together again in cultural, economic, political and other areas. Only then will Europe, free of internal tensions, be able to compete with other continents and world powers in order to secure a prominent position in the world for itself.

NOTES

1 Hugh Seton-Watson, What is Europe, Where is Europe? From Mystique to Politique, in George Schöpflin (ed), *In Search of Central Europe*, London, 1989, 30-46.

2 See Bruno Naarden, *Socialist Europe and Revolutionary Russia: Preception and Prejudice, 1848-1923*, Glasgow, 1992, Chpt. 1.

3 Stephen Borsody, *The New Central Europe*, New York, 1993, xiv, 67.

4 In this chapter, I shall base my conclusions on the following studies on Western images and national Hungarian stereotypes: Sándor Eckhardt, *A magyarság külföldi arcképe*, in: Gyula Szekfü, *Mi a magyar?*, Budapest, 1939 reprinted Budapest, 1992, 87-137; Kálmán Benda, *A törökkor német ujságirodalma*, a XV-XVII. századi német hírlapok magyar vonatkozásainak forráskritikájához, Budapest, 1942; Béla Köpeczi, *Magyarország a kereszténység ellensége*, a Thököly-felkelés az európai közvéleményben, Budapest, 1976; articles in Rákóczi-tanulmányok, B. Köpeczi, L. Hopp and A.R. Várkonyi (eds), Budapest, 1980; in particular Béla Köpeczi's *Rákóczi külpolitikája és a szabadságharc nemzetközi jelentősége*, 205-229; and Yves de Daruvar, *The Tragic Fate of Hungary*, a Country Carved-up Alive at Trianon, USA, second edition, translation of Le destin dramatique de la Hongrie, Paris, 1971; György Gömöri, *Angol-magyar kapcsolatok a XVI-XVII. században*, Budapest, 1989; György Gömöri, *Erdélyiek és angolok*, Budapest, 1990; Stephen Borsody, *The New Central Europe*, New York, 1993; György Gömöri, *Angol és skót utazók a régi Magyarországon 1542-1737*, Budapest, 1994 and Géza Jeszenszky, *Az elveszett presztízs, Magyarország megítélésének megváltozása Nagy-Britanniában 1914-1918*, Budapest, 1994

5 See Szabolcs de Vajay, *Der Eintritt des ungarischen Stämmenbundes in die europäischen Geschichte*, Mainz., 1968.

6 *Larousse Encyclopedia of Ancient & Medieval History*, Marcel Dunan (ed), London, 281. See Johannes Duft and Tibor Missura Sipos, *Hungarians in Sankt Gallen*, St. Gallen, 1992 for a description based on medieval sources of the plunderings carried out in the monastery of St. Gall in 926

7 Eckhardt, 91

8 Cited by C.A. Macartney, Britain and Eastern Europe, in Francis S. Wagner (ed), *Toward a New Central Europe*, Florida, 1970, 53.

9   See Mark Imre Major, *American Hungarian Relations 1918 1944*, Florida, 1974, 114-116.

10 Benda, 61

11 See for the positive and negative images of the uprising led by Imre Thököly, Béla Köpeczi, 1976. For Western images and stereotypes of the War of Independence led by Ferenc Rákóczi II see the articles in *Rákóczi-tanulmányok*, B. Köpeczi, L. Hopp and A.R. Várkonyi (eds), 1980; and for the negative images of Gábor Bethlen in British texts, Gömöri, 1989, 60-66

12 C.A. Macartney, 53

13 See for these arguments the study of the Marxist historian István Diószegi entitled *A magyar külpolitika útjai*, 1984, 214-218

14 In Yves de Daruvar, 54

15 See, for instance, the pamphlet *Détruisez l'Autriche-Hongrie! Le martyre des Tchécho-Slovaques a travers l'histoire*, Paris, 1916 written during the First World War by Eduard Benes

16 See Stephen Borsody, *State- and Nation-building in Central Europe*: the Origins of the Hungarian Problem, in Stephen Borsody (ed), *The Hungarians: A Divided Nation*, New Haven, 1988, 13

17 See Géza Jeszenszky, The Correspondence of Oszkár Jászi and R.W. Seton-Watson before World War I, in *Acta Historica Academiae Scientiarum Hungaricae* 26, Budapest, 1980, 437-445

18 Géza Jeszenszky, 1994, chapter one.

19 Cited in Hugh Seton-Watson, *R.W. Seton-Watson and the Trianon Settlement*, in B.K. Király, P. Pastor and I. Sanders (eds), War and Society in East Central Europe Vol. VI, Essays on World War I: Total War and Peacemaking, A Case Study on Trianon, New York, 1982, 3-15, 3

20 Cited by Hugh Seton-Watson, 1982, 6

21 See Bertrand Auerbach, *Les races et les nationalités en Autriche-Hongrie*, Paris, 1898, 311

22 As a child Harold Nicolson lived in Budapest for four years with his parents after his father, Arthur Nicolson, was appointed British

ambassador to Hungary in 1888. In his excellent book *Budapest 1900,* John Lukács wonders why it was that the Nicolsons disliked Budapest. See John Lukács, *Budapest 1900*: a historical portrait of a city and its culture, New York, 1988, Chpt. 2

23 Harold Nicolson, *Peacemaking 1919,* New Yok, 1933, 34

24 Count Carlo Sforza, *Makers of Modern Europe,* Portraits and Personal Impressions and Recollections, Indianapolis, 1928, Chapter VI, 66-78

25 Henry Bogdan, *From Warsaw to Sofia,* A History of Eastern Europe, Santa Fe, 1989, 150

26 Sforza, 69

27 Sforza, 68

28 Sforza, 70

29 Sforza, 72

30 Sforza, 70

31 Sforza, 66

32 Lukács, 1988

33 *Undiplomatic Diary,* by the American Member of the Inter-Allied Military Mission to Hungary 1919-1920 Maj. Gen. Harry Hill Bandholtz, USA, Fritz-Konrad Krüger (ed), New York, 1933, 362

34 See Ignác Romsics, *Bethlen István,* Budapest, 1991, 181-183

35 See for a similar interpretation István Bibó, *A mai külföld szemlélete a magyarságról,* 1936, in: válogatott tanulmányok 1935-1944, Budapest, 1986, 155

36 See De Daruvar, 178-179

37 See John Flourney Montgomery, *Hungary, the Unwilling Satellite,* New York, 1947

38 Montgomery, Chpt. 2.4

39 See Raul Hilberg, *The Destruction of the European Jews,* New York, 1985, 796-797

40 See on the end of the Second World War and on the persecu tion of the Jews in Hungary Perry Pierik, *Hungary 1944-1945, The Forgotten Tragedy*, Nieuwegein, 1996

41 See for more details the authoritative work on the Hungarian army during the Second World War by the Swiss-Hungarian historian Péter Gosztonyi, *A magyar honvédség a második világ háboruban*, Budapest, 1992, 152-155

42 Daniel Patrick Moynihan, *Pandeamonium*, Etnicity in International Politics, Oxford, 1993, 72

43 Előd Kincses, *Black Spring*, Budapest-München, 1992

44 Anthony D. Smith, *National Identity*, New York, 1991

45 Stephen Borsody, *The Hungarians: A Divided Nation*, New Haven, 1988

46 *Erdély népessége, anyanyelvi összetételének alakulása*, Statisztikai Szemle, October 1991

47 Endre Jónás, *A romániai magyarság és a Statisztikai Hivatal hamis adatai*, Kapu, 1992, nr. 12

48 K. Kocsis-E. Hodosi, *Magyarok a határainkon túl*, Tankönyv kiadó, Budapest, 1991

49 Count István Széchenyi, *Levél az akadémiához*, Felsődöbling No. 163, 6th November 1858

50 Thomas S. Kuhn, *The Structure of Scientific Revolutions*, Chigago, 1970

51 Frits Staal, *Universals*, Studies in Indian Logic and Linguistics, Chigago, 1988

52 László Götz, *Keleten kél a nap*, Budapest, 1991

53 Björn Collinder, *Comparative Grammar of the Uralic Languages*, Uppsala, 1960

54 Péter Hajdu, *Finnugor népek és nyelvek*, Budapest, 1962

55 Zsigmond Varga, *Ötezer év távlatából*, Debrecen, 1942; Kálmán Gosztonyi, *Dictionaire D'etymologie Sumerienne et Grammaire*, Sorbonne, Paris, 1975

56 Gyula Décsy, *Einführung in die Finnisch-Ugrische Sprachwissenschaft*, Wiesbaden, 1965

57 P. Hajdu-P.Domokos, *Uráli nyelvrokonaink*, Budapest, 1978, 127-128.

58 Péter Domokos, *Uralisztikai olvasókönyv*, Budapest, 1977

59 Compare the papers in: Eric Hobsbawm and Terence Ranger (eds), *The Invention of Tradition*, Cambridge, 1983

60 See for futher discussion of this issue: Elemér Illyés, *Ethnic Continuity in the Carpatho-Danubian Area*, New York, 1988, 41-46

61 André Du Nay, *The Early History of the Rumanian Language*, Edward Sapir Monograph Series in Language, Culture, and Cognition, Illinois, 1977

62 István Kiszely, *Honnan jöttünk?*, Budapest, 1992

63 A magyarok története, *Tárih-i Üngürüsz*, Madzsar Tárihi, József Blaskovics, Cleveland, 1988

64 Géza Varga, *Bronzkori magyar írásbeliség*, Budapest, 1993; Sándor Forrai, *Az ősi magyar rovásírás az ókortól napjainkig*, Lakitelek, 1994

65 Új Magyarország, 29th March 1994

66 Ferenc Kubinyi, *Fekete Lexicon*, Thousands Oaks California, 1994

67 Elemér Illyés, *Ethnic Continuity in the Carpatho-Danubian Area*, New York, 1988

68 László Marácz, De zigeuners in Hongarije, Harm Ramkema & Erik van Schaïk (red), *Tussen Recht en Repressie*, Minderheden in Oost-Europa, 1994, Amsterdam, 95-110

69 See for example, Lajos Csomor, *Magyarország szent koronája*, Budapest, 1986; István Szigeti, *A szent korona titkai*, Aachen, 1994; Gábor Pap, *A magyar szent korona*, Debrecen, to appear; *Sacra Corona Hungaricae*, Kornél Bakay (ed), Kőszeg, 1994

70 Ferenc Pecze, *A mai horvát alkotmány és a jus publicum croaticahungaricum utóélete,* Magyarság és Európa, 1994, 1, 39-59

71 Edward Chászár, *Decision in Vienna,* The Czechoslovak-Hungarian Border Dispute of 1938, Astor, 1978

72 András Rónai, *Térképezett történelem,* Budapest, 1989

73 Pál Hunfalvy, *Akadémiai Értesítő,* Budapest, 1851

74 See for the principles of Hungarian language and grammar László Marácz, *Asymmetries in Hungarian,* San Sebastian, 1991

75 Gergely Czuczor, A magyar nagyszótár ügyében, *Magyar Akadémiai Értesítő* I.IV, 1861, 403-445

76 See, for example, the recent work of the Hungarian linguist Sándor Győri-Nagy, Euroregionale Ökologie von Sprachen und Kulturen in der Heutigen Kommunikation zwischen Ost und West, *Kétnyelvüség,* II.1, 1994, 29-39.

77 Imre Pacsai, *A mellérendelő szóösszetételek areális vonásai,* Ms., Nyíregyháza, 1995

78 Gyula László, *Steppevolken en hun kunst,* Hongaarse schakel in de Volksverhuizing, Den Haag, 1970

79 See the excellent photographs in Gyula László and István Rácz, *Der Goldschatz von Nagyszentmiklós,* Budapest, 1977

80 Gyula László, *A Szent-László-legenda középkori falképei,* Budapest, 1993

81 *Székely népballadák,* Kőmives Kelemenné, Budapest, 1979, 63

82 Norman Stone, *Europe Transformed 1878-1919,* Glasgow, 1983, 59

83 See Abraham de Swaan, *Zorg en Staat,* Amsterdam, 1989, 73. The tension existing between various communication codes is a well-known problem in sociology. The code problem of the Hungarian kingdom may be described in terms of the flower figuration of languages

84 Henry Bogdan, *From Warsaw to Sofia,* A History of Eastern Europe, Santa Fe, 1989

85 François Fejtő, *Requiem pour un empire défunt, Historie de la destruction de l'Autriche-Hongrie*, Lieu Commun, 1988

86 Báró Miklós Wesselényi, *Szózat a magyar és szláv nemzetiség ügyében*, Budapest, 1843, reprinted in 1992

87 Henri Pozzi, *La guerre revient*, Paris, 1993; Henri Pozzi, *Les Coupables*, Paris, 1934; and Jeromos Szalay, *Igazságok Magyarország körül*, A magyar pör, Magyarország megcsonkítása Trianon-Párizs-1956, Paris, 1960, 28

88 Jeromos Szalay, *Igazságok Magyarország körül*, A magyar pör, Magyarország megcsonkítása Trianon-Párizs-1956, Paris, 1960

89 M. Butenschön, *Zarenhymne und Marseillaise: zur Geschichte der Russland-Ideologie in Frankreich (1870/71-1893/1894)*, Stuttgart, 1978

90 Zoltán Sztáray, *A bukaresti titkos szerződés, Hogyan adták el Erdélyt az antanthatalmak*, Uj látóhatár, 1980

91 Jan Willem Schulte Nordholt, *Woodrow Wilson, Een leven voor de wereldvrede*, Amsterdam, 1992

92 Harry Hill Bandholtz, *An Undiplomatic Diary*, New York, 1933

93 Count Albert Apponyi, *The Memoirs of Count Apponyi*, London, 1935

94 Zoltán Palotás, *A trianoni határok*, Budapest, 1990

95 For example Yves de Daruvar, *Le destin dramatique de la Hongrie*, Paris, 1989 and Stephen Borsody (ed), *The Hungarians: A Divided Nation*, New Haven, 1988

96 Ernő Raffay, *Trianon titkai*, Budapest, 1990

97 Henry Bogdan, *Les minorité nationales dans les pays danubiens, Les Dossiers de l'Histoire*, no. 27, 1980

98 Count Albert Apponyi, *The Memoirs of Count Apponyi*, London, 1935, 272-273

99 Henri Guillemin, *Nationalites et nationaux (1870-1940)*, Coll. Idées no. 321 NRF-Gallimard, 1974, 95

100 Count Albert Apponyi, 282-283

101 Henri Pozzi, *La guerre revient*, Paris, 1934

102 René Albrecht-Carrié, *A Diplomatic History of Europe,* since the Congress of Vienna (revised edition), New York, 1973, 409

103 Rapport au Congres de la Fédération de la Seine de la Ligue des Droits de l'Homme, 27th June 1920

104 Thomas Woodrow Wilson, *Twenty-Eighth President of the United States*, a Psychological Study, London, 1966, Sigmund Freud Copyrights Ltd. and William C. Bullit.

105 Miklós Zalka, *Mindenkihez!*, Budapest, 1978

106 Paul Teleki, *The Evolution of Hungary and Its Place in European History*, New York, 1923

107 Endre Jónás, *Trianon a European Problem*, Zürich, 1960

108 Henry Bogdan, *From Warsaw to Sofia*, A History of Eastern Europe, Santa Fe, 1989, 182

109 Henry Bogdan, *From Warsaw to Sofia*, A History of Eastern Europe, Santa Fe, 1989, 183

110 Henry Bogdan, *From Warsaw to Sofia*, A History of Eastern Europe, Santa Fe, 1989, 184

111 Gyula Popély, *A csehszlovákiai magyarság a népszámlálások tükrében 1918-1945*, Budapest, 1991, 95

112 Sándor Biró, *Kisebbségben és többségben: románok es magyarok (1867-1940)*, Bern, 1989

113 M. Millerand's letter, to be found in the Magyar Országos Levéltár, Dossier Embassy Bern, K. 84. 1920-19/5

114 The Hungarian Peace, *Speeches of the Members of the British House of Lords on the Trianon Peace Treaty*, Budapest, 1922, 11

115 The Hungarian Peace, *Speeches of the Members of the British House of Lords on the Trianon Peace Treaty*, Budapest, 1922, 25

116 The Hungarian Peace, *Speeches of the Members of the British House of Lords on the Trianon Peace Treaty*, Budapest, 1922, 27

117 Ignác Romsics, *Bethlen István*, Budapest, 1991, 181

118 See also the memoirs of the Hungarian Defence Minister Vilmos Nagybaczoni Nagy, *Végzetes Esztendők 1938-1945*, Budapest, 1986

119 Tibor Cseres, *Vérbosszú Bácskában*, Budapest, 1991; Perry Pierik, *Hungary 1944-1945, The Forgotten Tragedy*, Nieuwegein, 1995, 80

120 Márton Matuska, *A megtorlás napjai*, Újvidék, 1991. See English edition: Márton Matuska, *Retaliation*, Budapest, 1995; and Tibor Cseres, *Titoist Atrocities in Vojvodina 1944-1945*, Toronto, 1993

121 Mihály András Beke, *Illúziók kora Erdély*, párbeszéd Beke Györggyel Erdély ismeretlen tegnapjáról, Budapest, 1993, 33 See also István Ferenczes, *Székely apokalipszisz*, Csíkszereda, 1995

122 József Botlik-György Dupka, *Ez hát a hon...*, Budapest, 1991

123 Mihály András Beke, *Illúziók kora Erdély*, párbeszéd Beke Györggyel Erdély ismeretlen tegnapjáról, Budapest, 1993, 32

124 Kálmán Janics, *Czechoslovak Policy and the Hungarian Minority, 1945-1948*, New York, 1982

125 Imre Molnár-Kálmán Varga, *Hazahúzott a szülőföld*, Budapest, 1992

126 *Hungarians in Slovakia*, Political Movement Coexistence, Bratislava, 1992

127 Dalibor M. Krno, *A békéről tárgyaltunk Magyarországgal*, Budapest, 1992

128 Ignác Romsics, *A State Department és Magyarország*, 1942-1947, Valóság, 1992, 11, 32-67

129 See for Transylvania: *Witness to Cultural Genocide*, First Hand Reports on Rumania's Minority Policies Today, American Transylvanian Federation and Committee for Human Rights in Rumania, New York, 1979; *Rumania's Violations of Helsinki Final Act Provisions Protecting the Rights of National, Religious and Linguistic Minorities*, Study Prepared by the Committee for Human Rights in Rumania for the Conference on Security and Cooperation in Europe, Madrid, 1980-1981, New York, 1980; see for Slovakia: *Kettős elnyomásban*, Dokumentumok a csehszlovákiai magyarság helyzetéről és jogvédelméről 1978-1988 Hungarian Human Rights Foundation, New York, 1989

130 Mihai Fatu, Micea Musat (eds), Bucharest, 1985

131 Lajos Demény, *A román történetírásról a Ceausescu-érában,* Múltunk 33/1, Budapest, 85-99

132 Raul Hilberg, *The Destruction of the European Jews,* New York, 1985, 141. Péter Gosztonyi, *Magyarság,* október 1993.

133 See Mathias Bernath, *Habsburg und die Anfänge der Rumänisches Nationsbildung,* Leiden, 1972

134 *Jelentések a határon túli magyar kisebbségek helyzetéről,* Budapest, 1988, 225

135 István Tőkés, *A romániai magyar református egyház élete 1944-1989,* Budapest, 1990

136 László Tőkés, *De vonk in de Roemeense revolutie,* edited by David Porter, Leiden, 1991

137 László Tőkés, *"Ideje a szólásnak",* Nagyvárad, 1993

138 *Jelentések a határon túli magyar kisebbségek helyzetéről,* Budapest, 1988, 255

139 *Genocide in Transylvania; Nation on the Death Row a Documentary,* The Transylvanian World Federation and the Danubian Research and Information Center, Florida, 1985, 58

140 *Magyar Szó,* July 2, 1996

141 The above-mentioned facts on conditions for the Hungarians living in the Baranya Triangle and in Vojvodina derive from the following sources: Hungarians in Serbia are the victims, *NRC Handelsblad,* 12-7-1991; Conflict in Belgrade and Tirana escalates. Serbia tries to drown Albanians in river of blood, *NRC Handelsblad,* 17-7-1991; Ibrahim Rugova, Albanian leader in Kosovo: Kosovo could choose to unite with Albania, *NRC Handelsblad,* 19-7-1991; Threatened mass slaughter of Albanians in Kosovo, *Menschenrechte* 3/4, 1991; The "Democratic Party of Albania" demands that Kosovo unites with Albania in order to contribute to stability in the region, *Frankfurter Algemeine Zeitung,* 9-8-1991; Albanians killed on Albanian border, *NRC Handelsblad,* 13-8-1991; J. de Vogel, The time is now ripe for Kosovo to become independent, *NRC Handelsblad,* 3-10-1991; *Die Presse,* 30-10-1991, After more than 30 border infringements by Serbs, the Yugoslavian air force shot some 300 mortar-shells into the village of Barcs in Hungary. Serbia denies the attack and accuses

Hungary of lying; *Frankfurter Algemeine Zeitung,* 7-11-1991, approximately 42,000 refugees from Vojvodina and Croatia have sought refuge in Hungary; *Journal de Genéve,* 19-11-1991, Inhabitants of Vojvodina resist mobilization and calls to serve in the Serb army; *De Volkskrant,* 25-11-1991, Heavy fighting near the Croatian city of Osijek despite the truce. Reports have been received of massive destruction in the Hungarian village of Szentlászló (Laslovo) in East Slavonia; Amnesty International reveals that 21 civilians have been burned by Serbian fighters, *Neue Zürcher Zeitung,* 27-11-1991; in several Hungarian communities in Vojvodina there are protest rallies against the war, *Neue Zürcher Zeitung,* 28-11-1991; the federal army sends non-Serbian soldiers, like Hungarians, to the most dangerous front positions, *Frankfurter Algemeine Zeitung,* 29-11-1991; Hungarians trapped in Serbia, *NRC Handelsblad,* 5-12-1991; *Die Presse,* 10-12-1991, In Kosovo, Serbs try to break down the opposition of Albanian employees to Serbization by conducting large-scale dismissals. To date, more than 100,000 people, starting with the intelligentsia, like teachers and doctors, have been robbed of their livelihood; the Democratic Community of Hungarians in Vojvodina (VMDK) makes demands for the peace talks in The Hague to guarantee regional autonomy for Hungarians, *Frankfurter Algemeine Zeitung,* 13-12-1991; The US human rights group 'Helsinki Watch' accuses Serb leaders and the federal army of atrocities committed against civilians during the war with Croatia. In a brief report, mention is made of grave violations of war-law including mass executions, *Handelsblatt,* 24-1-1992, *Neue Zürcher Zeitung,* 25-1-1992; Registering of pupils for Hungarian schools is seen as separatism by the Serbs. Plans exist to make place and street names Serbian, *Le Monde Diplomatique,* January 1992; Five EU observers are killed by the Serbian air force, *Frankfurter Algemeine Zeitung,* 8-1-1992; The Serb army commits atrocities directed at the civilian population in the captured areas. Prisoners throats are cut, their eyes are poked out and ears and noses are amputated. Housing areas deserted by inhabitants are systematically plundered, *Frankfurter Algemeine Zeitung,* 18-1-1992; The ethnic Hungarian RC priest Tamás Velencei from Oroszlam is forced by Serbs to take up arms and fight at the front, *Magyar Nemzet,* 22-1-1992; Hungarian leaders are called to take up arms and send to the front, others are threatened with this, VMDK, press release, 29-1-1992, Hand grenade explodes on the land of Károly Tóth, vice-chairman of the local VMDK group in Kanizsa. Murder threats are issued for other Hungarian representatives, *Magyar Szó,* 13-2-1992; Helsinki Watch reports that 200 civilians have been publicly executed and a further 3,000 or more are missing. Hungarians and Croats of the Baranja (Croatia) are driven out of their villages to make way for Serbs, *Frankfurter Algemeine Zeitung,* 7-2-1992; The chief editor of the Hungarian language newspaper in Vojvodina *Magyar Szó* (The Hungarian Word), Béla

Csorda is arrested by the police. In the other regional newspaper, the Serbs have endeavoured to install a puppet chief editor. Radio and TV transmission times in Hungarian are heavily curtailed. The establishing of private schools - the only possibility for mother tongue education since state schools have been closed down - is hampered by the fact that lessons may only be given in Serbian, *Frankfurter Algemeine Zeitung,* 14-2-1992; Two thirds of all the people called up to serve in the federal army originate from Vojvodina (83,000 persons). Some 100,000 people manage to avoid being recruited by fleeing *Le Monde,* 29-2-1992; Serbs in East Slavonia (Croatia) forbid the return of Croatian and Hungarian refugees, *De Volkskrant,* 5-3-1992; Ference Csubela, Hungarian member of parliament in the Serb parliament representing the VMDK, Hungarians in Serbia have no rights, *De Volkskrant,* 21-3-1992; Letter from András Ágoston, chairman of the VMDK to Lord Carrington. Ágoston expresses fears about the threats and intimidations made by the chetnik leader Seselj addressed to Hungarians and Croats in Vojvodina, VMDK, 9-4-1992; Csubela acted in accordance with the interests of Vojvodinan Hungarians. Declaration released by the VMDK concerning the fate of 83 Hungarian conscientious objectors, VMDK, 16-4-1992; The Serb Foreign Affairs Minister Jovanovic rejects bids for territorial autonomy for Hungarians in Vojvodina arguing that Serbs constitute the majority in the province. At the same time, he calls Hungarians extremists and characterizes the federal army as a stabilizing factor in the region, *Frankfurter Algemeine Zeitung,* 24-4-1992; The West refuses to recognize the 'new Yugoslavia' under Serb rule. The new so-called 'Constitution' makes absolutely no mention of Kosovo and Vojvodina, not to speak of the specific rights of minorities, *NRC Handelsblad,* 28-4-1992; A Belgian EU observer is killed in Mostar (Hercegovina), *Le Monde,* 5-5-1992; Serbia sends huge troop divisions to Kosovo and distributes weapons to Serbian paramilitary units. The Albanian underground government in Kosovo expects the arrival of 200,000 Serb colonists. This will seriously disrupt ethnic Albanian homogeneity. Seselj, the chetnik leader, presses for the war to speedily extend to Kosovo, *Die Presse,* 4-5-1992; Berisha, the new president of Albania demands recognition of the right to self-determination for Albanians in Kosovo as the only way of averting a bloodbath, *Le Monde,* 7-5-1992; On the streets, Serb policemen shoot a young Albanian. This is an indication of the extent of the aggression felt towards Albanians in Kosovo, *Frankfurter Algemeine Zeitung,* 8-5-1992; VMDK calls for international protection and support. Serbia plans to force Hungarians to flee, *Népszabadság,* 9-5-1992; In different municipalities inhabited by Hungarians, peace meetings are organized and people call for soldiers to be released from the army and for refugees to be allowed to return home, *Uj Magyarország,* 11-5-1992; Despite the presence of UN troops whole communities of Hungarian, Croat and other non-Serb villagers are driven out of Baranja and East Slavonia. Tens of thousands are evacuated, *Die Presse*, 12-5-1992; The European Parliament passes a law demanding that autonomy be restored for Vojvodina and Kosovo, *Frankfurter Algemeine Zeitung*, 15-5-1992; Hungarian has been abolished as a compulsory language in Hungarian speaking areas of Vojvodina for some time. Serbian is the only recognized language, also compulsory for Hungarians, *De Volkskrant*, 20-5-1992; EU Foreign Affairs Ministers in Luxemburg state that the matter of the Kovoso population's legitimate struggle for autonomy must be raised during the conference on Yugoslavia; *De Volkskrant*, 16-6-1992; In Pristina, Serbs disrupt the first sitting of the recently elected Kosovo parliament. Seven Albanian politicians are arrested and also the director of the building in which they are sitting, *De Volkskrant*, 24-6-1992; In the Yugoslavia talks led by Lord Carrington, Milosevic refuses to be drawn into the discussion on the future of Kosovo, *De Volkskrant*, 26-6-1992.

142 Letter from Pál Csáky, member of the parliamentary assembly of the Council of Europe, Bratislava, 19th January 1994

143 Underinformed or disinformed?, *Kárpátalja* III/3, 11th February 1992

144 The work referred to here is the three-part *Erdély Története* 'The History of Transylvania' written as an assignment for the Hungarian Academy of Sciences and edited by Béla Köpeczi, Budapest, 1988. In this study, it is presumed that Transylvania belongs historically to three different nations: the Hungarians, the Rumanians and the Germans. For the first time in a long while, the Hungarians endeavoured to refute all the falsifications and anomalies produced by the Rumanians about Transylvania. The appearance of this three-part book gave rise to much anger of the Ceausescu regime. The Rumanians began a propaganda campaign against 'The History of Transylvania' but so far it has been unsuccessful

145 "Mit wirksamsten Mitteln": Das Manifest der "Vatra Romane asca", *Die Presse*, 11-4-1990; "Die Heilige Erde Rumäniens besudelt", *Frankfurter Algemeine Zeitung*, 12-4-1990; Rechts Roemenië dreigt met geweld, *De Volkskrant*, 14-4-1990

146 *Cuvîntul Liber*, 6th March 1990

147 News from Helsinki Watch, News from Romania: Ethnic Conflict in Tîrgu Mures, *U.S. Helsinki Watch Committee*, May 1990; *Hungarian Human Rights Foundation*, Resurgence of Ceausescu-Era Policies Prevents Genuine Democracy in Rumania, September 18, 1990, New

York; and *Hungarian Human Rights Foundation*, Criminal Injustice in Rumania, October.27, 1992, New York

148 Judea is now vice-chairman of the PUNR, the political wing of the neo-fascist organization Vatra Romaneasca

149 Március 19: A terror napja Marosvásárhelyen: Sütő András is súlyosan megsebesült, *Romániai Magyar Szó*, Bucharest, March 21, 1990. Véres Kedd, *Romániai Magyar Szó*, Bucharest, March 22, 1990

150 Előd Kincses, *Black Spring*, Budapest-Munich, 1992

151 Interview with László Pesty and Csaba Bátonyi, *Európai Idő*, 1/13, 2 and 7, April 20, 1990

152 Hungarian Human Rights Foundation, *Criminal Injustice in Rumania*, New York, October 27, 1992

153 *The Constitution of the Slovak Republic*, Press Agency of the Slovak Republic, Bratislava, 1992

154 László Szarka, Szlovák történészek Nagymorávia kiterjedéséről, *História*, 1986, 1, 17-18

155 Frits Schaling, Slowaken leiden de Donau om, *NRC Handelsblad*, October 26, 1995

156 Cees Zoon, Slowakije voltooit reactor desnoods met Russisch geld, *De Volkskrant*, February 18, 1995

157 Hamish Rae, *The World in 2010*, London, 1994

158 *Neue Zürcher Zeitung*, 10th January 1992

159 Letter from András Ágoston to Slobodan Milosevic, 14th April 1992, Novi Sad. Letter from András Ágoston to Lord Carrington, 19th April 1992, Novi Sad.

160 *Utrechts Nieuwsblad*, Bloemen en tranen aan grens Roemenië en Moldavië, May 7, 1990

161 Het Moldavische volk één dag herenigd, *NRC Handelsblad*, May 7, 1990

162 Oppositie Roemenië schiet Moldova te hulp, *De Volkskrant*, March 9 1992

163 Roemenië wil delen van Oekraïne terug, *NRC Handelsblad*, November 30, 1991

164 Roemeense naschokken, *Krant op Zondag*, December 8, 1991

165 Rumänischer Patriarch fordert die Rückgabe Bessarabiens und der nördlichen Bukowina an Rumänien, *Informationsdienst Osteuropäisches Christentum*, December 4, 1991

166 Slowaakse minister over de Hongaarse minderheid 'Problemen kunstmatig gecreëerd', Frits Schaling, *NRC Handelsblad*, February 17, 1993

167 In: Robert Aspeslagh/Hans Renner/Hans van der Meulen (eds), *Im historische Würgegriff*, Die Beziehungen zwischen Ungarn und der Slowakei in der Vergangenheit, Gegenwart und Zukunft, Baden-Baden, 1994, 113-121

168 Letter from Max van der Stoel to Géza Jeszenszky, reference: No 1331/93/L, The Hague, 8th November 1993

169 Letter from Géza Jeszenszky to Max van der Stoel, Budapest, 29th November 1993

170 *RMDSZ declaration*, 3rd August 1993

171 David B. Funderburk, *Pinstripes and Reds*: an American Ambassador Caught between the State Department and the Romanian Communists 1981-1985, Washington, 1987, 21

172 *Press conference*, 23rd July 1993

173 *László Tőkés, the RMDSZ court case*, 21st September 1993

174 *RMDSZ memo*, 13th August 1993

175 *Orient Express*, 20th September 1993

176 *RMDSZ memo*, 22nd July 1993. *Népújság*, 22nd July 1993

177 *New York Times*, 20th July 1993. Munich, 21st July 1993

178 Jacques Decornoy, *Le Monde Diplomatique*, November 1992 *RMDSZ memo*, 13th July 1993

179 Letter from Attila Bégány to the MDF congress, 3rd December 1993, Budapest

180 KMKSZ presidium decision pertaining to the law on Ukrainian national minorities, 6th July 1992, *Kárpáti Igaz Szó*, 16th July 1992

181 Letter from Attila Bégány to the MDF congress, 3rd December 1993, Budapest

182 Editions Odile Jacob, 1995

183 *Magyar Nemzet*, 28th February 1995

184 *Népszabadság*, 28th February 1995. Not only has Rumania rejected the resolution of the Council of Europe, but it has also ignored the decisions of its own Constitutional Court. The Court resolution of 21st December 1994 on free border crossing traffic is ignored by customs authorities. Despite this ruling, people are required to pay 10,000-15,000 lei on leaving Rumania.

185 Wenzel Jaksch, *Der Weg nach Potsdam*, 1958 Stuttgart. In a resolution of 8th March 1995, the Constitutional Court at Brno declared the Benes decrees valid with the argument that the decrees were, in hindsight, ratified by the (communist) parliament.

186 London, 1987, 144

187 *Committee for Human Rights in Rumania*, Rumania's Violations of Helsinki Final Act Provisions Protecting the Rights of National, Religious and Linguistic Minorities, New York, 1980; American Transylvanian Federation and Committee for Human Rights in Rumania, *Witness to Cultural Genocide*, First-Hand Reports on Rumania's Minority Policies Today, New York, 1979

188 *Kettős elnyomásban*, Dokumentumok a csehszlovákiai magyarság helyzetéről és jogvédelméről 1978-1988, Miklós Duray (ed), New York, 1989

189 Transylvanian World Federation and The Danubian Research and Information Center, *Genocide in Transylvania*, Nation on the Death Row, a documentary, Florida, 1986; Memorandum of the *Transylvanian World Federation* to the Congress and the Government of the United States of America, Washington, March 1987

190 Hungary's Romanian Time-Bomb..., Peter Keresztes, *The Wall Street Journal*, 12th July 1988

191 *Magyar Tükör*, Közép-Európai Intézet, Budapest, 1995

192 Most is aggódom... Szűrös Mátyással tegnapi küzdelemekről és mai kétségekről beszélget Ablonczy László, *Tiszatáj*, June 1990

193 *Erdélyi Napló*, Feketelista-halállista?, 18th January 1995

194 László Tőkés, *Nyilatkozat*, 7th February 1995

195 *News from the Carter Center*, Atlanta, 15th February 1995

196 *Final Agreement*, Atlanta, 15th February 1995

197 *Declaration of the World Federation of Hungarians on the Hungarian-Slovak and the Hungarian-Rumanian friendship treaties*, Budapest, 3rd March 1995

198 "A magyar kormányzat félrevezette a közvéleményt", *Magyarország*, 31st March 1995, Mihály András Beke

199 Letter from László Lábody to the Federation of Hungarians in the Netherlands, Budapest, 13th April 1995

200 Letter from László Lábody to the Federation of Hungarians in the Netherlands, Budapest, 13th April 1995

201 László Marácz, Hongarije's Democratie in Verwording?, Midden-Europa in Beweging, *Jason*, 1995, 23-27

202 Harry Hill Bandholtz, *An Undiplomatic Diary by the American Member of the Inter-Allied Military Mission to Hungary*, 1919-1920, Fritz-Konrad Krüger (ed), New York, 1933, 226

203 *Nobel Prize Winners*, From Hungary for Humanity, Ferenc Nagy (ed), Budapest, 1994

204 Ferenc Pecze, A mai horváth alkotmány és a jus publicum croatica-hungaricum utóélete, *Magyarság és Európa*, 1994, 1, 39-50

205 Hungarians are Looking East, Far East for Their Roots, John Pomfret, *International Herald Tribune*, 8th February 1995

206 Kladje Zjirinovski belooft revolutie, *De Volkskrant*, 1st February 1994

207 Alfred Reisch, *Hungarian-Russian Relations Enter a New Era*, 8th December 1992

208 J.W. van der Meulen, *Bescherming van minderheden in Oost- en West-Europa*, Nederlands Instituut voor Internationale Betrekkingen 'Clingendael', The Hague, February 1995

209 Auf dem Weg zu neuen Grenzen in Osteuropa, *Neue Zürcher Zeitung*, 30th June 1991

210 John D. Harborn, Time to Bring Back the Empire, *Toronto Globe and Mail*; Joseph C. Harsch, A Solution for Eastern Europe, *Christian Science Monitor*; Thomas Schreiber, Trianon 1992, Paris quoted in *Amerikai Magyarság*, 15th August 1992

211 Gusztáv Molnár, Miért kell a konfederáció?, *Limes*, 1992, 7/8, 56-60

BIBLIOGRAPHICAL NOTES

1) The first chapter *'Western Images and Stereotypes of the Hungarians'* was published as a separate chapter in André Gerrits' and Nanci Adler's (eds.), *Vampires Unstaked, National Images, Stereotypes and Myths in East Central Europe*, Amsterdam, 1995, p. 25-40.

2) See for views other than the one defended here with respect to the position of non-Magyar nationalities in Hungary during the era of dualism and the Hungarian policy of 'Magyarization' and for the views of the non-Hungarian nations of the Carpathian Basin the following references: Janos C. Andrew, *The Politics of Backwardness in Hungary*, 1825-1945, Princeton, 1982. Robert Aspeslagh, Hans Renner, Hans van der Meulen (eds.), *Im historischen Würgegriff*, Die Beziehungen zwischen Ungarn und der Slowakei in der Vergangenheit, Gegenwart und Zukunft, Baden-Baden, 1994. Compare for the Slovak view on Hungarian-Slovak relations and the policy of Magyarization the papers of D. Kovác and J. Fabian. Cornelia Bodea and Virgil Candea, *Transylvania in the History of the Romanians*, New York, 1982. See this book for the Rumanian view of Hungarian-Rumanian relations and the Rumanian interpretation of the policy of Magyarization. R.J. Crampton, *Eastern Europe in the Twentieth Century*, London, 1994. Crampton's discussion on Hungary before the twentieth century dwells almost exclusively on Magyarization, much in the same way that R.W. Seton-Watson (p.11-12) does. Misha Glenny, *The Rebirth of History*, Eastern Europe in the Age of Democracy, London, 1990, p. 72-96. Glenny's interpretation of Hungarian history is deeply influenced by the work of R.W. Seton-Watson. Keith Hitchins, *The Nationality Problem in Austria-Hungary*, Leiden, 1974. See this volume for information on the Rumanian grievances against the Magyarization policy. Jörg K. Hoensch, *A History of Modern Hungary 1867-1986*, London, 1988, p. 28-36. See this volume for critical notes on Magyarization. Robert A. Kann, *A History of the Habsburg Empire 1526-1918*, University of California Press, 1974, p. 406-461 for a critical evaluation of the different nationalities and their relations under Hungarian rule. Joseph Rothschild, *East Central Europe between the two World Wars*, University of Washington, 1989. I very much agree with Rothschild's statement (p.118):"While the Hungarians' goal here was clearly the dubious one of ultimately denationalizing an entire [Slovak, LM] people, it should be recalled that their intolerance was exclusively cultural and linguistic, not racial and ethnic." Norman Stone, *Europe Transformed 1878-1919*, Glasgow, 1983, p.303-325. Compare this study for a critical review of the political situation in Hungary during the time of dualism. Peter F. Sugar and I.J.Lederer, *Nationalism in Eastern Europe*, University of Washington Press, 1994. See for a clearly defined opinion on Hungarian nationalism the paper of G. Barany. Zoltán Szász, From the Empire to Civic Hungary (Part Five), in *History of Transylvania*, B. Köpeczi (ed.),

Budapest, 1994, p. 525-643. A Marxist view of the nationality conflict in Transylvania under Hungarian rule is defended in this chapter. A.J.P. Taylor, *The Habsburg Monarchy 1809-1918*, London, 1990. Taylor's analysis of Hungary under dualist rule is very much influenced by R.W. Seton-Watson's work.

3) In the text not much is said about Hungary's role in World War II and its alliance with Nazi Germany. Though I am critical of Hungary's collaboration with the destructive Nazi forces the Hungarian leaders - Admiral Horthy included - had little choice in the matter. In the inter-war period Hungary was not a western-style democracy, but one may not assert that the Hungarians embraced German fascism. By the end of the inter-war period, Hungary's conservative political system rather resembled Mussolini's model. For the Hungarians, especially the ones living in the successor states, the Vienna Awards came as a relief after the nightmare caused by the Trianon constellation. See the following references on these issues:

Péter Hanák, *Hungary on a Fixed Course: An Outline of Hungarian History, 1918-1945*, In: Joseph Held's (ed.), *The Columbia History of Eastern Europe in the Twentieth Century*, New York, 1992, p. 164-204. See this chapter for a description of Hungary's internal political system and its alliance with Nazi Germany. Jörg. K. Hoensch, *A History of Modern Hungary 1867-1986*, London, 1988, p. 84-131. See this chapter for a critical, though somewhat biased, analysis of Hungary between the wars. Macartney, C.A. *October Fifteenth: A History of Modern Hungary, 1929-1945*, 2 vols, Edinburgh, 1956. This is an objective study of Hungary in the inter-war period. Perry Pierik, *Hungary 1944-1945, The Forgotten Tragedy, Nieuwegein, 1996*. See this volume and the references cited for details of the tragedies that took place in Hungary at the end of World War II. Also, for information on the destruction of Europe's last remaining Jewish community and on the assistance provided by Hungarian members of the Arrow Cross movement in the process of exterminating the Hungarian Jews.

INDEX OF NAMES

Aczél 77
Ady 48
Ágoston 254, 255, 294
Ajtony 104
Albrecht-Carrié 141
Alekszij II 320, 321
Alexander the Great 253
Álmos 105
Andrássy 42
Andreas II 87, 88
Anghelescu 169
Antall 52, 258
Apáczai Csere
Apponyi 137, 139
Armstrong 175
Árpád 104, 250
Ata Turk 127
Attila 46
Auerbach 45

Bach 66, 98
Bacsa 187
Balassa 145
Balladur 269, 270, 298, 302
Bandholtz 48, 49, 52, 129, 312
Barabás 237
Barki 286, 292
Bátonyi 233, 234
Béla IV 87
Bem 85
Beneš 124, 133, 136, 137, 150, 151, 173, 174, 175, 274, 275, 301
Berthelot 137, 139
Bethlen, G. 39, 220
Bethlen, M. 147
Binder 265
Bíró 155, 156, 157
Bismarck 42, 117
Blaauw 282
Blaauw, J.D. 306
Bocskai 39, 97, 144
Borbély, I. 261
Borbély, L. 261

Borsody 60
Bryce 168, 169
Budenz 66, 67, 100
Bull 141
Byrnes 176

Carp 181
Carrington 80, 254, 294, 329
Carter 243
Ceausescu 57, 108, 149, 178, 182, 217, 221, 261, 262, 263, 278, 282, 283, 285, 287
Chamberlain 32
Charlemagne 31
Chebeleu 262
Chirac 270
Clemenceau 129, 131, 333
Clinton 305
Coexistence 203, 204
Cofariu 237
Collinder 68
Constantin 180
Coolidge 175
Corvinus 146
Crnojević III 88
Csapó 292
Cseresznyés 237, 238
Csomor 91
Csoóri 320, 321
Csörgits 190
Curzon of Keddleston 168
Cyril 325
Czuczor 101, 102

Dalai Lama 293, 319
Dalmay 212, 213
Damianus 32
Dankavics 212
Dávid 146
Davis 262, 265, 266
Deák, I. 119
Deák, F. 93
Deák, L. 259
Décsy 69
Demény 57, 180

359

Demetrius 92
Denis 137
Dohotaru 257
Domokos 70
Ducas 92
Dufourcq 273
Du Nay 76
Duray 278, 280

Eckhardt 35
Eide 264
Eisenmann 137
Emese 105
Eötvös 42, 116

Faragó 191
Feketehalmy-Czeydner 171
FKGP (Independent Smallholders' Party) 299, 300, 308
Foch 151
Fogarasi 101, 102
Franz Ferdinand 46, 122
Franz Joseph 41, 115, 119, 122, 129
Frunda 261
Funar 146, 149
Funderburk 262
Füzesi 238

Gabor 306
Gál 333
Galaczi 238
Geerts 226
George 92, 131
Gertrud 148
Ghiulea 165
Giscard d'Estaing 272
Glatz 63
Gob 145
Goebbels 58
Göncz 71
Gorbachev 98, 270, 271, 283
Gosztonyi 181
Grassy 171
Grósz 287
Győrffi 225

Hajdu 69

Hamos 282
Hanzi 238
Herder 65, 100
Hilberg 50, 181
Hitler 95, 136
Hobsbawm 71
Hodosi 63
Holbrooke 273
Holy Virgin Mary 92
Horn 274, 290, 299, 300, 309
Horthy 50, 51, 129, 170, 180
Hunfalvy 66, 67, 100
Hunyadi 146
Hussein 272

Iancu 220
Iliescu 218, 262, 286, 328
Imre 86
Iorga 156
Iotsaldus 36
Iswolski 123

Janics 173
Jászi 48, 79, 127, 175
Jesus 92
Jeszenszky 79, 80, 260, 261, 268, 269, 290
Jónás 62, 63
Judea 230, 236
Juppé 302

Kádár 51, 54
Karadzic 245
Károlyi 79, 126, 127, 128
Katona, Á. 289, 290, 292
Katona, J. 148
Kávássy 307, 308
Kazár 73, 74
Kazinczy 145
Kennedy, J.F. 309
Kennedy, P. 119
Kincses 233
Király 277, 278, 280
Kis de Misztótfalu 147
Kiszely 77, 320
KMKSZ (Hungarian Cultural Federation of Subcarpathia) 212, 269, 289

Knazko 259
Kocsis, I. 284, 284
Kocsis, K. 63
Kolozsvári 148
Kőrösi Csoma 77, 319
Kosma 92
Kossuth 38, 41, 44, 85, 97, 115, 166, 212
Kovács 307, 308
Kubinyi 80
Kuhn 67
Kun 128
Kusztos 226
Lábody 303
Laroche 137
László 76, 97, 104', 105
László, St. 105, 106, 107, 166
Lenau 37
Lenin 128
Leopold I 88
Leopold II 89
Linder 127
Lipták 251
List 37
Louiş XIV 118
Lubbers 255
Ludwig 87
Macartney 40, 136
Maczó-Nagy 308
Maet, Van der 147
Maléter 98
Maniu 172
Margerie, De 137
Markó 261
Masaryk 124, 130, 137, 151, 154
Matthias 144, 146
Matuska 171
MDF (Hungarian Democratic Forum) 268, 300, 301, 311
Mečiar 300
Mester 332
Method 325
Meulen, Van der 333, 334
Mierlo, Van 306
Mikes 147
Millerand 139, 168

Milosevic 80, 245, 254, 255, 272
Mindszenty 51
Mitterand 270, 271
MKDM (Hungaria nChristian Democratic Movement, Slovakia) 295, 300
MNP (Hungarian People's Party) 296
Molnár, E. 76
Molnár, G. 335
Molotov 95
Montgomery 50, 52, 175
Moses 273
Moynihan 51
MPP (Hungarian Civic Party) 203, 295
Münninghoff 184
Mussolini 136

Nagy 98, 308
Napoleon I 118
Németh, M. 99
Németh, Zs. 302
Nicholas I 115
Nicolson 45
Nimrod 72
Nyers 99

Odilo 36
Otto III 37

Pacepa 277
Pacsai 103
Palmerstone 38, 40
Palotás 132
Panini 68
Pap 92
Papp 238
Pataki 321
Paunescu
Pázmány 145
Petőfi 85, 97, 166, 212
Petru 237
Philippe II 118
Plaks 265
Poincaré 122, 139, 141
Pompidou 272
Pop-Cicio 167

361

Pozsgay 99
Pozzi 141

Raffay 136
Rákóczi II 38, 97, 144, 145, 147
Rákosi 53
Révai 92
RMDSZ (Democratic Union of Hungarians in Rumania) 223, 230, 235, 236, 261, 263, 265, 266, 269, 288, 290, 291, 292, 293
Robin 272
Roman 234
Rónai 95
Rothermere 49, 169
Rubik 316

Sancho 37
Schiller 37
Schreiber 333
Sebestyén 145
Seselj 201, 295
Seton-Watson, H.31, 337
Seton-Watson, R.W. 44, 48, 79, 117, 123
Sforza 46, 47, 48
Sigismund 148
Smith 59
Stalin 136
Stanasila 219
Stein 264
Stephen, St. 37, 65, 66, 85, 87, 91, 93, 94
Stoel, Van der 260, 261, 264
Sulijman I 77, 87, 312
Sulijman II 85
Sütő 219, 230
Sylvester II 37, 91
Szabadi 237, 238
Szaczvay 147
Szamuely 128
Széchenyi 37, 66, 82, 99, 166
Székely 226
Szent-Iványi 302

Szombathelyi 171
Szűrös 99, 287

Tardieu 137, 140
Teleki 50, 95, 135, 170
Teocrist 258
Thököly 39
Thyssen-Bornemisza 282
Tisza, K. 42
Tisza, I./S. 46, 47, 122, 126, 132
Tito 171
Tokay 261
Tőkés 99, 182, 183, 220, 221, 227, 258, 262, 263, 264, 265, 266, 292, 293, 319
Toszó 183
Tóth 289
Traianus 74, 89

Ujvárossy 183

Vaida-Voevod 167
Vajay 33, 78
Vajda 238
Vatra Romaneasca 219, 220, 221, 222, 234, 236, 290
VMDK (Democratic Community of Hungarians in Vojvodina) 294, 295
Vyx 128

Wesselényi 121
Wickham-Steed 137
Wijnaendts 255
Wilders 307
Willis 142
Wilson 51, 125, 129, 131, 134, 141

Zapolyai 39, 144
Zjirinovski 324
Zolcsák 281
Zrínyi, I. 144
Zrínyi, M./N. 38, 84
Zsigmond 89

PERRY PIERIK
Hungary 1944-1945
The Forgotten Tragedy

German's final offensives during World War II

The destruction of Europe's last Jewish community

ASPEKT

The book describes Hungary during World War II on the basis of Hitler's most important political principles, namely the acquisition of Lebensraum (Living space) in which raw materials, oil in particular, were vital. Another tragic subject discussed is the destruction of the last remaining Jewish community in Europe.

The author considers the case of Hungary to be the final manifestation of a long and tragic policy. At the end of the war, Hitler was obsessed by the Hungarian oilfields of Nagykanizsa, the last natural oil wonder reserves of the Third Reich. This thoroughly influenced Hitler s strategies and involved enormous military efforts. In January 1945, the Army Group South started an offensive, known as the three Operations Konrad, followed by Operation Südwind in February 1945 and the large scale and mostly forgotten Operation Frühligserwachen, also know as the Ardennes Offensive of the East in spring. During the last months of the war, Hitler ordered the 6th SS Panzer Army from the Ardennes to Hungary, and Budapest was sacrificed als a Festung (stronghold). The aim of the operation was not only the preservation of the Hungarian oilfields, but also the recapture the Rumanian oilfields. The operation developed dramatically. Ten days after the beginning of Frühlingserwachen, the Red Army started the Vienna operation and broke through the German front.

Another tragedy is the extradition of the Hungarian Jews, the last remaining Jewish community in Europe, by SS-Commander Adolf Eichmann, who claimed the Hungarian operation to be the most successful one in his career. The author thoroughly investigated how at the end of the war such an extensive destruction campaign could still have taken place. While the SS appeared to be prepared to come to an agreement to spare Jews in Western Europe, most Hungarian Jews died in Auschwitz or during marches to Hegyeshalom. The dubious part played by the Hungarian authorities, Horthy and Szálasi, and the rescue attempts by Wallenberg, Kastner, Lutz and Perlasca, are also investigated.

The book is a political and military study, focusing largely on the economic politics of the Third Reich, which have been neglected in historiography.
Research has been based on thousands of documents from German, American and Hungarian archives. The photographes have never been used before.

How to order:

**Pery Pierik, Hungary 1944-1945, The Forgotten Tragedy
ISBN: 90-75323-10-7**

Mail/fax your name, adress, country, telephonenumber, titel and ISBN number to:

Aspekt
P.O. BOX 7081
3430 JB-Nieuwegein/ The Netherlands
Aspekt@knoware.nl
fax: +31-306056409
tel: +31-306051196

Methods of payment:

1) Cash by post
2) VISA
3) American Express
4) Bank account: ABN/AMRO 454071485 P.O. Box 2300, 3430 DM Nieuwegein /The Nethrelands

The book will be sent postage paid to your adress
Delivery 3 to 5 weeks

Price: Argentina USD 26, Australia AUD 33, Austria ATS 270, Belgium BEF 785, Brasil USD 26, Canada CAD 35, France FRF 130, Germany DEM 38, Great Britain GBP 18, Hungary HUF 3250, Japan JYP 2750, Kroatia USD 26, The Netherlands NLG 42,50, Romania ROL 43250, Slovakia SLK 730, Sweden SEK 185, Switzerland CHF 33, USA USD 26.

How to order:

**László Marácz, Hungarian Revival,
Political Reflectins on Central Europe.**
ISBN: 90-75323-11-5

Mail/fax your name, adress, country, telephonenumber, titel and ISBN number to:

Aspekt
P.O. BOX 7081
3430 JB-Nieuwegein/ The Netherlands
Aspekt@knoware.nl
fax: +31-306056409
tel: +31-306051196

Methods of payment:

1) Cash by post
2) VISA
3) American Express
4) Bank account: ABN/AMRO 454071485 P.O. Box 2300, 3430 DM Nieuwegein /The Nethrelands

The book will be sent postage paid to your adress
Delivery 3 to 5 weeks

Price: Argentina USD 28, Australia AUD 36, Austria ATS 300, Belgium BEF 850, Brasil USD 28, Canada CAD 38, France FRF 140, Germany DEM 40, Great Britain GBP 20, Hungary HUF 3500, Japan JYP 3000, Kroatia USD 28, The Netherlands NLG 45, Romania ROL 47000, Slovakia SLK 790, Sweden SEK 200, Switzeland CHF 36, USA USD 28.